Elements of Data Science

Getting Started with Data Science and Python

Allen B. Downey

Green Tea Press

Needham, Massachusetts

Elements of Data Science
Getting Started with Data Science and Python
by Allen B. Downey

Version 1.0.1

Green Tea Press
9 Washburn Ave
Needham MA 02492

Copyright © 2024 Allen B. Downey.

Permission is granted to copy, distribute, transmit and adapt this work under the Creative Commons Attribution-NonCommercial-ShareAlike 4.0 International License: https://creativecommons.org/licenses/by-nc-sa/4.0.

If you are interested in distributing a commercial version of this work, please contact the author.

Cover Design by Liana Moisescu
https://99designs.com/profiles/lianam

ISBN 978-0-9716775-1-7

Contents

I		**From Python to Pandas**	1
1		**Variables and Values**	**3**
	1.1	Numbers	3
	1.2	Arithmetic	4
	1.3	Math Functions	5
	1.4	Variables	7
	1.5	Calculating with Variables	8
	1.6	Summary	9
2		**Times and Places**	**11**
	2.1	Strings	11
	2.2	Representing Dates and Times	13
	2.3	Timedelta	15
	2.4	Representing Location	17
	2.5	Calculating Distance	18
	2.6	Defining Functions	19
	2.7	Haversine Distance	20
	2.8	Geopandas	21
	2.9	Summary	23
3		**Lists and Arrays**	**25**
	3.1	Tuples	25
	3.2	Lists	26
	3.3	Sandwich Prices	27
	3.4	NumPy Arrays	28
	3.5	Statistical Summaries	30
	3.6	Relative Difference	30
	3.7	Summarizing Relative Differences	31
	3.8	Debugging	32
	3.9	Summary	34
4		**Loops and Files**	**35**
	4.1	Loops	35
	4.2	Counting with Loops	36
	4.3	Files	38

	4.4	if Statements	38
	4.5	The `break` Statement	40
	4.6	Whitespace	40
	4.7	Counting Words	41
	4.8	Summary	43
5	**Dictionaries**	**45**
	5.1	Indexing	45
	5.2	Dictionaries	47
	5.3	Counting Unique Words	50
	5.4	Dealing with Capitalization	51
	5.5	Removing Punctuation	52
	5.6	Counting Word Frequencies	54
	5.7	Summary	56
6	**Plotting**	**57**
	6.1	Keyword Arguments	57
	6.2	Graphing Religious Affiliation	59
	6.3	Decorating the Axes	62
	6.4	Plotting Sandwich Prices	63
	6.5	Zipf's Law	67
	6.6	Logarithmic Scales	71
	6.7	Summary	73

II Exploratory Data Analysis 75

7	**DataFrames and Series**	**77**
	7.1	Reading the Data	78
	7.2	Series	80
	7.3	Validation	81
	7.4	Summary Statistics	84
	7.5	Series Arithmetic	85
	7.6	Histograms	85
	7.7	Boolean Series	86
	7.8	Filtering Data	88
	7.9	Weighted Means	89
	7.10	Making an Extract	91
	7.11	Summary	92
8	**Distributions**	**93**
	8.1	Distributions	93
	8.2	The General Social Survey	94
	8.3	Distribution of Education	95
	8.4	Cumulative Distribution Functions	98
	8.5	CDF of Age	100

		8.6	Comparing Distributions	103
		8.7	Comparing Incomes	105
		8.8	Modeling Distributions	107
		8.9	Kernel Density Estimation	109
		8.10	Summary	112

9 Relationships — 113
- 9.1 Exploring relationships 113
- 9.2 Visualizing relationships 119
- 9.3 Quantifying Correlation 123
- 9.4 Simple Linear Regression 127
- 9.5 Regression of Height and Weight 130
- 9.6 Summary 134

10 Regression — 135
- 10.1 Regression with StatsModels 136
- 10.2 Multiple Regression 137
- 10.3 Grouping by Age 138
- 10.4 Visualizing regression results 139
- 10.5 Categorical Variables 143
- 10.6 Logistic Regression 144
- 10.7 Summary 147

III Statistical Inference — 149

11 Resampling — 151
- 11.1 Vaccine Testing 151
- 11.2 Simulating One Group 153
- 11.3 Simulating the Trial 156
- 11.4 Estimating Means 158
- 11.5 The Resampling Framework 160
- 11.6 Summary 162

12 Bootstrap Sampling — 163
- 12.1 Estimating Average Income 163
- 12.2 Estimating Percentiles 167
- 12.3 Bootstrapping 169
- 12.4 Working with Bigger Data 171
- 12.5 Weighted Bootstrapping 174
- 12.6 Correlation and Regression 176
- 12.7 Limitations of Bootstrapping 177
- 12.8 Resampling with KDE 179
- 12.9 Summary 181

13 Hypothesis Testing — 185

	13.1	Testing Medical Treatments	186
	13.2	Computing p-values	189
	13.3	Are First Babies More Likely To Be Late?	190
	13.4	The Hypothesis Testing Framework	193
	13.5	Testing Correlation	195
	13.6	Testing Regression Models	199
	13.7	Controlling for Age	201
	13.8	Summary	204

IV Case Study: Political Alignment — 207

14 Political Alignment and Polarization — 209
	14.1	Political Alignment	210
	14.2	Visualizing Distributions	212
	14.3	Plotting a Time Series	214
	14.4	Smoothing the Curve	216
	14.5	Cross Tabulation	218
	14.6	Color Palettes	220
	14.7	Plotting a Cross Tabulation	220
	14.8	Summary	223

15 Political Alignment and Outlook — 225
	15.1	Are People Fair?	226
	15.2	Fairness Over Time	227
	15.3	Political Views on a 3-point Scale	228
	15.4	Fairness by Group	229
	15.5	Fairness over Time by Group	229
	15.6	Plotting the Results	230
	15.7	Simulating Possible Datasets	232
	15.8	Summary	234

V Case Study: Algorithmic Fairness — 235

16 Predicting Crime — 237
	16.1	Machine Bias	237
	16.2	Replicating the Analysis	239
	16.3	Data Bias	243
	16.4	Arranging the confusion matrix	244
	16.5	Accuracy	244
	16.6	Predictive Value	245
	16.7	Sensitivity and Specificity	246
	16.8	False Positive and Negative Rates	247
	16.9	All Metrics	250

17	**Algorithmic Fairness**		**253**
	17.1	The Response	253
	17.2	Calibration	254
	17.3	Matrices and Metrics	256
	17.4	What Would It Take?	258
	17.5	ROC Curve	263
	17.6	Concordance	265
	17.7	Summary	266
	17.8	Discussion	267

Further Reading   **269**

Index   **271**

Preface

Introduction

The goal of this book is to give you the tools you need to execute a data science project from beginning to end, including these steps:

- Choosing questions, data, and methods that go together

- Finding data or collecting it yourself

- Cleaning and validating data

- Exploring datasets and visualizing distributions and relationships between variables

- Modeling data and generating predictions

- Designing data visualizations that tell a compelling story

- Communicating results effectively

We'll start with basic Python programs and work our way up. My goal is to present a small, powerful subset of Python that allows you to do real work in data science as quickly as possible.

I won't assume you know anything about programming, statistics, or data science. When I use a term, I'll define it immediately, and when I use a programming feature, I'll explain it.

For each chapter in this book, there is a Jupyter notebook you can access from https://allendowney.github.io/ElementsOfDataScience. Jupyter is a software development tool you can run in a web browser, so you don't have to install any software. A Jupyter notebook is a document that contains text, Python code, and results. You can read it like a book, but you can also run the code, develop new programs, and test them.

The notebooks contain exercises where you can practice what you learn. Most of the exercises are meant to be quick, but a few are more substantial.

Book Overview

This book is organized in five parts.

Part I is an introduction to Python with emphasis on concepts and tools for working with data. It introduces Python data structures like lists and dictionaries, NumPy arrays, and Pandas DataFrames.

Part II is about exploratory data analysis, starting with the ways we represent and summarize the distribution of a variable, moving on to relationships between variables, and ending with linear and logistic regression.

Part III is about statistical inference – that is, using a sample to infer the properties of a population. It introduces randomization methods, especially bootstrap resampling, as a tool for estimating a quantity, describing the precision of the estimate, and testing hypotheses.

Part IV is the first of two case studies, an exploration of data from the General Social Survey related to political alignment and beliefs. In introduces tools for describing changes over time and differences between groups, including cross tabulations and pivot tables.

Part V is the second case study, which introduces classification algorithms and the metrics we use to evaluate their performance. It presents a particularly challenging topic in the criminal justice system, the use of algorithms to predict who is most likely to commit future crimes.

Here are more detailed descriptions of the chapters:

Chapter 1 introduces variables, values, and numerical computation.

Chapter 2 shows how to represent times, dates, and locations in Python, and uses the GeoPandas library to plot points on a map.

Chapter 3 presents lists and NumPy arrays. It discusses absolute, relative, and percent errors, and ways to summarize them.

Chapter 4 presents the `for` loop and the `if` statement; then it uses them to speed-read *War and Peace* and count the words.

Chapter 5 presents one of the most powerful features of Python, dictionaries, and uses them to count the unique words in a text and their frequencies.

Chapter 6 introduces a plotting library, Matplotlib, and uses it to generate a few common data visualizations and one less common one, a Zipf plot.

Chapter 7 presents Pandas DataFrames, which are used to represent tables of data. As an example, it uses data from the National Survey of Family Growth to find the average weight of babies in the U.S.

Chapter 8 explains what a distribution is and presents 3 ways to represent one: a PMF, CDF, or PDF. It also shows how to compare a distribution to another distribution or a mathematical model.

Chapter 9 explores relationships between variables using scatter plots, violin plots, and box plots. It quantifies the strength of a relationship using correlation, and uses simple regression to estimate the slope of a line.

Chapter 10 presents multiple regression and uses it to explore the relationship between age, education, and income. It uses visualization to interpret multivariate models. It also presents binary variables and logistic regression.

Chapter 11 presents computational methods we can use to quantify variation due to random sampling, which is one of several sources of error in statistical estimation.

Chapter 12 introduces bootstrapping, a kind of resampling that is well suited to computational statistics.

Chapter 13 uses a computational approach to explain hypothesis testing, which is the bugbear of classical statistics.

Chapter 14 is the beginning of a case study that uses data from the General Social Survey. It uses survey responses to explore political polarization in the United States over the last 50 years.

Chapter 15 is the second part of the case study – it explores the relationship between political alignment (conservative, moderate, or liberal) and other attitudes and beliefs.

Chapter 16 introduces the second case study, related to an algorithm used in the criminal justice system to predict crime. It replicates analysis reported in 2016 to evaluate the performance of the algorithm and its fairness between racial groups.

Chapter 17 extends the analysis in the previous chapter to address fairness between men and women, and explores different definitions of fairness and why they are hard to achieve.

Acknowledgments

This book started as a collaboration with an interdisciplinary team at Harvard University, assembled to develop a new data science course. I am grateful to my collaborators, Liberty Vittert, Hanspeter Pfister, Joe Blitzstein, Salma Abu Ayyash, Xiao-Li Meng, Aditya Ranganathan, Robert Haussman, Nishant Sule and Salma Abdel Magid. Special thanks to Aditya Ranganathan for also serving as a technical reviewer.

Part II is based on an online course I developed for DataCamp, called "Exploratory Data Analysis in Python". The course was retired recently after five very successful years. Thanks to the people at DataCamp who worked on it, including Chester Ismay and Yashas Roy.

Part III is based on material I created for my data science course at Olin College. As always, I am grateful to my former colleagues for their support, and to my students for their suggestions and corrections.

The case studies in Part IV are based on material I developed at Olin College and as a visiting lecturer at Ashesi University in Ghana. These chapters benefited from the students' diverse perspectives and insights.

This book was in development at No Starch Press, where Alex Freed provided valuable editorial guidance. I am also grateful to Jill Franklin and Bill Pollock.

Part I

From Python to Pandas

Chapter 1

Variables and Values

The topics in this chapter are:

- Basic programming features in Python: variables and values.
- Translating formulas from math notation to Python.

You don't need a lot of math to do data science, but and the end of this chapter I'll review one topic that comes up a lot: logarithms.

1.1 Numbers

Python provides tools for working with many kinds of data, including numbers, words, dates, times, and locations (latitude and longitude). Let's start with numbers. Python can work with several types of numbers, but the two most common are:

- `int`, which represents integer values like 3, and
- `float`, which represents numbers that have a fraction part, like 3.14159.

Most often, we use `int` to represent counts and `float` to represent measurements.

Here's an example of an `int`:

```
3
```
3

When you run a cell that contains a value like this, Jupyter displays the value.

Here's an example of a `float`:

```
3.14159
```
```
3.14159
```

`float` is short for "floating-point", which is the name for the way these numbers are stored. Floating-point numbers can also be written in a format similar to scientific notation:

```
1.2345e3
```
```
1234.5
```

This value is equivalent to 1.2345×10^3, so the result is `1234.5`. The `e` in `1.2345e3` stands for "exponent".

1.2 Arithmetic

Python provides operators that perform arithmetic. The operators that perform addition and subtraction are + and -:

```
3 + 2 - 1
```
```
4
```

The operators that perform multiplication and division are * and /:

```
2 * 3
```
```
6
```

```
2 / 3
```
```
0.6666666666666666
```

And the operator for exponentiation is **:

```
2 ** 3
```
```
8
```

Unlike math notation, Python does not allow implicit multiplication. For example, in math notation, if you write $3(2+1)$, that's understood to be the same as $3 \times (2+1)$. In Python, that's an error.

1.3 Math Functions

NOTE: The following example uses %%expect, which is a Jupyter "magic command" that means we expect an error.

```
%%expect TypeError

3 (2 + 1)
```

```
TypeError: 'int' object is not callable
```

In this example, the error message is not very helpful, which is why I am warning you now. If you want to multiply, you have to use the * operator.

The arithmetic operators follow the rules of precedence you might have learned as "PEMDAS":

- Parentheses before

- Exponentiation before

- Multiplication and division before

- Addition and subtraction.

So in this expression:

```
1 + 2 * 3
```

```
7
```

The multiplication happens first. If that's not what you want, you can use parentheses to make the order of operations explicit:

```
(1 + 2) * 3
```

```
9
```

Exercise: Write a Python expression that raises 1+2 to the power 3*4. The answer should be 531441.

1.3 Math Functions

Python provides functions that compute mathematical functions like `sin` and `cos`, `exp` and `log`. However, they are not part of Python itself, but they are available from a **library**, which is a collection of values and functions. The one we'll use is called NumPy, which stands for "Numerical Python", and is pronounced "num pie". Before you can use a library, you have to **import** it.

Here's how we import NumPy:

```
import numpy as np
```

This line of code imports `numpy` as `np`, which means we can refer to it by the short name `np` rather than the longer name `numpy`. Names like this are case-sensitive, which means that `numpy` is not the same as `NumPy`. So even though the name of the library is NumPy, when we import it we have to call it `numpy`.

```
%%expect ModuleNotFoundError

import NumPy as np
```

```
ModuleNotFoundError: No module named 'NumPy'
```

This error message might be confusing if you don't pay attention to the difference between uppercase and lowercase. But assuming we import `np` correctly, we can use it to read the value `pi`, which represents the mathematical constant π.

```
np.pi
```

```
3.141592653589793
```

The result is a `float` with 16 digits. As you might know, we can't represent π with a finite number of digits, so this result is only approximate.

NumPy provides `log`, which computes the natural logarithm

```
np.log(100)
```

```
4.605170185988092
```

NumPy also provides `exp`, which raises the constant `e` to a power.

```
np.exp(1)
```

```
2.718281828459045
```

Exercise: Use these functions to check the identity $\log(e^x) = x$. Mathematically, it is true for any value of x. With floating-point values, it only holds for values of x between -700 and 700. What happens when you try it with larger and smaller values?

1.4 Variables

Floating-point numbers are finite approximations, which means they don't always behave like math. As another example, let's see what happens if we add up `0.1` three times:

```
0.1 + 0.1 + 0.1
```

0.30000000000000004

The result is close to `0.3`, but not exact. When you work with floating-point numbers, remember that they are only approximately correct.

1.4 Variables

A **variable** is a name that refers to a value. The following statement assigns the value 5 to a variable named `x`:

```
x = 5
```

The variable we just created has the name `x` and the value 5.

If we use `x` as part of an arithmetic operation, it represents the value 5:

```
x + 1
```

6

```
x ** 2
```

25

We can also use a variable when we call a function:

```
np.exp(x)
```

148.4131591025766

Notice that the result from `exp` is a `float`, even though the value of `x` is an `int`.

Exercise: If you have not programmed before, one of the things you have to get used to is that programming languages are picky about details. Natural languages, like English, and semi-formal languages, like math notation, are more forgiving.

As an example, in math notation, parentheses and square brackets mean the same thing, you can write $\sin(\omega t)$ or $\sin[\omega t]$ – either one is fine. And you can leave out the parentheses altogether, as long as the meaning is clear, as in $\sin \omega t$. In Python, every character counts. For example, the following are all different, and only the first one works:

```
np.exp(x)
np.Exp(x)
np.exp[x]
np.exp x
```

While you are learning, I encourage you to make mistakes on purpose to see what goes wrong. Read the error messages carefully. Sometimes they are helpful and tell you exactly what's wrong. Other times they can be misleading. But if you have seen the message before, you might remember some likely causes.

Exercise: The NumPy function that computes square roots is `sqrt`. Use it to compute a floating-point approximation of the golden ratio, $\phi = \frac{1}{2}(1 + \sqrt{5})$. Hint: The result should be close to `1.618`.

1.5 Calculating with Variables

Now we'll use variables to solve a problem involving compound interest. It might not be the most exciting example, but it uses everything we have done so far, and it reviews exponentiation and logarithms, which we are going to need.

If we invest an amount of money, P, in an account that earns compounded interest, the total accumulated value, V, after an interval of time, t, is:

$$V = P\left(1 + \frac{r}{n}\right)^{nt}$$

where r is the annual interest rate and n is the compounding frequency. For example, if you deposit $2,100 in a bank paying an annual interest rate of 3.4% compounded four times a year, we can compute the balance after 7 years by defining these variables:

```
P = 2100
r = 0.034
n = 4
t = 7
```

And computing the total accumulated value like this.

```
P * (1 + r/n)**(n*t)
```

2661.6108980682593

Exercise: Continuing the previous example, suppose you start with the same principle and the same interest rate, but interest is compounded twice per year, so `n = 2`. What would the total value be after 7 years? Hint: we expect the answer to be a bit less than the previous answer.

Exercise: If interest is compounded continuously, the value after time t is $V = P\,e^{rt}$. Translate this equation into Python and use it compute the value of the investment in the previous example with continuous compounding. Hint: we expect the answer to be a bit more than the previous answers.

1.6 Summary

This chapter introduces variables, which are names that refer to values, and two kinds of values, integers and floating-point numbers.

It presents mathematical operators, like + for addition and * for multiplication, and mathematical functions like `log` for logarithms and `exp` for raising `e` to a power.

In the next chapter, we'll see additional data types for representing letters and words, dates and times, and latitude and longitude.

Chapter 2

Times and Places

The previous chapter introduces variables and two kinds of values: integers and floating-point numbers. This chapter presents these additional types:

- Strings, which represent text.
- Time stamps, which represent dates and times.
- And several ways to represent and display geographical locations.

Not every data science project uses all of these types, but many projects use at least one.

2.1 Strings

A **string** is a sequence of letters, numbers, and punctuation marks. In Python you can create a string by enclosing text between single or double quotation marks.

```
'Elements'
```
'Elements'

```
"of"
```
'of'

And you can assign string values to variables.

```
first = 'Data'
last = "Science"
```

Some arithmetic operators work with strings, but they might not do what you expect. For example, the + operator **concatenates** two strings – that is, it creates a new string that contains the first string followed by the second string:

```
first + last
```

'DataScience'

If you want to put a space between the words, you can use a string that contains a space:

```
first + ' ' + last
```

'Data Science'

Strings are used to store text data like names, addresses, titles, etc. When you read data from a file, you might see values that look like numbers, but they are actually strings, like this:

```
not_actually_a_number = '123'
```

If you try to do math with these strings, you *might* get an error.

```
%%expect TypeError

not_actually_a_number + 1
```

TypeError: can only concatenate str (not "int") to str

But you might not – instead, you might get a surprising result. For example:

```
not_actually_a_number * 3
```

'123123123'

If you multiply a string by an integer, Python repeats the string the given number of times.

If you have a string that contains only digits, you can convert it to an integer using the `int` function:

```
int('123')
```

123

2.2 Representing Dates and Times

Or you can convert it to a floating-point number using `float`:

```
float('12.3')
```
12.3

But if the string contains a decimal point, you can't convert it to an `int`.

```
%%expect ValueError

int('12.3')
```
ValueError: invalid literal for int() with base 10: '12.3'

Going in the other direction, you can convert any type of value to a string using `str`:

```
str(123)
```
'123'

```
str(12.3)
```
'12.3'

Exercise: When personal names are stored in a database, they might be stored in variables representing one or more given names, family names, and maybe additional middle names. For example, a list of early statisticians might include:

```
given = 'William'
middle = 'Sealy'
family = 'Gosset'
```

But names are often displayed different ways in different contexts. For example, the first time you mention someone in a book, you might give all three names, like "William Sealy Gosset". But in the index, you might put the family name first, like "Gosset, William Sealy". Write Python expressions that use the variables `given`, `middle`, and `family` to display Gosset's name in these two formats.

2.2 Representing Dates and Times

When you read data from a file, you might find that dates and times are represented with strings.

```
not_really_a_date = 'June 4, 1989'
```

To check the type of a value, we can use the `type` function.

```
type(not_really_a_date)
```

str

The result indicates that the value of `not_really_a_date` is a string.

We get the same result with `not_really_a_time`, below:

```
not_really_a_time = '6:30:00'
type(not_really_a_time)
```

str

Strings that represent dates and times are readable for people, but they are not useful for computation. Fortunately, Python provides libraries for working with date and time data – the one we'll use is called Pandas. As always, we have to import a library before we use it. It is conventional to import Pandas with the abbreviated name `pd`:

```
import pandas as pd
```

Pandas provides a type called `Timestamp`, which represents a date and time. If we have a string that contains a time or date, we can convert it to a `Timestamp` like this:

```
pd.Timestamp('6:30:00')
```

Timestamp('2024-05-18 06:30:00')

Or we can do the same thing using the variable defined above.

```
pd.Timestamp(not_really_a_time)
```

Timestamp('2024-05-18 06:30:00')

In this example, the string specifies a time but no date, so Pandas fills in today's date. A `Timestamp` is a value, so you can assign it to a variable.

```
date_of_birth = pd.Timestamp('May 11, 1967')
date_of_birth
```

Timestamp('1967-05-11 00:00:00')

If the string specifies a date but no time, Pandas fills in midnight as the default time.

2.3 Timedelta

If you assign the `Timestamp` to a variable, you can use the variable name to get the year, month, and day, like this:

```
date_of_birth.year, date_of_birth.month, date_of_birth.day
```

(1967, 5, 11)

You can also get the name of the month and the day of the week.

```
date_of_birth.day_name(), date_of_birth.month_name()
```

('Thursday', 'May')

`Timestamp` provides a function called `now` that returns the current date and time.

```
now = pd.Timestamp.now()
now
```

Timestamp('2024-05-18 15:04:03.507085')

Exercise: Use the value of `now` to display the name of the current month and day of the week.

2.3 Timedelta

`Timestamp` values support some arithmetic operations. For example, you can compute the difference between two `Timestamp` objects:

```
age = now - date_of_birth
age
```

Timedelta('20827 days 15:04:03.507085')

The result is a `Timedelta` that represents the current age of someone born on `date_of_birth`. The `Timedelta` contains `components` that store the number of days, hours, etc. between the two `Timestamp` values.

```
from utils import wrap

wrap(age.components)
```

Components(days=20827, hours=15, minutes=4, seconds=3,
    milliseconds=507, microseconds=85, nanoseconds=0)

You can get one of the components like this:

```
age.days
```

20827

It might seem strange to measure a large interval in days rather than years. The problem is that the duration of a year is not clearly defined. Most years are 365 days, but some are 366. The average calendar year is 365.24 days, which is a very good approximation of a solar year, but even that's not exact.

Expressing a duration in days is clearly defined – but it is not easy to interpret. To express `age` in years, we can divide by 365.24:

```
age.days / 365.24
```

57.022779542218814

But people usually report their ages in integer years. We can use the Numpy `floor` function to round down:

```
import numpy as np

np.floor(age.days / 365.24)
```

57.0

Or the `ceil` function (which stands for "ceiling") to round up:

```
np.ceil(age.days / 365.24)
```

58.0

We can also compare `Timestamp` values to see which comes first. For example, let's see if a person with a given birthdate has already had a birthday this year. Here's a new `Timestamp` with the year from `now` and the month and day from `date_of_birth`.

```
bday_this_year = pd.Timestamp(now.year,
                              date_of_birth.month,
                              date_of_birth.day)
bday_this_year
```

Timestamp('2024-05-11 00:00:00')

The result represents the person's birthday this year.

2.4 Representing Location

Now we can use the "greater than" operator, >, to check whether `now` is later than the birthday:

```
now > bday_this_year
```

True

The result is either `True` or `False`. These values belong to a type called `bool`. The name comes from "Boolean algebra", which is a branch of algebra where all values are either true or false.

```
type(True)
```

bool

```
type(False)
```

bool

Exercise: Any two people with different birthdays have a "Double Day" when one is twice as old as the other. Suppose you are given two `Timestamp` values, `d1` and `d2`, that represent birthdays for two people. Use `Timestamp` arithmetic to compute their double day. With the following dates, the result should be December 19, 2009.

```
d1 = pd.Timestamp('2003-07-12')
d2 = pd.Timestamp('2006-09-30')
```

2.4 Representing Location

In addition to times and dates, we might also want to represent locations, especially if we are working with geographical data. There are many ways to represent locations, but the most common, at least for global data, is latitude and longitude. When stored in a string, latitude and longitude are expressed in degrees with compass directions N, S, E, and W. For example, this string represents the location of Boston, Massachusetts, USA:

```
lat_lon_string = '42.3601° N, 71.0589° W'
```

But for purposes of computation it is more common to represent longitude and latitude with two floating-point numbers, with

- Positive latitude for locations in the northern hemisphere, negative latitude for the southern hemisphere, and

- Positive longitude locations in the eastern hemisphere and negative longitude for the western hemisphere.

The location of the origin and the orientation of positive and negative are arbitrary choices that were made for historical reasons.

Here's how we might represent the location of Boston with two variables.

```
lat = 42.3601
lon = -71.0589
```

It is also possible to combine two numbers into a composite value and assign it to a single variable:

```
boston = lat, lon
boston
```

(42.3601, -71.0589)

The type of this variable is `tuple`, which is a mathematical term for a value that contains a sequence of elements. Math people pronounce it "tuh' ple", but computational people usually say "too' ple". Either is fine.

```
type(boston)
```

tuple

If you have a tuple with two elements, you can assign them to two variables, like this:

```
y, x = boston
y
```

42.3601

```
x
```

-71.0589

Notice that I assigned latitude to `y` and longitude to `x`, because a `y` coordinate usually goes up and down like latitude, and an `x` coordinate usually goes side-to-side like longitude.

Exercise: Find the latitude and longitude of the place you were born or someplace you think of as your "home town". Make a tuple of floating-point numbers that represents that location.

2.5 Calculating Distance

If you are given two tuples that represent locations, you can compute the approximate distance between them, along the surface of the globe, using the haversine function:

$$\text{haversine}(\theta) = \sin^2(\theta/2)$$

where θ is an angle in radians.

2.6 Defining Functions

We can compute this function in Python like this:

```python
import numpy as np

θ = 1
np.sin(θ/2)**2
```

0.22984884706593015

You can use Greek letters in variable names, but there is currently no way to type them in Jupyter/Colab, so I usually copy them from a web page and paste them in. To avoid the inconvenience, it is common to write out letter names, like this:

```python
theta = 1
np.sin(theta/2)**2
```

0.22984884706593015

Remember that the operator for exponentiation is `**`. In some other languages it's `^`, which is also an operator in Python, but it performs another operation altogether.

2.6 Defining Functions

If we are planning to use an expression like `np.sin(theta/2)**2` more than a few times, we can define a new function that computes it, like this:

```python
def haversine(theta):
    """Compute the haversine function of theta."""
    return np.sin(theta/2)**2
```

On the first line, `def` indicates that we are defining a function. The second line is a triple-quoted string, which is a **comment**: it describes what the function does, but has no effect when the program runs. On the third line, `return` indicates the result of the function.

When you run the previous cell, it creates a new variable called `haversine`. You can display its value like this:

```python
haversine
```

<function __main__.haversine(theta)>

And you can display its type like this:

```python
type(haversine)
```

function

So `haversine` is a variable that refers to a function. To run the function and compute a result, we have to **call** the function and provide a value for `theta`:

```
haversine(1)
```

```
0.22984884706593015
```

When you define a function, you create a new variable. But the function doesn't actually run until you call it.

2.7 Haversine Distance

Now we can use `haversine` as part of a function that computes haversine distances. I won't explain this function in as much detail, but if you read through it, you can get a sense of how it works.

```python
def haversine_distance(coord1, coord2):
    """Haversine distance between two locations.
    
    coord1: lat-lon as tuple of float
    coord2: lat-lon as tuple of float
    
    returns: distance in km
    """
    R = 6372.8   # Earth radius in km
    lat1, lon1 = coord1
    lat2, lon2 = coord2
    
    phi1, phi2 = np.radians(lat1), np.radians(lat2)
    dphi = np.radians(lat2 - lat1)
    dlambda = np.radians(lon2 - lon1)
    
    a = haversine(dphi) + np.cos(phi1) * np.cos(phi2) * haversine(dlambda)
    
    distance = 2 * R * np.arctan2(np.sqrt(a), np.sqrt(1 - a))
    
    return distance
```

When we call this function, we provide two tuples – each is a latitude-longitude pair. We already have a tuple that represents the location of Boston. Now here's a tuple that represents the location of London, England, UK:

```
london = 51.5074, -0.1278
```

2.8 Geopandas

And here's the haversine distance between Boston and London.

```
haversine_distance(boston, london)
```

5265.656325981015

The actual geographic distance is slightly different because Earth is not a perfect sphere. But the error of this estimate is less than 1%.

Exercise: Use `haversine_distance` to compute the distance between Boston and your home town from the previous exercise. If possible, use an online map to check the result.

2.8 Geopandas

Python provides libraries for working with geographical data. One of the most popular is Geopandas, which is based on Pandas and another library called Shapely. Shapely provides `Point` and `LineString` values, which we'll use to represent geographic locations and lines between them.

```python
from shapely.geometry import Point, LineString
```

We can use the tuples we defined in the previous section to create Shapely `Point` values, but we have to reverse the order of the coordinates, providing them in `x-y` order rather than `lat-lon` order, because that's the order the `Point` function expects.

```python
lat, lon = boston
p1 = Point(lon, lat)
```

```python
lat, lon = london
p2 = Point(lon, lat)
```

We can use the points we just defined to create a `LineString`:

```python
line = LineString([p1, p2])
```

Now we can use Geopandas to show these points and lines on a map. The following cells load a map of the world and plot it.

```python
from geodatasets import fetch

fetch('naturalearth.land')
```

```python
from geodatasets import get_path

path = get_path('naturalearth.land')
```

```
import geopandas as gpd
world = gpd.read_file(path)
world.plot(color='white', edgecolor='gray');
```

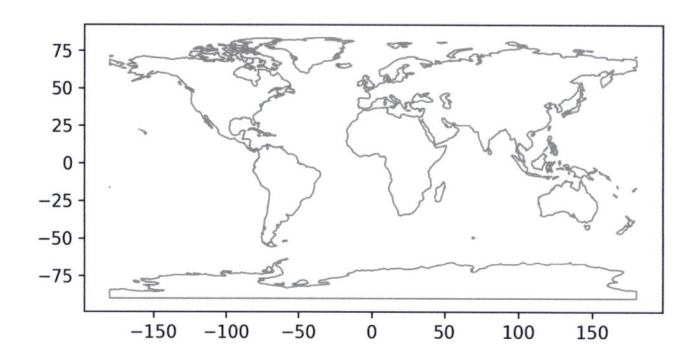

By default, Geopandas uses an equirectangular projection, which provides a misleading picture of relative land areas. Other projections are available that show land areas accurately, but they can be misleading in other ways. You can't make a map without making visualization decisions.

Now let's put dots on the map for Boston and London. First, we have to put the `Point` values and the `LineString` into a `GeoSeries`.

```
t = [p1, p2, line]
series = gpd.GeoSeries(t)
```

Here's a first attempt to plot the maps and the lines together:

```
# plot the map
world.plot(color='white', edgecolor='gray')

# plot Boston, London, and the line
series.plot();
```

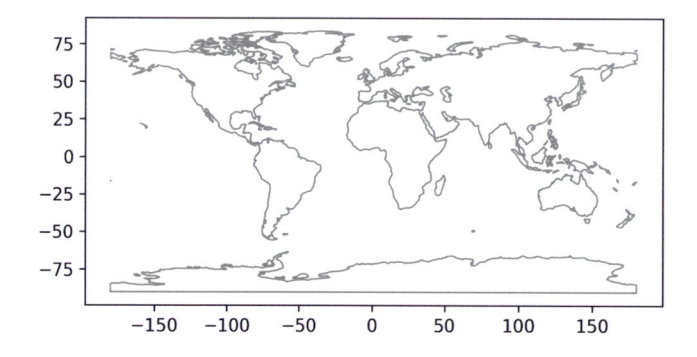

2.9 Summary

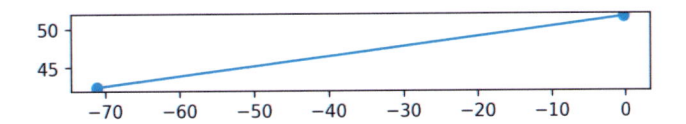

The two plots are on different axes, which is not what we want in this case.

To get the points and the map on the same axes, we have to use a function from Matplotlib, which is a visualization library we will use extensively. We'll import it like this.

```
import matplotlib.pyplot as plt
```

From Matplotlib, we'll use the function `gca`, which stands for "get current axes". With the result we can tell `plot` to put the points and lines on the current axes, rather than create a new one.

```
ax = plt.gca()
world.plot(color='white', edgecolor='gray', ax=ax)
series.plot(ax=ax);
```

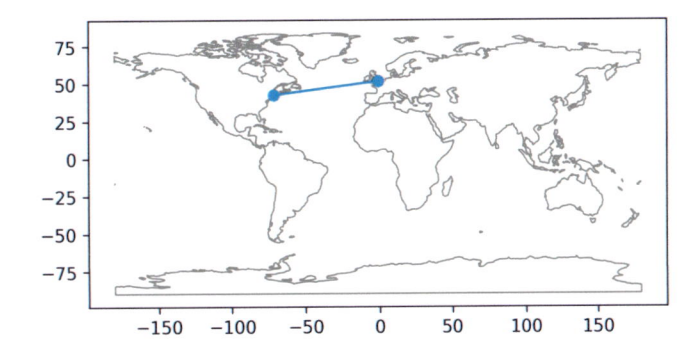

Exercise: Modify the code in this section to plot a point that shows the home town you chose in a previous exercise and a line from there to Boston.

2.9 Summary

This chapter presents three new data types: strings to represent letters and words, `Timestamp` objects to represent dates and times, and tuples to represent latitude, longitude pairs. It also introduces Geopandas, a library for working with location data.

In the next chapter we'll see two ways to represent a collection of data, a Python list and a Numpy array.

Chapter 3

Lists and Arrays

In the previous chapter we used tuples to represent latitude and longitude. In this chapter, we'll use tuples more generally to represent a sequence of values. And we'll see two more ways to represent sequences: lists and arrays.

You might wonder why we need three ways to represent the same thing. Most of the time we don't, but each of them has different capabilities. For work with data, we will use arrays most of the time.

As an example, we will use a small dataset from an article in *The Economist* about the price of sandwiches. It's a silly example, but I'll use it to introduce relative differences and ways to summarize them.

3.1 Tuples

A tuple is a sequence of elements. When we use a tuple to represent latitude and longitude, the sequence only contains two elements, and they are both floating-point numbers. But in general a tuple can contain any number of elements, and the elements can be values of any type. For example, here's a tuple of two strings.

```
('Data', 'Science')
```

('Data', 'Science')

The elements don't have to be the same type. Here's a tuple with a string, an integer, and a floating-point number.

```
('one', 2, 3.14159)
```

('one', 2, 3.14159)

When you create a tuple, the parentheses are optional, but the commas are required. So how do you think you create a tuple with a single element? You might be tempted to write:

```
x = (5)
x
```

```
5
```

But you will find that the result is just a number, not a tuple. To make a tuple with a single element, you need a comma:

```
t = (5,)
t
```

```
(5,)
```

That might look funny, but it does the job.

If you have a string, you can convert it to a tuple using the `tuple` function:

```
tuple('DataScience')
```

```
('D', 'a', 't', 'a', 'S', 'c', 'i', 'e', 'n', 'c', 'e')
```

The result is a sequence of single-character strings. You can also use the `tuple` function to make an empty tuple – that is, one that has no elements.

```
tuple()
```

```
()
```

3.2 Lists

Python provides another way to store a sequence of elements: a **list**. To create a list, you put a sequence of elements in square brackets.

```
[1, 2, 3]
```

```
[1, 2, 3]
```

Lists and tuples are very similar. They can contain any number of elements, the elements can be any type, and the elements don't have to be the same type. The difference is that you can modify a list and you can't modify a tuple – that is, tuples are **immutable**. This difference will matter later, but for now we can ignore it.

3.3 Sandwich Prices

When you make a list, the brackets are required, but if there is a single element, you don't need a comma. So you can make a list like this:

```
single = [5]
```

It is also possible to make a list with no elements, like this:

```
empty = []
```

The `len` function returns the length (number of elements) in a list or tuple.

```
len([1, 2, 3]), len(single), len(empty)
```

(3, 1, 0)

There's more we could do with lists, but that's enough to get started. In the next section, we'll use lists to store data about sandwich prices.

Exercise: Create a list with 4 elements. Then use `type` to confirm that it's a list, and `len` to confirm that it has 4 elements.

3.3 Sandwich Prices

In September 2019, *The Economist* published an article comparing sandwich prices in Boston and London, called "Why Americans pay more for lunch than Britons do".

It includes this graph showing prices of several sandwiches in the two cities:

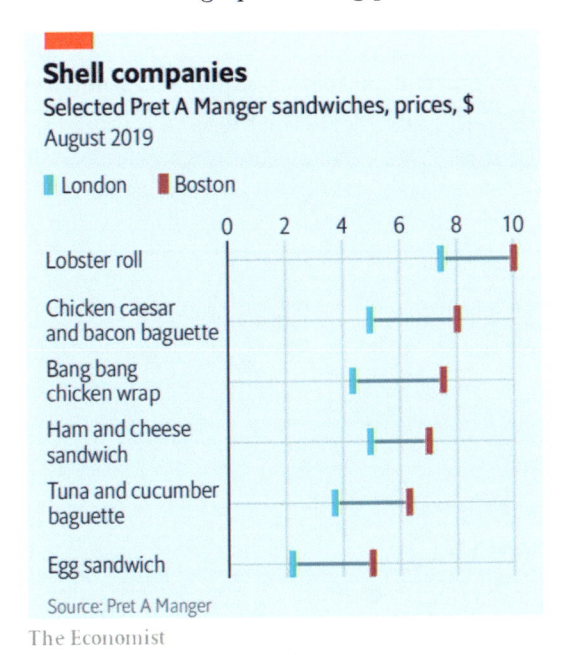

Shell companies
Selected Pret A Manger sandwiches, prices, $
August 2019

London   Boston

Sandwich	
Lobster roll	
Chicken caesar and bacon baguette	
Bang bang chicken wrap	
Ham and cheese sandwich	
Tuna and cucumber baguette	
Egg sandwich	

Source: Pret A Manger

The Economist

Here are the sandwich names from the graph, as a list of strings.

```
name_list = [
    'Lobster roll',
    'Chicken caesar',
    'Bang bang chicken',
    'Ham and cheese',
    'Tuna and cucumber',
    'Egg'
]
```

I contacted *The Economist* to ask for the data they used to create that graph, and they were kind enough to share it with me. Here are the sandwich prices in Boston:

```
boston_price_list = [9.99, 7.99, 7.49, 7.00, 6.29, 4.99]
```

Here are the prices in London, converted to dollars at $1.25 / £1.

```
london_price_list = [7.5, 5, 4.4, 5, 3.75, 2.25]
```

Lists provide some arithmetic operators, but they might not do what you want. For example, the + operator works with lists:

```
boston_price_list + london_price_list
```

[9.99, 7.99, 7.49, 7.0, 6.29, 4.99, 7.5, 5, 4.4, 5, 3.75, 2.25]

But it concatenates the two lists, which is not very useful in this example. To compute differences between prices, you might try subtracting lists, but it doesn't work.

We can solve this problem with NumPy.

3.4 NumPy Arrays

We've already seen that the NumPy library provides math functions. It also provides a type of sequence called an **array**. You can create a new array with the `np.array` function, starting with a list or tuple.

```
import numpy as np

boston_price_array = np.array(boston_price_list)
london_price_array = np.array(london_price_list)
```

3.4 NumPy Arrays

The type of the result is `numpy.ndarray`.

```
type(boston_price_array)
```

numpy.ndarray

The "nd" stands for "n-dimensional", which indicates that NumPy arrays can have any number of dimensions. But for now we will work with one-dimensional sequences. If you display an array, Python displays the elements:

```
boston_price_array
```

array([9.99, 7.99, 7.49, 7. , 6.29, 4.99])

You can also display the **data type** of the array, which is the type of the elements:

```
boston_price_array.dtype
```

dtype('float64')

`float64` means that the elements are floating-point numbers that take up 64 bits each. The elements of a NumPy array can be any type, but they all have to be the same type. Most often the elements are numbers, but you can also make an array of strings.

```
name_array = np.array(name_list)
name_array
```

array(['Lobster roll', 'Chicken caesar', 'Bang bang chicken',
       'Ham and cheese', 'Tuna and cucumber', 'Egg'], dtype='<U17')

In this example, the `dtype` is `<U17`. The `U` indicates that the elements are Unicode strings. Unicode is the standard Python uses to represent strings. The number 17 is the length of the longest string in the array.

Now, here's why NumPy arrays are useful – they can do arithmetic. For example, to compute the differences between Boston and London prices, we can write:

```
differences = boston_price_array - london_price_array
differences
```

array([2.49, 2.99, 3.09, 2. , 2.54, 2.74])

Subtraction is done **elementwise** – that is, NumPy lines up the two arrays and subtracts corresponding elements. The result is a new array.

3.5 Statistical Summaries

NumPy provides functions that compute statistical summaries like the mean:

```
np.mean(differences)
```

2.6416666666666666

So we could describe the difference in prices like this: "Sandwiches in Boston are more expensive by $2.64, on average". We could also compute the means first, and then compute their difference:

```
np.mean(boston_price_array) - np.mean(london_price_array)
```

2.6416666666666675

And that turns out to be the same thing – the difference in means is the same as the mean of the differences.

As an aside, many of the NumPy functions also work with lists, so we could also do this:

```
np.mean(boston_price_list) - np.mean(london_price_list)
```

2.6416666666666675

Exercise: Standard deviation is way to quantify the variability in a set of numbers. The NumPy function that computes standard deviation is `np.std`.

Compute the standard deviation of sandwich prices in Boston and London. By this measure, which set of prices is more variable?

3.6 Relative Difference

In the previous section we computed differences between prices. But often when we make this kind of comparison, we are interested in **relative differences**, which are differences expressed as a fraction or percentage of a quantity. Taking the lobster roll as an example, the difference in price is:

```
9.99 - 7.5
```

2.49

We can express that difference as a fraction of the London price, like this:

```
(9.99 - 7.5) / 7.5
```

0.332

3.7 Summarizing Relative Differences

Or as a *percentage* of the London price, like this:

```
(9.99 - 7.5) / 7.5 * 100
```

33.2

So we might say that the lobster roll is 33% more expensive in Boston. But putting London in the denominator was an arbitrary choice. We could also compute the difference as a percentage of the Boston price:

```
(9.99 - 7.5) / 9.99 * 100
```

24.924924924924927

If we do that calculation, we might say the lobster roll is 25% cheaper in London. When you read this kind of comparison, you should make sure you understand which quantity is in the denominator, and you might want to think about why that choice was made. In this example, if you want to make the difference seem bigger, you might put London prices in the denominator.

If we do the same calculation with the arrays of prices, we can compute the relative differences for all sandwiches:

```
differences = boston_price_array - london_price_array
relative_differences = differences / london_price_array
relative_differences
```

array([0.332   , 0.598   , 0.70227273, 0.4   , 0.67733333,
       1.21777778])

And the percent differences.

```
percent_differences = relative_differences * 100
percent_differences
```

array([33.2   , 59.8   , 70.22727273, 40.   ,
        67.73333333, 121.77777778])

3.7 Summarizing Relative Differences

Now let's think about how to summarize an array of percentage differences. One option is to report the range, which we can compute with `np.min` and `np.max`.

```
np.min(percent_differences), np.max(percent_differences)
```

(33.2, 121.77777777777779)

The lobster roll is only 33% more expensive in Boston; the egg sandwich is 121% percent more (that is, more than twice the price).

Exercise: What are the percent differences if we put the Boston prices in the denominator? What is the range of those differences? Write a sentence that summarizes the results.

Another way to summarize percentage differences is to report the mean.

```
np.mean(percent_differences)
```

65.4563973063973

So we might say that sandwiches are 65% more expensive in Boston, on average.

Another way to summarize the data is to compute the mean price in each city, and then compute the percentage difference of the means:

```
boston_mean = np.mean(boston_price_array)
london_mean = np.mean(london_price_array)

(boston_mean - london_mean) / london_mean * 100
```

56.81003584229393

Based on this calculation we might say that the average sandwich price is 56% higher in Boston. As this example demonstrates:

- With relative and percentage differences, the mean of the differences is not the same as the difference of the means.

- When you report data like this, you should think about different ways to summarize the data.

- When you read a summary of data like this, make sure you understand what summary was chosen and what it means.

In this example, I think the second option (the relative difference in the means) is more meaningful, because it reflects the difference in price between "baskets of goods" that include one of each sandwich.

3.8 Debugging

So far, most of the exercises have only required a few lines of code. If you made errors along the way, you probably found them quickly. As we go along, the exercises will be more substantial, and you may find yourself spending more time debugging.

3.8 Debugging

Here are a couple of suggestions to help you find errors quickly – and avoid them in the first place.

- Most importantly, you should develop code incrementally – that is, you should write a small amount of code and test it. If it works, add more code; otherwise, debug what you have.

- Conversely, if you have written too much code, and you are having a hard time debugging it, split it into smaller chunks and debug them separately.

For example, suppose you want to compute, for each sandwich in the sandwich list, the midpoint of the Boston and London prices.

As a first draft, you might write something like this:

```
boston_price_list = [9.99, 7.99, 7.49, 7, 6.29, 4.99]
london_price_list = [7.5, 5, 4.4, 5, 3.75, 2.25]

midpoint_price = np.mean(boston_price_list + london_price_list)
midpoint_price
```

5.970833333333334

This code runs, and it produces an answer, but the answer is a single number rather than the list we were expecting.

You might have already spotted the error, but let's suppose you did not. To debug this code, I would start by splitting the computation into smaller steps and displaying the intermediate results. For example, we might add the two lists and display the result, like this.

```
total_price = boston_price_list + london_price_list
total_price
```

[9.99, 7.99, 7.49, 7, 6.29, 4.99, 7.5, 5, 4.4, 5, 3.75, 2.25]

Looking at the result, we see that it did not add the sandwich prices elementwise, as we intended. Because the arguments are lists, the + operator concatenates them rather than adding the elements. We can solve this problem by using the arrays rather than the lists.

```
total_price_array = boston_price_array + london_price_array
total_price_array
```

array([17.49, 12.99, 11.89, 12. , 10.04, 7.24])

And then computing the midpoint of each pair of prices, like this:

```
midpoint_price_array = total_price_array / 2
midpoint_price_array
```

array([8.745, 6.495, 5.945, 6.   , 5.02 , 3.62])

As you gain experience, you will be able to write bigger chunks of code before testing. But while you are getting started, keep it simple! As a general rule, each line of code should perform a small number of operations, and each cell should contain a small number of statements.

3.9 Summary

This chapter presents three ways to represent a sequence of values: tuples, lists, and Numpy arrays. Working with data, we will primarily use arrays.

It also introduces three ways to represent differences: absolute, relative, and percentage – and several ways to summarize a set of values: minimum, maximum, mean, and standard deviation.

In the next chapter we'll start working with data files, and we'll use loops to process letters and words.

Chapter 4

Loops and Files

This chapter presents loops, which are used to perform repeated computation, and files, which are used to store data. As an example, we will download the famous book *War and Peace* and write a loop that reads the book and counts the words. This example presents some new computational tools – it is also an introduction to working with textual data.

4.1 Loops

One of the most important elements of computation is repetition, and the most common way to perform repetitive computations is a `for` loop. As a simple example, suppose we want to display the elements of a tuple. Here's a tuple of three integers:

```
t = (1, 2, 3)
```

And here's a `for` loop that prints the elements.

```
for x in t:
    print(x)
```

```
1
2
3
```

The first line of the loop is a **header** that specifies the tuple, `t`, and a variable name, `x`. The tuple must already exists, but if `x` does not, the loop will create it. Note that the header ends with a colon, :.

Inside the loop is a `print` statement, which displays the value of `x`. So here's what happens:

1. When the loop starts, it gets the first element of `t`, which is 1, and assigns it to `x`. It executes the `print` statement, which displays the value 1.

2. Then it gets the second element of `t`, which is 2, and displays it.

3. Then it gets the third element of `t`, which is 3, and displays it.

After printing the last element of the tuple, the loop ends. We can also loop through the letters in a string:

```
word = 'Data'

for letter in word:
    print(letter)
```
```
D
a
t
a
```

When the loop begins, `word` already exists, but `letter` does not. Again, the loop creates `letter` and assigns values to it. The variable created by the loop is called the **loop variable**. You can give it any name you like – in this example, I chose `letter` to remind me what kind of value it contains. After the loop ends, the loop variable contains the last value.

```
letter
```
```
'a'
```

Exercise: Create a list called `sequence` with four elements of any type. Write a `for` loop that prints the elements. Call the loop variable `element`.

4.2 Counting with Loops

Inside a loop, it is common to use a variable to count the number of times something happens. We've already seen that you can create a variable and give it a value, like this:

```
count = 0
count
```
```
0
```

4.2 Counting with Loops

If you assign a different value to the same variable, the new value replaces the old one.

```
count = 1
count
```

1

You can increase the value of a variable by reading the old value, adding 1, and assigning the result back to the original variable.

```
count = count + 1
count
```

2

Increasing the value of a variable is called **incrementing** and decreasing the value is called **decrementing**. These operations are so common that there are special operators for them.

```
count += 1
count
```

3

In this example, the `+=` operator reads the value of `count`, adds 1, and assigns the result back to `count`. Python also provides `-=` and other update operators like `*=` and `/=`.

Exercise: The following is a number trick from the website *Learn With Math Games*:

> *Finding Someone's Age*
>
> - Ask the person to multiply the first number of their age by 5.
> - Tell them to add 3.
> - Now tell them to double this figure.
> - Finally, have the person add the second number of their age to the figure and have them tell you the answer.
> - Deduct 6 and you will have their age.

Test this algorithm using your age. Use a single variable and update it using `+=` and other update operators.

4.3 Files

Now that we know how to count, let's see how to read words from a file. As an example, we'll read a file that contains the text of Tolstoy's famous novel, *War and Peace*. We can download it from Project Gutenberg, which is a repository of free books. Instructions are in the notebook for this chapter.

In order to read the contents of the file, you have to **open** it, which you can do with the `open` function.

```
fp = open('2600-0.txt')
fp
```

```
<_io.TextIOWrapper name='2600-0.txt' mode='r' encoding='UTF-8'>
```

The result is a `TextIOWrapper`, which is a type of **file pointer**. It contains the name of the file, the mode (which is `r` for "reading") and the encoding (which is `UTF` for "Unicode Transformation Format"). A file pointer is like a bookmark – it keeps track of which parts of the file you have read.

If you use a file pointer in a `for` loop, it loops through the lines in the file. So we can count the number of lines like this:

```
fp = open('2600-0.txt')
count = 0
for line in fp:
    count += 1
```

And then display the result.

```
count
```

```
66050
```

There are about 66,000 lines in this file.

4.4 if Statements

`if` statements are used to check whether a condition is true and, depending on the result, perform different computations. A condition is an expression whose value is either `True` or `False`. For example, the following expression compares the final value of `count` to a number:

```
count > 60000
```

```
True
```

For *War and Peace*, the result is `True`.

4.4 if Statements

We can use this condition in an `if` statement to display a message, or not, depending on the result.

```
if count > 60000:
    print('Long book!')
```
Long book!

The first line specifies the condition we're checking for. Like the header of a `for` statement, the first line of an `if` statement has to end with a colon.

If the condition is true, the indented statement runs; otherwise, it doesn't. In the previous example, the condition is true, so the `print` statement runs. In the following example, the condition is false, so the `print` statement doesn't run.

```
if count < 1000:
    print('Short book!')
```

We can put an `if` statement inside a `for` loop. The following example only prints a line from the book when `count` is 0. The other lines are read, but not displayed.

```
fp = open('2600-0.txt')
count = 0
for line in fp:
    if count == 0:
        print(line)
    count += 1
```
The Project Gutenberg EBook of War and Peace, by Leo Tolstoy

Notice that we use == to compare values and check if they are equal, not =, which is used in assignment statements. Also, notice the indentation in this example:

- Statements inside the `for` loop are indented.

- The statement inside the `if` statement is indented.

- The statement `count += 1` is **outdented** from the previous line, so it ends the `if` statement. But it is still inside the `for` loop.

It is legal in Python to use spaces or tabs for indentation, but the most common convention is to use four spaces, never tabs.

4.5 The `break` Statement

If we display the final value of `count`, we see that the loop reads the entire file, but only prints one line:

```
count
```

```
66050
```

We can avoid reading the whole file by using a `break` statement, like this:

```python
fp = open('2600-0.txt')
count = 0
for line in fp:
    print(line)
    count += 1
    if count == 1:
        break
```

```
The Project Gutenberg EBook of War and Peace, by Leo Tolstoy
```

The `break` statement ends the loop immediately, skipping the rest of the file, as we can confirm by checking the final value of `count`.

```
count
```

```
1
```

Exercise: Write a loop that prints the first 5 lines of the file and then breaks out of the loop.

4.6 Whitespace

If we run the loop again and display the final value of `line`, we see the special sequence `\n` at the end.

```python
fp = open('2600-0.txt')
count = 0
for line in fp:
    count += 1
    if count == 1:
        break

line
```

```
'The Project Gutenberg EBook of War and Peace, by Leo Tolstoy\n'
```

4.7 Counting Words

This sequence represents a single character, called a **newline**, that puts vertical space between lines. If we use a `print` statement to display `line`, we don't see the special sequence, but we do see extra space after the line.

```
print(line)
```

```
The Project Gutenberg EBook of War and Peace, by Leo Tolstoy
```

In other strings, you might see the sequence `\t`, which represents a tab character. When you print a tab character, it adds enough space to make the next character appear in a column that is a multiple of 8.

```
print('|       ' * 6)
print('a\tbc\tdef\tghij\tklmno\tpqrstu')
```

```
|       |       |       |       |       |
a       bc      def     ghij    klmno   pqrstu
```

Newline characters, tabs, and spaces are called **whitespace** because when they are printed they leave white space on the page (assuming that the background color is white).

4.7 Counting Words

So far we've counted the lines in a file – now let's count the words. To split a line into words, we can use a function called `split` that takes a string and returns a list of words. To be more precise, `split` doesn't actually know what a word is – it just splits the line wherever there's a space or other whitespace character.

```
line.split()
```

```
['The',
 'Project',
 'Gutenberg',
 'EBook',
 'of',
 'War',
 'and',
 'Peace,',
 'by',
 'Leo',
 'Tolstoy']
```

Notice that the syntax for `split` is different from other functions we have seen. Normally when we call a function, we name the function and provide values in parentheses. So you might have expected to write `split(line)`.

Sadly, that doesn't work.

```
%%expect NameError

split(line)
```

```
NameError: name 'split' is not defined
```

The problem is that the `split` function belongs to the string `line`. In a sense, the function is attached to the string, so we can only refer to it using the string and the **dot operator**, which is the period between `line` and `split`. For historical reasons, functions like this are called **methods**.

Now that we can split a line into a list of words, we can use `len` to get the number of words in each list, and increment `count` accordingly.

```
fp = open('2600-0.txt')
count = 0
for line in fp:
    count += len(line.split())

count
```

566316

By this count, there are more than half a million words in *War and Peace*.

Actually, there aren't quite that many, because the file we got from Project Gutenberg has some introductory material before the text and some license information at the end. To mark the beginning and end of the text, the file includes special lines that begin with `'***'`. We can identify these lines with the `startswith` function, which checks whether a string begins with a particular sequence of characters.

```
line = '*** START OF THIS PROJECT GUTENBERG EBOOK WAR AND PEACE ***'
line.startswith('***')
```

True

To skip the front matter, we can use a loop to read lines until it finds the first line that starts with this sequence.

Then we can use a second loop to read lines and count words until it finds the second line that starts with this sequence.

```
fp = open('2600-0.txt')
for line in fp:
    if line.startswith('***'):
        print(line)
        break

count = 0
for line in fp:
    if line.startswith('***'):
        print(line)
        break
    count += len(line.split())
```

*** START OF THIS PROJECT GUTENBERG EBOOK WAR AND PEACE ***

*** END OF THIS PROJECT GUTENBERG EBOOK WAR AND PEACE ***

When the second loop exits, `count` contains the number of words in the text.

```
count
```

563299

4.8 Summary

This chapter presents loops, `if` statements, and the `break` statement. It also introduces tools for working with letters and words, and a simple kind of textual analysis, word counting.

In the next chapter we'll continue this example, counting the number of unique words in a text and the number of times each word appears. And we'll see another way to represent a collection of values, a Python dictionary.

Chapter 5

Dictionaries

In the previous chapter we used a `for` loop to read a file and count the words. In this chapter we'll count the number of *unique* words and the number of times each one appears. To do that, we'll use one of Python's most useful features, a **dictionary**.

You will also see how to select an element from a sequence (tuple, list, or array). And you will learn a little about Unicode, which is used to represent letters, numbers, and punctuation for almost every language in the world.

5.1 Indexing

Suppose you have a variable named `t` that refers to a list or tuple. You can select an element using the **bracket operator**, `[]`. For example, here's a tuple of strings:

```
t = ('zero', 'one', 'two')
```

To select the first element, we put `0` in brackets:

```
t[0]
```

```
'zero'
```

To select the second element, we put `1` in brackets:

```
t[1]
```

```
'one'
```

To select the third element, we put `2` in brackets:

```
t[2]
```

```
'two'
```

The number in brackets is called an **index** because it indicates which element we want. Tuples and lists use zero-based numbering – that is, the index of the first element is 0. Some other programming languages use one-based numbering.

The index in brackets can also be a variable:

```
i = 1
t[i]
```

```
'one'
```

Or an expression with variables, values, and operators:

```
t[i+1]
```

```
'two'
```

But if the index goes past the end of the sequence, you get an error.

```
%%expect IndexError

t[3]
```

```
IndexError: tuple index out of range
```

Also, the index has to be an integer – if it is any other type, you get an error.

```
%%expect TypeError

t[1.5]
```

```
TypeError: tuple indices must be integers or slices, not float
```

5.2 Dictionaries

```
%%expect TypeError

t['1']
```

```
TypeError: tuple indices must be integers or slices, not str
```

Exercise: You can use negative integers as indices. Try using `-1` and `-2` as indices, and see if you can figure out what they do.

5.2 Dictionaries

A dictionary is similar to a tuple or list, but in a dictionary, the index can be almost any type, not just an integer. We can create an empty dictionary like this:

```
d = {}
```

Then we can add elements like this:

```
d['one'] = 1
d['two'] = 2
```

In this example, the indices are the strings, `'one'` and `'two'`. If you display the dictionary, it shows each index and the corresponding value.

```
d
```

```
{'one': 1, 'two': 2}
```

Instead of creating an empty dictionary and then adding elements, you can create a dictionary and specify the elements at the same time:

```
d = {'one': 1, 'two': 2, 'three': 3}
d
```

```
{'one': 1, 'two': 2, 'three': 3}
```

When we are talking about dictionaries, an index is usually called a **key**. In this example, the keys are strings and the corresponding values are integers. A dictionary is also called a **map**, because it represents a correspondence or "mapping", between keys and values. So we might say that this dictionary maps from English number names to the corresponding integers.

You can use the bracket operator to select an element from a dictionary, like this:

```
d['two']
```

2

But don't forget the quotation marks. Without them, Python looks for a variable named `two` and doesn't find one.

```
%%expect NameError

d[two]
```

NameError: name 'two' is not defined

To check whether a particular key is in a dictionary, you can use the `in` operator:

```
'one' in d
```

True

```
'zero' in d
```

False

Because the word `in` is an operator in Python, you can't use it as a variable name.

```
%%expect SyntaxError

in = 5
```

    Cell In[22], line 1
        in = 5

SyntaxError: invalid syntax

Each key in a dictionary can only appear once. Adding the same key again has no effect:

```
d['one'] = 1
d
```

{'one': 1, 'two': 2, 'three': 3}

5.2 Dictionaries

But you can change the value associated with a key:

```
d['one'] = 100
d
```

```
{'one': 100, 'two': 2, 'three': 3}
```

You can loop through the keys in a dictionary like this:

```
for key in d:
    print(key)
```

```
one
two
three
```

If you want the keys and the values, one way to get them is to loop through the keys and look up the values:

```
for key in d:
    print(key, d[key])
```

```
one 100
two 2
three 3
```

Or you can loop through both at the same time, like this:

```
for key, value in d.items():
    print(key, value)
```

```
one 100
two 2
three 3
```

The `items` method loops through the key-value pairs in the dictionary. Each time through the loop, they are assigned to `key` and `value`.

Exercise: Make a dictionary with the integers 1, 2, and 3 as keys and strings as values. The strings should be the words "one", "two", and "three" or their equivalents in any language you know.

Write a loop that prints just the values from the dictionary.

5.3 Counting Unique Words

In the previous chapter we downloaded *War and Peace* from Project Gutenberg and counted the number of lines and words. Now that we have dictionaries, we can also count the number of unique words and the number of times each one appears.

As we did in the previous chapter, we can read the text of *War and Peace* and count the number of words.

```
fp = open('2600-0.txt')
count = 0
for line in fp:
    count += len(line.split())

count
```

566316

To count the number of unique words, we'll loop through the words in each line and add them as keys in a dictionary:

```
fp = open('2600-0.txt')
unique_words = {}
for line in fp:
    for word in line.split():
        unique_words[word] = 1
```

This is the first example we've seen with one loop **nested** inside another.

- The outer loop runs through the lines in the file.

- The inner loops runs through the words in each line.

Each time through the inner loop, we add a word as a key in the dictionary, with the value 1. If a word that is already in the dictionary appears again, adding it to the dictionary again has no effect. So the dictionary gets only one copy of each unique word in the file. At the end of the loop, we can display the first eight keys like this.

```
list(unique_words)[:8]
```

['The', 'Project', 'Gutenberg', 'EBook', 'of', 'War', 'and', 'Peace,']

The `list` function puts the keys from the dictionary in a list. In the bracket operator, :8 is a special index called a *slice* that selects the first eight elements.

Each word only appears once, so the number of keys is the number of unique words.

5.4 Dealing with Capitalization

```
len(unique_words)
```

41990

There are about 42,000 different words in the book, which is substantially less than the total number of words, about 560,000. But this count is not correct yet, because we have not taken into account capitalization and punctuation.

Exercise: Before we deal with those problems, let's practice with nested loops – that is, one loop inside another. Suppose you have a list of words, like this:

```
line = ['War', 'and', 'Peace']
```

Write a nested loop that iterates through each word in the list, and each letter in each word, and prints the letters on separate lines.

5.4 Dealing with Capitalization

When we count unique words, we probably want to treat `The` and `the` as the same word. We can do that by converting all words to lower case, using the `lower` function:

```
word = 'The'
word.lower()
```

'the'

`lower` creates a new string; it does not modify the original string.

```
word
```

'The'

However, you can assign the new string back to the existing variable, like this:

```
word = word.lower()
```

Now if we can display the new value of `word`, we get the lowercase version:

```
word
```

'the'

Exercise: Modify the previous loop so it makes a lowercase version of each word before adding it to the dictionary. How many unique words are there, if we ignore the difference between uppercase and lowercase?

5.5 Removing Punctuation

To remove punctuation from the words, we can use `strip`, which removes characters from the beginning and end of a string. Here's an example:

```
word = 'abracadabra'
word.strip('ab')
```

```
'racadabr'
```

In this example, `strip` removes all instances of `a` and `b` from the beginning and end of the word, but not from the middle. Like `lower`, this function makes a new word – it doesn't modify the original:

```
word
```

```
'abracadabra'
```

To remove punctuation, we can use the `string` library, which provides a variable named `punctuation`.

```
import string

string.punctuation
```

```
'!"#$%&\'()*+,-./:;<=>?@[\\]^_`{|}~'
```

`string.punctuation` contains the most common punctuation marks, but as we'll see, not all of them. Nevertheless, we can use it to handle most cases. Here's an example:

```
line = "It's not given to people to judge what's right or wrong."

for word in line.split():
    word = word.strip(string.punctuation)
    print(word)
```

```
It's
not
given
to
people
to
judge
what's
right
or
wrong
```

5.5 Removing Punctuation

`strip` removes the period at the end of `wrong`, but not the apostrophes in `It's`, `don't` and `what's`. That's good, because we want to treat an apostrophe as part of a word. But we have one more problem to solve. Here's another line from the book.

```
line = 'anyone, and so you don't deserve to have them."'
```

Here's what happens when we try to remove the punctuation.

```
for word in line.split():
    word = word.strip(string.punctuation)
    print(word)
```

```
anyone
and
so
you
don't
deserve
to
have
them."
```

The comma after `anyone` is removed, but not the quotation mark at the end of the last word. The problem is that this kind of quotation mark is not in `string.punctuation`, so `strip` doesn't remove it. To fix this problem, we'll use the following loop, which

1. Reads the file and builds a dictionary that contains all punctuation marks that appear in the book, then

2. It uses the `join` function to concatenate the keys of the dictionary in a single string.

You don't have to understand everything about how it works, but I suggest you read it and see how much you can figure out.

```
import unicodedata

fp = open('2600-0.txt')
punc_marks = {}
for line in fp:
    for x in line:
        category = unicodedata.category(x)
        if category[0] == 'P':
            punc_marks[x] = 1

all_punctuation = ''.join(punc_marks)
```

```
print(all_punctuation)
```

,.-:[#]*/"'-'!?";()%@

The result is a string containing all of the punctuation characters that appear in the document, in the order they first appear.

Exercise: Modify the word-counting loop from the previous section to convert words to lower case *and* strip punctuation before adding them to the dictionary. Now how many unique words are there?

5.6 Counting Word Frequencies

In the previous section we counted the number of unique words, but we might also want to know how often each word appears. Then we can find the most common and least common words in the book. To count the frequency of each word, we'll make a dictionary that maps from each word to the number of times it appears.

Here's an example that loops through a string and counts the number of times each letter appears.

```
word = 'Mississippi'

letter_counts = {}
for x in word:
    if x in letter_counts:
        letter_counts[x] += 1
    else:
        letter_counts[x] = 1

letter_counts
```

{'M': 1, 'i': 4, 's': 4, 'p': 2}

The `if` statement includes a feature we have not seen before, an `else` clause. Here's how it works.

1. First, it checks whether the letter, `x`, is already a key in the dictionary, `letter_counts`.

2. If so, it runs the first statement, `letter_counts[x] += 1`, which increments the value associated with the letter.

3. Otherwise, it runs the second statement, `letter_counts[x] = 1`, which adds `x` as a new key, with the value 1 indicating that we have seen the new letter once.

5.6 Counting Word Frequencies

The result is a dictionary that maps from each letter to the number of times it appears. To get the most common letters, we can use a `Counter`, which is similar to a dictionary. To use it, we have to import a library called `collections`:

```
import collections
```

Then we use `collections.Counter` to convert the dictionary to a `Counter`:

```
counter = collections.Counter(letter_counts)
type(counter)
```

collections.Counter

`Counter` provides a function called `most_common` we can use to get the most common characters:

```
counter.most_common(3)
```

[('i', 4), ('s', 4), ('p', 2)]

The result is a list of tuples, where each tuple contains a character and count, sorted by count.

Exercise: Modify the loop from the previous exercise to count the frequency of the words in *War and Peace*. Then print the 20 most common words and the number of times each one appears.

Exercise: You can run `most_common` with no value in parentheses, like this:

```
word_freq_pairs = counter.most_common()
```

The result is a list of tuples, with one tuple for every unique word in the book. Use it to answer the following questions:

1. How many times does the #1 ranked word appear (that is, the first element of the list)?
2. How many times does the #10 ranked word appear?
3. How many times does the #100 ranked word appear?
4. How many times does the #1000 ranked word appear?
5. How many times does the #10000 ranked word appear?

Do you see a pattern in the results? We will explore this pattern more in the next chapter.

Exercise: Write a loop that counts how many words appear 200 times. What are they? How many words appear 100 times, 50 times, and 20 times?

Optional: If you know how to define a function, write a function that takes a `Counter` and a frequency as arguments, prints all words with that frequency, and returns the number of words with that frequency.

5.7 Summary

This chapter introduces dictionaries, which are collections of keys and corresponding values. We used a dictionary to count the number of unique words in a file and the number of times each one appears.

It also introduces the bracket operator, which selects an element from a list or tuple, or looks up a key in a dictionary and finds the corresponding value.

We saw some new methods for working with strings, including `lower` and `strip`. Also, we used the `unicodedata` library to identify characters that are considered punctuation.

Chapter 6

Plotting

This chapter presents ways to create figures and graphs, more generally called **data visualizations**. As examples, we'll generate three figures:

- We'll replicate a figure from the Pew Research Center that shows changes in religious affiliation in the United States over time.

- We'll replicate a figure from *The Economist* that shows the prices of sandwiches in Boston and London (we saw this data back in Chapter 3).

- We'll make a plot to test Zipf's law, which describes the relationship between word frequencies and their ranks.

With the tools in this chapter, you can generate a variety of simple graphs. We will see more visualization tools in later chapters. But before we get started with plotting, we need a new feature: keyword arguments.

6.1 Keyword Arguments

When you call most functions, you have to provide values. For example, when you call `np.exp`, you provide a number.

```
import numpy as np

np.exp(1)
```
2.718281828459045

When you call `np.power`, you provide two numbers.

```
np.power(10, 6)
```

```
1000000
```

The values you provide are called **arguments**. Specifically, the values in these examples are **positional arguments** because their position determines how they are used. In the second example, `power` computes `10` to the sixth power, not `6` to the tenth power – because of the order of the arguments.

Many functions also take **keyword arguments**, which are identified by name. For example, we have previously used `int` to convert a string to an integer. Here's how we use it with a string as a positional argument:

```
int('21')
```

```
21
```

By default, `int` assumes that the number is in base 10. But you can provide a keyword argument that specifies a different base. For example, the string `'21'`, interpreted in base 8, represents the number 2 * 8 + 1 = 17. Here's how we do this conversion using `int`.

```
int('21', base=8)
```

```
17
```

The integer value 8 is a keyword argument, with the keyword `base`. Specifying a keyword argument looks like an assignment statement, but it does not create a new variable. And when you provide a keyword argument, you don't choose the variable name – it is specified by the function. If you provide a name that is not specified by the function, you get an error.

```
%%expect TypeError

int('123', bass=11)
```

```
TypeError: 'bass' is an invalid keyword argument for int()
```

Exercise: The `print` function takes a keyword argument called `end` that specifies the character it prints at the end of the line. By default, `end` is the newline character, `\n`.

6.2 Graphing Religious Affiliation   59

So if you call `print` more than once, the outputs normally appear on separate lines, like this:

```
for x in [1, 2, 3]:
    print(x)
```

```
1
2
3
```

Modify the previous example so the outputs appear on one line with spaces between them. Then modify it to print an open bracket at the beginning and a close bracket and newline at the end.

6.2 Graphing Religious Affiliation

Now we're ready to make some graphs. In October 2019 the Pew Research Center published "In U.S., Decline of Christianity Continues at Rapid Pace". It includes this figure, which shows changes in religious affiliation among adults in the U.S. over the previous 10 years.

As an exercise, we'll replicate this figure. It shows results from two sources, Religious Landscape Studies and Pew Research Political Surveys. The political surveys provide data from more years, so we'll focus on that.

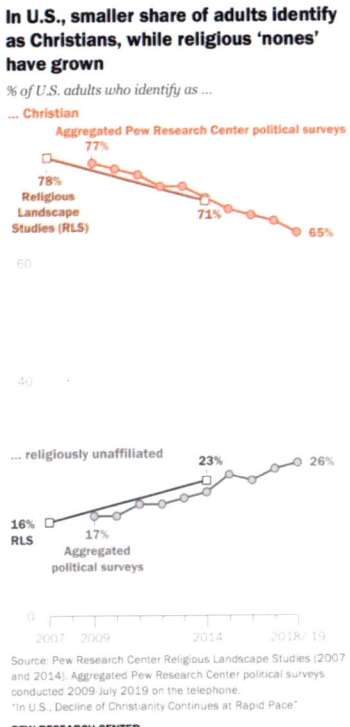

In U.S., smaller share of adults identify as Christians, while religious 'nones' have grown

% of U.S. adults who identify as ...

... Christian
Aggregated Pew Research Center political surveys
77%
78%
Religious Landscape Studies (RLS)
71%
65%

60

40

... religiously unaffiliated   23%   26%
16% RLS   17%
Aggregated political surveys

0
2007 2009   2014   2018/19

Source: Pew Research Center Religious Landscape Studies (2007 and 2014). Aggregated Pew Research Center political surveys conducted 2009-July 2019 on the telephone.
"In U.S., Decline of Christianity Continues at Rapid Pace"

PEW RESEARCH CENTER

The data from the figure are available from Pew Research, but they are in a PDF document. It is sometimes possible to extract data from PDF documents, but for now we'll enter the data by hand.

```
year = [2009, 2010, 2011, 2012, 2013, 2014, 2015, 2016, 2017, 2018]
```

```
christian = [77, 76, 75, 73, 73, 71, 69, 68, 67, 65]
```

```
unaffiliated = [17, 17, 19, 19, 20, 21, 24, 23, 25, 26]
```

The library we'll use for plotting is Matplotlib – more specifically, we'll use a part of it called Pyplot, which we'll import with the shortened name `plt`.

```
import matplotlib.pyplot as plt
```

Pyplot provides a function called `plot` that makes a line plot. It takes two sequences as arguments, the `x` values and the `y` values. The sequences can be tuples, lists, or arrays.

```
plt.plot(year, christian);
```

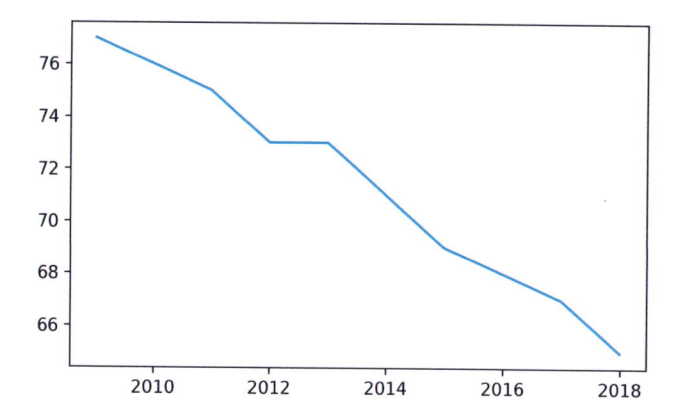

The semi-colon at the end of the line prevents the return value from `plot`, which is an object representing the line, from being displayed.

6.2 Graphing Religious Affiliation

If you plot multiple lines in a single cell, they appear on the same axes.

```
plt.plot(year, christian)
plt.plot(year, unaffiliated);
```

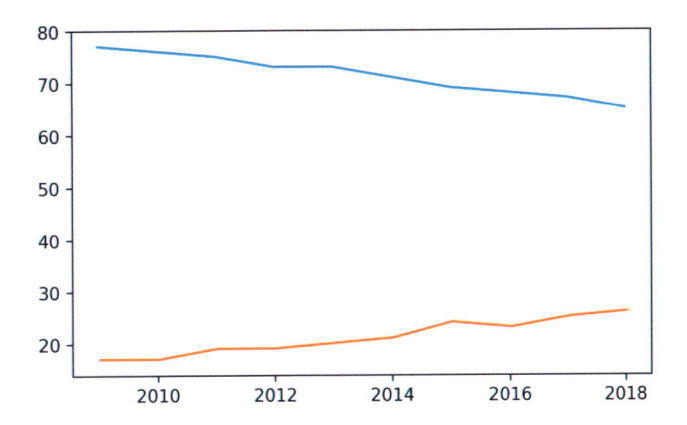

Plotting them on the same axes makes it possible to compare them directly. However, notice that Pyplot chooses the range for the axes automatically. In this example the y-axis starts around 15, not zero.

As a result, it provides a misleading picture, making the ratio of the two lines look bigger than it really is. We can set the limits of the y-axis using the function `plt.ylim` – the arguments are the lower bound and the upper bounds.

```
plt.plot(year, christian)
plt.plot(year, unaffiliated)

plt.ylim(0, 80);
```

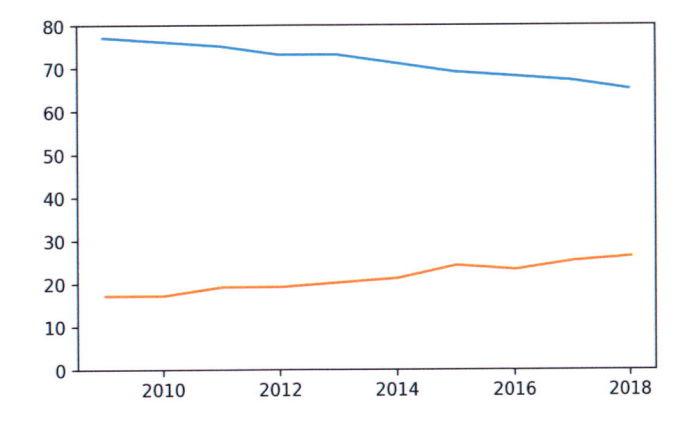

That's better, but this graph is missing some important elements: labels for the axes, a title, and a legend.

6.3 Decorating the Axes

To label the axes and add a title, we'll use Pyplot functions `xlabel`, `ylabel`, and `title`. All of them take strings as arguments.

```
plt.plot(year, christian)
plt.plot(year, unaffiliated)

plt.ylim(0, 80)
plt.xlabel('Year')
plt.ylabel('% of adults')
plt.title('Religious affiliation of U.S adults');
```

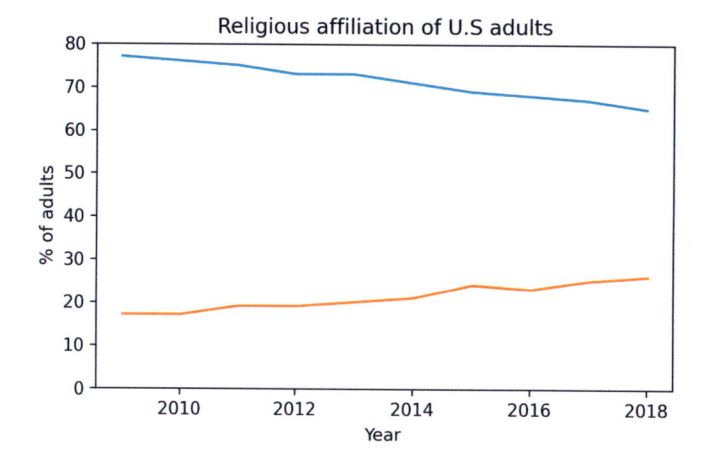

To add a legend, first we add a label to each line, using the keyword argument `label`. Then we call `plt.legend` to create the legend.

```
plt.plot(year, christian, label='Christian')
plt.plot(year, unaffiliated, label='Unaffiliated')

plt.ylim(0, 80)
plt.xlabel('Year')
plt.ylabel('% of adults')
plt.title('Religious affiliation of U.S adults')
plt.legend();
```

6.4 Plotting Sandwich Prices

[Figure: Religious affiliation of U.S adults — line plot showing Christian (declining from ~77% to ~66%) and Unaffiliated (rising from ~17% to ~27%) from 2009 to 2018]

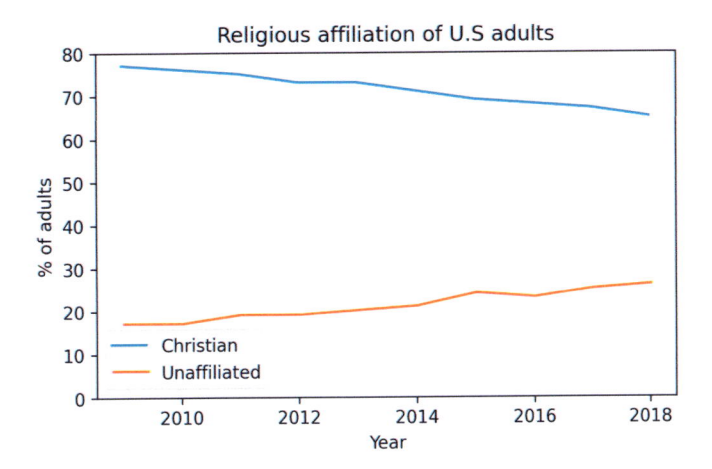

The legend shows the labels we provided when we created the lines.

Exercise: The original figure plots lines between the data points, but it also plots markers showing the location of each data point. It is good practice to include these markers, especially if data are not available for every year.

Modify the previous example to include a keyword argument `marker` with the string value `'.'`, which indicates that you want to plot small circles as markers.

Exercise: In the original figure, the line labeled `'Christian'` is red and the line labeled `'Unaffiliated'` is gray.

Find the online documentation of `plt.plot`, or ask a virtual assistant like ChatGPT, and figure out how to use keyword arguments to specify colors. Choose colors to (roughly) match the original figure.

The `legend` function takes a keyword argument that specifies the location of the legend. Read the documentation of this function and move the legend to the center left of the figure.

6.4 Plotting Sandwich Prices

In Chapter 3 we used data from an article in *The Economist* comparing sandwich prices in Boston and London: "Why Americans pay more for lunch than Britons do".

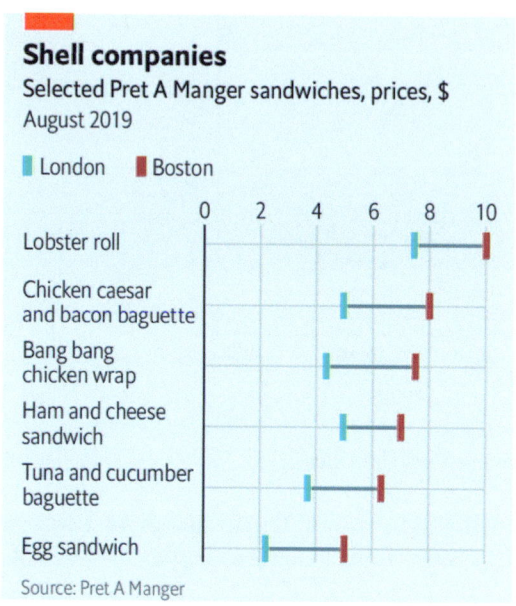

The article includes this graph showing prices of several sandwiches in the two cities:

As an exercise, let's see if we can replicate this figure. Here's the data from the article again.

```
name_list = [
    'Lobster roll',
    'Chicken caesar',
    'Bang bang chicken',
    'Ham and cheese',
    'Tuna and cucumber',
    'Egg'
]
```

```
boston_price_list = [9.99, 7.99, 7.49, 7, 6.29, 4.99]
london_price_list = [7.5, 5, 4.4, 5, 3.75, 2.25]
```

In the previous section we plotted percentages on the y-axis versus time on the x-axis. Now we want to plot the sandwich names on the y-axis and the prices on the x-axis. Here's how:

```
plt.plot(boston_price_list, name_list)
plt.xlabel('Price in USD');
```

6.4 Plotting Sandwich Prices

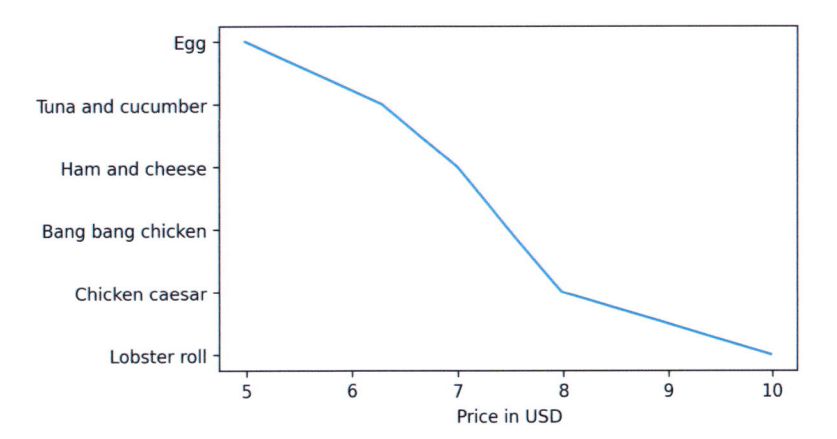

By default Pyplot connects the points with lines, but in this example the lines don't make sense because the sandwich names are discrete – that is, there are no intermediate points between an egg sandwich and a tuna sandwich. We can remove the lines and add markers with the keywords `linestyle` and `marker`.

```
plt.plot(boston_price_list, name_list, linestyle='', marker='o')
plt.xlabel('Price in USD');
```

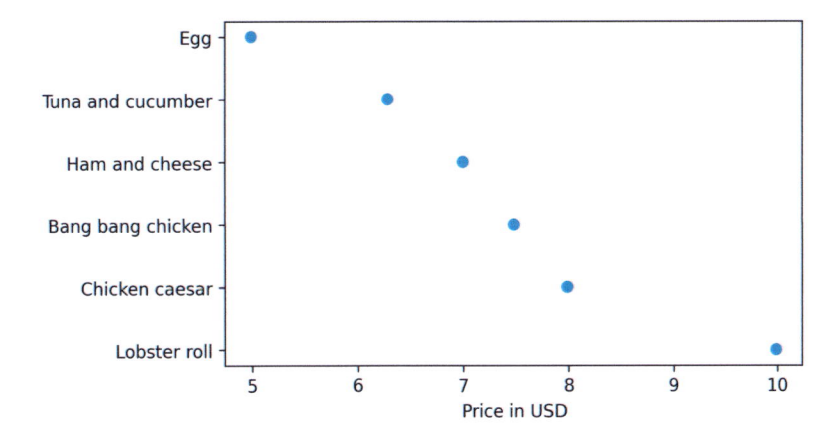

Or we can do the same thing more concisely by providing a **format string** as a positional argument. In the following examples, `'o'` indicates a circle marker and `'s'` indicates a square. You can read the documentation of `plt.plot` to learn more about format strings.

```
plt.plot(boston_price_list, name_list, 'o')
plt.plot(london_price_list, name_list, 's')

plt.xlabel('Price in USD')
plt.title('Pret a Manger prices in Boston and London');
```

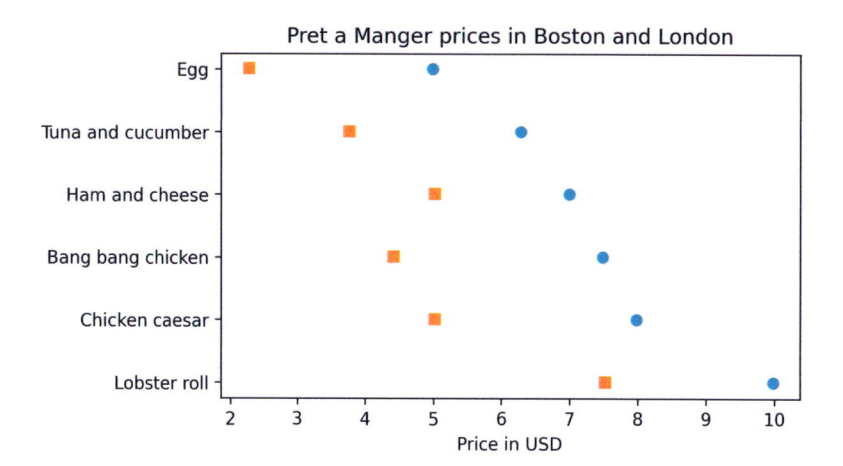

[Figure: Pret a Manger prices in Boston and London — scatter plot with orange squares and blue circles]

Now, to approximate the colors in the original figure, we can use the strings `'C3'` and `'C0'`, which specify colors from the default color sequence.

```
plt.plot(boston_price_list, name_list, 'o', color='C3')
plt.plot(london_price_list, name_list, 's', color='C0')

plt.xlabel('Price in USD')
plt.title('Pret a Manger prices in Boston and London');
```

[Figure: Pret a Manger prices in Boston and London — scatter plot with blue squares and red/orange circles]

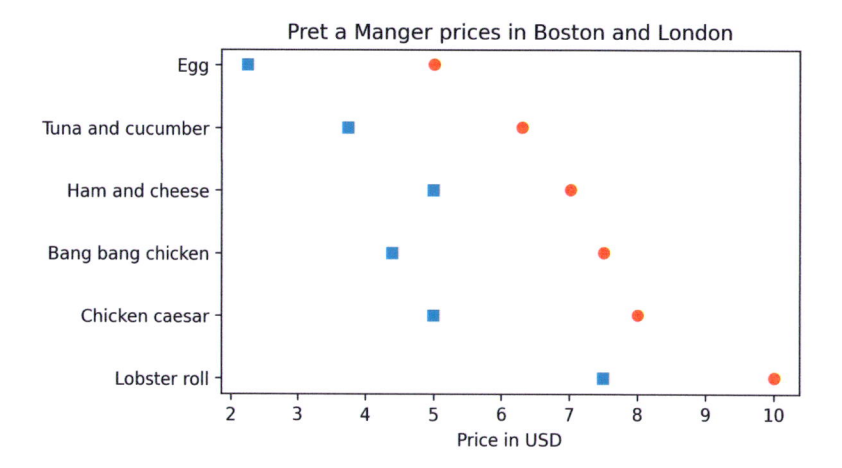

To connect the dots with lines, we'll use `plt.hlines`, which draws horizontal lines. It takes three arguments: a sequence of values on the y-axis, which are the sandwich names in this example, and two sequences of values on the x-axis, which are the London prices and Boston prices.

6.5 Zipf's Law

```
plt.hlines(name_list, london_price_list, boston_price_list, color='gray')

plt.plot(boston_price_list, name_list, 'o', color='C3')
plt.plot(london_price_list, name_list, 's', color='C0')

plt.xlabel('Price in USD')
plt.title('Pret a Manger prices in Boston and London');
```

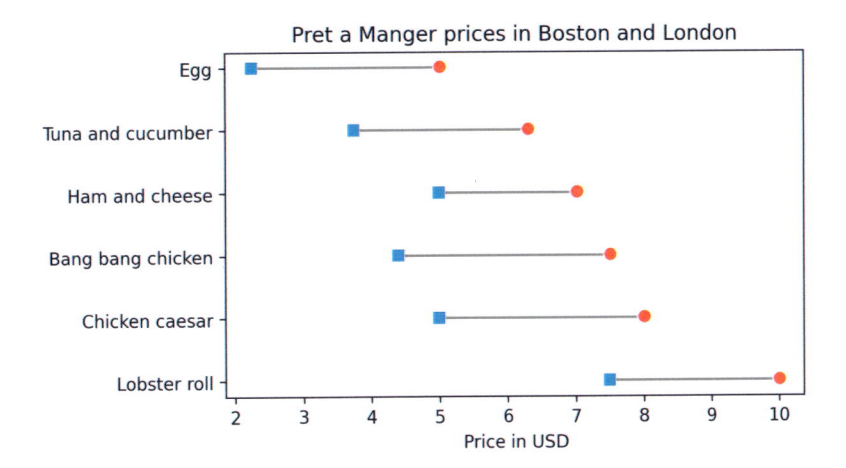

Exercise: To finish off this example, add a legend that identifies the London and Boston prices. Remember that you have to add a `label` keyword each time you call `plt.plot`, and then call `plt.legend`.

Notice that the sandwiches in our figure are in the opposite order of the sandwiches in the original figure. There is a Pyplot function that inverts the y-axis; see if you can find it and use it to reverse the order of the sandwich list.

6.5 Zipf's Law

In almost any book, in almost any language, if you count the number of unique words and the number of times each word appears, you will find a remarkable pattern: the most common word appears twice as often as the second most common – at least approximately – three times as often as the third most common, and so on.

In general, if we sort the words in descending order of frequency, there is an inverse relationship between the rank of the words – first, second, third, etc. – and the number of times they appear. This observation was most famously made by George Kingsley Zipf, so it is called Zipf's law.

To see if this law holds for the words in *War and Peace*, we'll make a Zipf plot, which shows:

- The frequency of each word on the y-axis, and

- The rank of each word on the x-axis, starting from 1.

In the previous chapter, we looped through the book and made a string that contains all punctuation characters. Here are the results, which we will need again.

```
all_punctuation = ',.-:[#]*/"'-'!?";()%@'
```

The following program reads through the book and makes a dictionary that maps from each word to the number of times it appears.

```
fp = open('2600-0.txt')
for line in fp:
    if line.startswith('***'):
        break

unique_words = {}
for line in fp:
    if line.startswith('***'):
        break

    for word in line.split():
        word = word.lower()
        word = word.strip(all_punctuation)
        if word in unique_words:
            unique_words[word] += 1
        else:
            unique_words[word] = 1
```

In `unique_words`, the keys are words and the values are their frequencies. We can use the `values` function to get the values from the dictionary. The result has the type `dict_values`:

```
freqs = unique_words.values()
type(freqs)
```
```
dict_values
```

6.5 Zipf's Law

Before we plot them, we have to sort them, but the `sort` function doesn't work with `dict_values`.

```
%%expect AttributeError

freqs.sort()
```

```
AttributeError: 'dict_values' object has no attribute 'sort'
```

We can use `list` to make a list of frequencies:

```
freq_list = list(unique_words.values())
type(freq_list)
```

```
list
```

And now we can use `sort`. By default it sorts in ascending order, but we can pass a keyword argument to reverse the order.

```
freq_list.sort(reverse=True)
```

Now, for the ranks, we need a sequence that counts from 1 to `n`, where `n` is the number of elements in `freq_list`. We can use the `range` function, which returns a value with type `range`. As a small example, here's the range from 1 to 5.

```
range(1, 5)
```

```
range(1, 5)
```

However, there's a catch. If we use the range to make a list, we see that "the range from 1 to 5" includes 1, but it doesn't include 5.

```
list(range(1, 5))
```

```
[1, 2, 3, 4]
```

That might seem strange, but it is often more convenient to use `range` when it is defined this way, rather than what might seem like the more natural way. Anyway, we can get what we want by increasing the second argument by one:

```
list(range(1, 6))
```

```
[1, 2, 3, 4, 5]
```

So, finally, we can make a range that represents the ranks from 1 to n:

```
n = len(freq_list)
ranks = range(1, n+1)
ranks
```

range(1, 20484)

And now we can plot the frequencies versus the ranks:

```
plt.plot(ranks, freq_list)

plt.xlabel('Rank')
plt.ylabel('Frequency')
plt.title("War and Peace and Zipf's law");
```

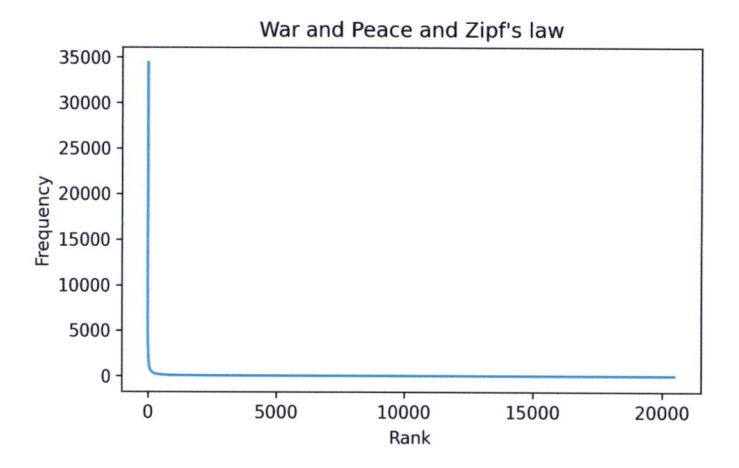

According to Zipf's law, these frequencies should be inversely proportional to the ranks. If that's true, we can write:

$$f = k/r$$

where r is the rank of a word, f is its frequency, and k is an unknown constant of proportionality. If we take the logarithm of both sides, we get

$$\log f = \log k - \log r$$

This equation implies that if we plot f versus r on a log-log scale, we expect to see a straight line with intercept at $\log k$ and slope -1.

6.6 Logarithmic Scales

We can use `plt.xscale` to plot the x-axis on a log scale.

```
plt.plot(ranks, freq_list)

plt.xlabel('Rank')
plt.ylabel('Frequency')
plt.title("War and Peace and Zipf's law")
plt.xscale('log')
```

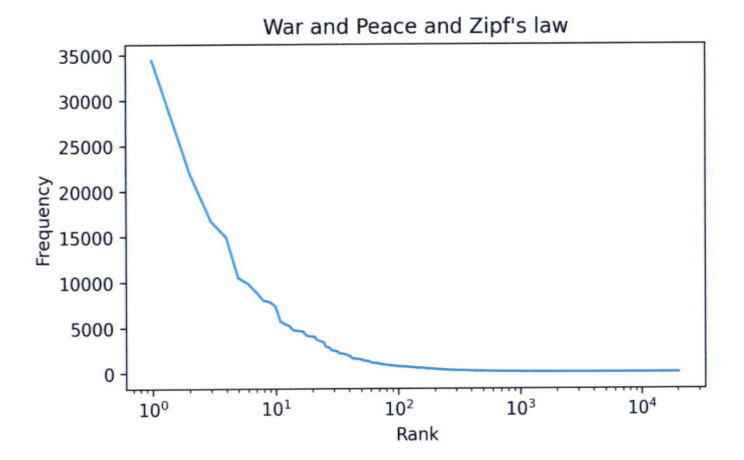

And `plt.yscale` to plot the y-axis on a log scale.

```
plt.plot(ranks, freq_list)

plt.xlabel('Rank')
plt.ylabel('Frequency')
plt.title("War and Peace and Zipf's law")
plt.xscale('log')
plt.yscale('log')
```

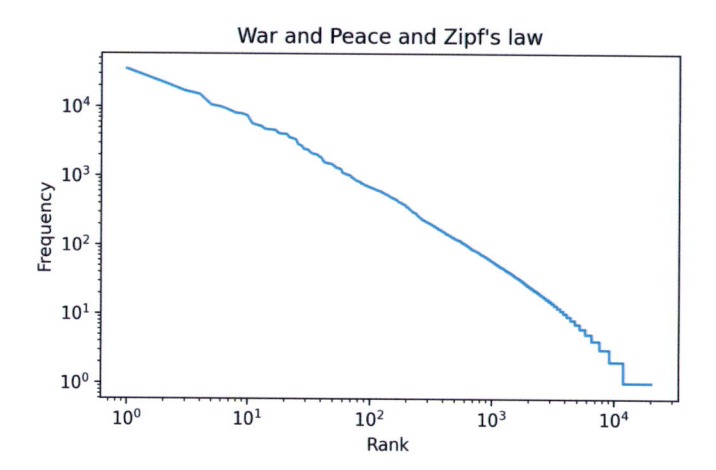

War and Peace and Zipf's law

The result is not quite a straight line, but it is close. We can get a sense of the slope by connecting the end points with a line. First, we'll select the first and last elements from `xs`.

```
xs = ranks[0], ranks[-1]
xs
```

(1, 20483)

And the first and last elements from `ys`.

```
ys = freq_list[0], freq_list[-1]
ys
```

(34389, 1)

And plot a line between them.

```
plt.plot(xs, ys, color='gray')
plt.plot(ranks, freq_list)

plt.xlabel('Rank')
plt.ylabel('Frequency')
plt.title("War and Peace and Zipf's law")
plt.xscale('log')
plt.yscale('log')
```

6.7 Summary

War and Peace and Zipf's law

[Figure: log-log plot of Frequency vs Rank for War and Peace showing Zipf's law]

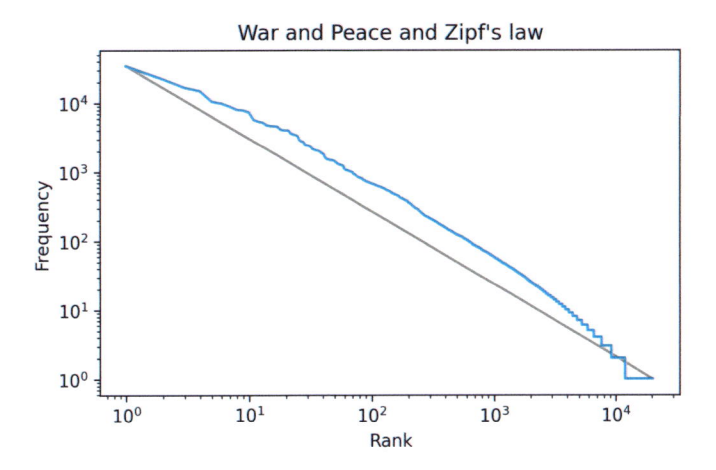

The slope of this line is the "rise over run", that is, the difference on the y-axis divided by the difference on the x-axis. We can compute the rise using `np.log10` to compute the log base 10 of the first and last values:

```
np.log10(ys)
```

```
array([4.53641955, 0.        ])
```

Then we can use `np.diff` to compute the difference between the elements:

```
rise = np.diff(np.log10(ys))
rise
```

```
array([-4.53641955])
```

Exercise: Use `log10` and `diff` to compute the run, that is, the difference on the x-axis. Then divide the rise by the run to get the slope of the grey line. Is it close to −1, as Zipf's law predicts?

6.7 Summary

This chapter introduces Pyplot, which is part of the Matplotlib library. We used to replicate two figures and make a Zipf plot. These examples demonstrate the most common elements of data visualization, including lines and markers, values and labels on the axes, a legend and a title. The Zipf plot also shows the power of plotting data on logarithmic scales.

Part II

Exploratory Data Analysis

Chapter 7

DataFrames and Series

This chapter introduces Pandas, a Python library that provides functions for reading and writing data files, exploring and analyzing data, and generating visualizations. And it provides two new types for working with data, `DataFrame` and `Series`.

We will use these tools to answer a data question – what is the average birth weight of babies in the United States? This example will demonstrate important steps in almost any data science project:

1. Identifying data that can answer a question.

2. Obtaining the data and loading it in Python.

3. Checking the data and dealing with errors.

4. Selecting relevant subsets from the data.

5. Using histograms to visualize a distribution of values.

6. Using summary statistics to describe the data in a way that best answers the question.

7. Considering possible sources of error and limitations in our conclusions.

Let's start by getting the data.

7.1 Reading the Data

To estimate average birth weight, we'll use data from the National Survey of Family Growth (NSFG), which is available from the National Center for Health Statistics. To download the data, you have to agree to the Data User's Agreement. URLs for the data and the agreement are in the notebook for this chapter.

You should read the terms carefully, but let me draw your attention to what I think is the most important one:

> Make no attempt to learn the identity of any person or establishment included in these data.

NSFG respondents answer questions of the most personal nature with the expectation that their identities will not be revealed. As ethical data scientists, we should respect their privacy and adhere to the terms of use.

Respondents to the NSFG provide general information about themselves, which is stored in the respondent file, and information about each time they have been pregnant, which is stored in the pregnancy file.

We will work with the pregnancy file, which contains one row for each pregnancy and one column for each question on the NSFG questionnaire.

The data is stored in a fixed-width format, which means that every row is the same length and each column spans a fixed range of characters. For example, the first six characters in each row represent a a unique identifier for each respondent; the next two characters indicate whether a pregnancy is the respondent's first, second, etc.

To read this data, we need a **data dictionary**, which specifies the names of the columns and the index where each one begins and ends. The data and the data dictionary are available in separate files. Instructions for downloading them are in the notebook for this chapter.

```
dict_file = '2015_2017_FemPregSetup.dct'
data_file = '2015_2017_FemPregData.dat'
```

Pandas can read data in most common formats, including CSV, Excel, and fixed-width format, but it cannot read the data dictionary, which is in Stata format. For that, we'll use a Python library called `statadict`.

7.1 Reading the Data

From `statadict`, we'll import `parse_stata_dict`, which reads the data dictionary.

```
from statadict import parse_stata_dict

stata_dict = parse_stata_dict(dict_file)
stata_dict
```

<statadict.base.StataDict at 0x7f0727940ad0>

The result is an object that contains

- `names`, which is a list of column names, and

- `colspecs`, which is a list of tuples, where each tuple contains the first and last index of a column.

These values are exactly the arguments we need to use `read_fwf`, which is the Pandas function that reads a file in fixed-width format.

```
import pandas as pd

nsfg = pd.read_fwf(data_file,
                   names=stata_dict.names,
                   colspecs=stata_dict.colspecs)
type(nsfg)
```

pandas.core.frame.DataFrame

The result is a `DataFrame`, which is the primary type Pandas uses to store data. `DataFrame` has a method called `head` that shows the first 5 rows:

```
nsfg.head()
```

	CASEID	PREGORDR	HOWPREG_N	HOWPREG_P	MOSCURRP	NOWPRGDK	PREGEND1
0	70627	1	NaN	NaN	NaN	NaN	6
1	70627	2	NaN	NaN	NaN	NaN	1
2	70627	3	NaN	NaN	NaN	NaN	6
3	70628	1	NaN	NaN	NaN	NaN	6
4	70628	2	NaN	NaN	NaN	NaN	6

The first two columns are `CASEID` and `PREGORDR`, which I mentioned earlier. The first three rows have the same `CASEID`, which means this respondent reported three pregnancies. The values of `PREGORDR` indicate that they are the first, second, and third pregnancies, in that order. We will learn more about the other columns as we go along.

In addition to methods like `head`, a `Dataframe` object has several **attributes**, which are variables associated with the object. For example, `nsfg` has an attribute called `shape`, which is a tuple containing the number of rows and columns:

```
nsfg.shape
```

```
(9553, 248)
```

There are 9553 rows in this dataset, one for each pregnancy, and 248 columns, one for each question. `nsfg` also has an attribute called `columns`, which contains the column names:

```
nsfg.columns
```

```
Index(['CASEID', 'PREGORDR', 'HOWPREG_N', 'HOWPREG_P', 'MOSCURRP', 'NOWPRGDK',
       'PREGEND1', 'PREGEND2', 'HOWENDDK', 'NBRNALIV',
       ...
       'SECU', 'SEST', 'CMINTVW', 'CMLSTYR', 'CMJAN3YR', 'CMJAN4YR',
       'CMJAN5YR', 'QUARTER', 'PHASE', 'INTVWYEAR'],
      dtype='object', length=248)
```

The column names are stored in an `Index`, which is another Pandas type, similar to a list.

Based on the names, you might be able to guess what some of the columns are, but in general you have to read the documentation. When you work with datasets like the NSFG, it is important to read the documentation carefully. If you interpret a column incorrectly, you can generate nonsense results and never realize it.

So, before we start looking at data, let's get familiar with the NSFG codebook, which describes every column. Instructions for downloading it are in the notebook for this chapter.

If you search that document for "weigh at birth" you should find these columns related to birth weight.

- `BIRTHWGT_LB1`: Birthweight in Pounds - 1st baby from this pregnancy

- `BIRTHWGT_OZ1`: Birthweight in Ounces - 1st baby from this pregnancy

There are similar columns for a 2nd or 3rd baby, in the case of twins or triplets. For now we will focus on the first baby from each pregnancy, and we will come back to the issue of multiple births.

7.2 Series

In many ways a `DataFrame` is like a Python dictionary, where the column names are the keys and the columns are the values. You can select a column from a `DataFrame` using the bracket operator, with a string as the key.

7.3 Validation

```
pounds = nsfg['BIRTHWGT_LB1']
type(pounds)
```

pandas.core.series.Series

The result is a Series, which is a Pandas type that represents a single column of data. In this case the Series contains the birth weight, in pounds, for each live birth.

head shows the first five values in the Series, the name of the Series, and the data type:

```
pounds.head()
```

```
0    7.0
1    NaN
2    9.0
3    6.0
4    7.0
Name: BIRTHWGT_LB1, dtype: float64
```

One of the values is NaN, which stands for "Not a Number". NaN is a special value used to indicate invalid or missing data. In this example, the pregnancy did not end in live birth, so birth weight is inapplicable.

Exercise: The column BIRTHWGT_OZ1 contains the ounces part of birth weight. Select this column from nsfg and assign it to a new variable called ounces. Then display the first 5 elements of ounces.

7.3 Validation

At this point we have identified the columns we need to answer the question and assigned them to variables named pounds and ounces.

```
pounds = nsfg['BIRTHWGT_LB1']
ounces = nsfg['BIRTHWGT_OZ1']
```

Before we do anything with this data, we have to validate it. One part of validation is confirming that we are interpreting the data correctly.

We can use the `value_counts` method to see what values appear in `pounds` and how many times each value appears. With `dropna=False`, it includes NaNs. By default, the results are sorted with the highest count first, but we can use `sort_index` to sort them by value instead, with the lightest babies first and heaviest babies last.

```
pounds.value_counts(dropna=False).sort_index()
```

```
BIRTHWGT_LB1
0.0        2
1.0       28
2.0       46
3.0       76
4.0      179
5.0      570
6.0     1644
7.0     2268
8.0     1287
9.0      396
10.0      82
11.0      17
12.0       2
13.0       1
14.0       1
98.0       2
99.0      89
NaN     2863
Name: count, dtype: int64
```

The values are in the left column and the counts are in the right column. The most frequent values are 6-8 pounds, but there are some very light babies, a few very heavy babies, and two special values, 98, and 99. According to the codebook, these values indicate that the respondent declined to answer the question (98) or did not know (99).

7.3 Validation

We can validate the results by comparing them to the codebook, which lists the values and their frequencies.

Value	Label	Total
.	INAPPLICABLE	2863
0-5	UNDER 6 POUNDS	901
6	6 POUNDS	1644
7	7 POUNDS	2268
8	8 POUNDS	1287
9-95	9 POUNDS OR MORE	499
98	Refused	2
99	Don't know	89
Total		9553

The results from `value_counts` agree with the codebook, so we can be confident that we are reading and interpreting the data correctly.

Exercise: In `nsfg`, the `OUTCOME` column encodes the outcome of each pregnancy as shown below:

Value	Meaning
1	Live birth
2	Induced abortion
3	Stillbirth
4	Miscarriage
5	Ectopic pregnancy
6	Current pregnancy

Use `value_counts` to display the values in this column and how many times each value appears. Are the results consistent with the codebook?

7.4 Summary Statistics

Another way to validate the data is with `describe`, which computes statistics that summarize the data, like the mean, standard deviation, minimum, and maximum. Here are the results for `pounds`.

```
pounds.describe()
```
```
count    6690.000000
mean        8.008819
std        10.771360
min         0.000000
25%         6.000000
50%         7.000000
75%         8.000000
max        99.000000
Name: BIRTHWGT_LB1, dtype: float64
```

`count` is the number of values, not including `NaN`. `mean` and `std` are the mean and standard deviation. `min` and `max` are the minimum and maximum values, and in between are the 25th, 50th, and 75th percentiles. The 50th percentile is the median.

The mean is about 8.05, but that doesn't mean much because it includes the special values 98 and 99. Before we can really compute the mean, we have to replace those values with `NaN` to identify them as missing data. The `replace` method does what we want:

```
import numpy as np

pounds_clean = pounds.replace([98, 99], np.nan)
```

`replace` takes a list of the values we want to replace and the value we want to replace them with. `np.nan` means we are getting the special value `NaN` from the NumPy library, which is imported as `np`. The result is a new `Series`, which I assign to `pounds_clean`. If we run `describe` again, we see that `count` is smaller now because it includes only the valid values.

```
pounds_clean.describe()
```
```
count    6599.000000
mean        6.754357
std         1.383268
min         0.000000
25%         6.000000
50%         7.000000
75%         8.000000
max        14.000000
Name: BIRTHWGT_LB1, dtype: float64
```

7.5 Series Arithmetic

The mean of the new `Series` is about 6.7 pounds. Remember that the mean of the original `Series` was more than 8 pounds. It makes a big difference when you remove a few 99-pound babies!

The effect on standard deviation is even more dramatic. If we include the values 98 and 99, the standard deviation is 10.8. If we remove them – as we should – the standard deviation is 1.4.

Exercise: Use `describe` to summarize `ounces`. Then use `replace` to replace the special values 98 and 99 with `NaN`, and assign the result to `ounces_clean`. Run `describe` again. How much does this cleaning affect the results?

7.5 Series Arithmetic

Now we want to combine `pounds` and `ounces` into a single `Series` that contains total birth weight. With `Series` objects, the arithmetic operators work elementwise, as they do with NumPy arrays.

So, to convert `pounds` to ounces, we can write `pounds * 16`. Then, to add in `ounces` we can write `pounds * 16 + ounces`.

Exercise: Use `pounds_clean` and `ounces_clean` to compute the total birth weight expressed in kilograms (there are roughly 2.2 pounds per kilogram). What is the mean birth weight in kilograms?

7.6 Histograms

Let's get back to the original question: what is the average birth weight for babies in the U.S.? As an answer we *could* take the results from the previous section and compute the mean:

```
pounds_clean = pounds.replace([98, 99], np.nan)
ounces_clean = ounces.replace([98, 99], np.nan)

birth_weight = pounds_clean + ounces_clean / 16
birth_weight.mean()
```

7.180217889908257

But it is risky to compute a summary statistic, like the mean, before we look at the whole distribution of values. A **distribution** is a set of possible values and their frequencies. One way to visualize a distribution is a **histogram**, which shows values on the x-axis and their frequencies on the y-axis.

`Series` provides a `hist` method that makes histograms, and we can use Pyplot to label the axes.

```
import matplotlib.pyplot as plt

birth_weight.hist(bins=30)
plt.xlabel('Birth weight in pounds')
plt.ylabel('Number of live births')
plt.title('Distribution of U.S. birth weight');
```

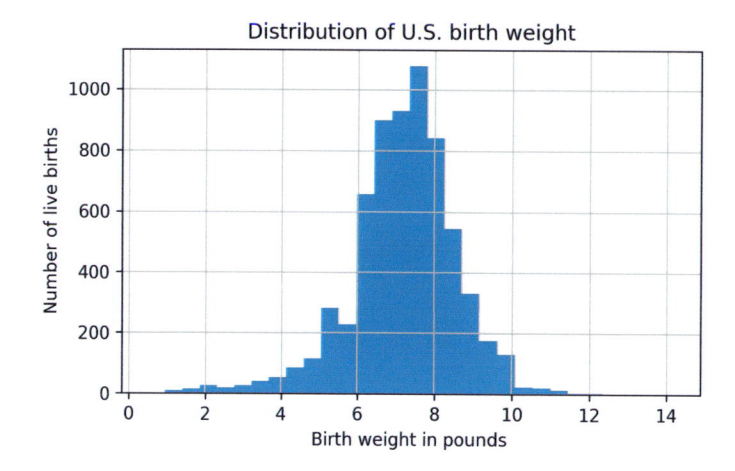

The keyword argument, `bins`, tells `hist` to divide the range of weights into 30 intervals, called **bins**, and count how many values fall in each bin. The x-axis is birth weight in pounds; the y-axis is the number of births in each bin.

The distribution looks like a bell curve, but the tail is longer on the left than on the right – that is, there are more light babies than heavy babies. That makes sense, because the distribution includes some babies that were born preterm.

Exercise: The NSFG dataset includes a column called `AGECON` that records a woman's age at conception for each pregnancy. Select this column from the `DataFrame` and plot the histogram of the values with 20 bins. Label the axes and add a title.

7.7 Boolean Series

We have seen that the distribution of birth weights is **skewed** to the left – that is, the left tail extends farther from the center than the right tail. That's because preterm babies tend to be lighter.

7.7 Boolean Series

To see which babies are preterm, we can use the `PRGLNGTH` column, which records pregnancy length in weeks. A baby is considered preterm if it is born prior to the 37th week of pregnancy.

```
preterm = (nsfg['PRGLNGTH'] < 37)
preterm.dtype
```

dtype('bool')

When you compare a `Series` to a value, the result is a Boolean `Series` – that is, a `Series` where each element is a Boolean value, `True` or `False`. In this case, it's `True` for each preterm baby and `False` otherwise. We can use `head` to see the first 5 elements.

```
preterm.head()
```

```
0    False
1     True
2    False
3    False
4    False
Name: PRGLNGTH, dtype: bool
```

For a Boolean `Series`, the `sum` method treats `True` as 1 and `False` as 0, so the result is the number of `True` values, which is the number of preterm babies.

```
preterm.sum()
```

3675

If you compute the mean of a Boolean `Series`, the result the *fraction* of `True` values. In this case, it's about 0.38 – which means about 38% of the pregnancies are less than 37 weeks in duration.

```
preterm.mean()
```

0.38469590704490736

However, this result is misleading because it includes all pregnancy outcomes, not just live births. We can use the `OUTCOME` column to create another Boolean `Series` to indicate which pregnancies ended in live birth.

```
live = (nsfg['OUTCOME'] == 1)
live.mean()
```

0.7006176070344394

Now we can use the `&` operator, which represents the logical AND operation, to identify pregnancies where the outcome is a live birth *and* preterm:

```
live_preterm = (live & preterm)
live_preterm.mean()
```

0.08929132209777034

About 9% of all pregnancies resulted in a preterm live birth.

The other common logical operators that work with `Series` objects are:

- `|`, which represents the logical OR operation – for example, `live | preterm` is true if either `live` is true, or `preterm` is true, or both.

- `~`, which represents the logical NOT operation – for example, `~live` is true if `live` not true.

The logical operators treat `NaN` the same as `False`, so you should be careful about using the NOT operator with a Series that contains `NaN` values. For example, `~preterm` would include not just full term pregnancies, but also pregnancies with unknown duration.

Exercise: Of all pregnancies, what fraction are live births at full term (37 weeks or more)? Of all live births, what fraction are full term?

7.8 Filtering Data

We can use a Boolean `Series` as a filter – that is, we can select only rows that satisfy a condition or meet some criterion. For example, we can use `preterm` and the bracket operator to select values from `birth_weight`, so `preterm_weight` gets birth weights for preterm babies.

```
preterm_weight = birth_weight[preterm]
preterm_weight.mean()
```

5.480958781362007

To select full-term babies, we can create a Boolean `Series` like this:

```
fullterm = (nsfg['PRGLNGTH'] >= 37)
```

And use it to select birth weights for full term babies:

```
full_term_weight = birth_weight[fullterm]
full_term_weight.mean()
```

7.429609416096791

7.9 Weighted Means

As expected, full term babies are heavier, on average, than preterm babies. To be more explicit, we could also limit the results to live births, like this:

```
full_term_weight = birth_weight[live & fullterm]
full_term_weight.mean()
```

7.429609416096791

But in this case we get the same result because `birth_weight` is only valid for live births.

Exercise: Let's see if there is a difference in weight between single births and multiple births (twins, triplets, etc.). The column `NBRNALIV` represents the number of babies born alive from a single pregnancy.

```
nbrnaliv = nsfg['NBRNALIV']
nbrnaliv.value_counts()
```

```
NBRNALIV
1.0    6573
2.0     111
3.0       6
Name: count, dtype: int64
```

Use `nbrnaliv` and `live` to create a Boolean series called `multiple` that is true for multiple live births. Of all live births, what fraction are multiple births?

Exercise: Make a Boolean series called `single` that is true for single live births. Of all single births, what fraction are preterm? Of all multiple births, what fraction are preterm?

Exercise: What is the average birth weight for live, single, full-term births?

7.9 Weighted Means

We are almost done, but there's one more problem we have to solve: oversampling. The NSFG sample is not exactly representative of the U.S. population. By design, some groups are more likely to appear in the sample than others – that is, they are **oversampled**. Oversampling helps to ensure that you have enough people in every group to get reliable statistics, but it makes data analysis a little more complicated.

Each pregnancy in the dataset has a **sampling weight** that indicates how many pregnancies it represents. In `nsfg`, the sampling weight is stored in a column named `wgt2015_2017`.

Here's what it looks like.

```
sampling_weight = nsfg['WGT2015_2017']
sampling_weight.describe()
```

```
count      9553.000000
mean      13337.425944
std       16138.878271
min        1924.916000
25%        4575.221221
50%        7292.490835
75%       15724.902673
max      106774.400000
Name: WGT2015_2017, dtype: float64
```

The median value (50th percentile) in this column is about 7292, which means that a pregnancy with that weight represents 7292 total pregnancies in the population. But the range of values is wide, so some rows represent many more pregnancies than others.

To take these weights into account, we can compute a **weighted mean**. Here are the steps:

1. Multiply the birth weights for each pregnancy by the sampling weights and add up the products.

2. Add up the sampling weights.

3. Divide the first sum by the second.

To do this correctly, we have to be careful with missing data. To help with that, we'll use two `Series` methods, `isna` and `notna`. `isna` returns a Boolean `Series` that is `True` where the corresponding value is `NaN`.

```
missing = birth_weight.isna()
missing.sum()
```

3013

In `birth_weight` there are 3013 missing values (mostly for pregnancies that did not end in live birth). `notna` returns a Boolean `Series` that is `True` where the corresponding value is *not* `NaN`.

```
valid = birth_weight.notna()
valid.sum()
```

6540

7.10 Making an Extract

We can combine `valid` with the other Boolean `Series` we have computed to identify single, full term, live births with valid birth weights.

```
single = (nbrnaliv == 1)
selected = valid & live & single & fullterm
selected.sum()
```

5648

You can finish off this computation as an exercise.

Exercise: Use `selected`, `birth_weight`, and `sampling_weight` to compute the weighted mean of birth weight for live, single, full term births. You should find that the weighted mean is a little higher than the unweighted mean we computed in the previous section. That's because the groups that are oversampled in the NSFG tend to have lighter babies, on average.

7.10 Making an Extract

The NSFG dataset is large, and reading a fixed-width file is relatively slow. So now that we've read it, let's save a smaller version in a more efficient format. When we come back to this dataset in Chapter 13, here are the columns we'll need.

```
variables = ['CASEID', 'OUTCOME', 'BIRTHWGT_LB1', 'BIRTHWGT_OZ1',
             'PRGLNGTH', 'NBRNALIV', 'AGECON', 'AGEPREG', 'BIRTHORD',
             'HPAGELB', 'WGT2015_2017']
```

And here's how we can select just those columns from the `DataFrame`.

```
subset = nsfg[variables]
subset.shape
```

(9553, 11)

`DataFrame` provides several methods for writing data to a file – the one we'll use is `to_hdf`, which creates an HDF file. The parameters are the name of the new file, the name of the object we're storing in the file, and the compression level, which determines how effectively the data are compressed.

```
filename = 'nsfg.hdf'
nsfg.to_hdf(filename, key='nsfg', complevel=6)
```

The result is much smaller than the original fixed-width file, and faster to read.

We can read it back like this.

```
nsfg = pd.read_hdf(filename, key='nsfg')
```

7.11 Summary

This chapter poses what seems like a simple question: what is the average birth weight of babies in the United States?

To answer it, we found an appropriate dataset and downloaded the files. We used Pandas to read the files and create a `DataFrame`. Then we validated the data and dealt with special values and missing data. To explore the data, we used `value_counts`, `hist`, `describe`, and other methods. And to select relevant data, we used Boolean `Series` objects.

Along the way, we had to think more about the question. What do we mean by "average", and which babies should we include? Should we include all live births or exclude preterm babies or multiple births?

And we had to think about the sampling process. By design, the NSFG respondents are not representative of the U.S. population, but we can use sampling weights to correct for this effect.

Even a simple question can be a challenging data science project.

A note on vocabulary: In a dataset like the one we used in this chapter, we could say that each column represents a "variable", and what we called column names might also be called variable names. I avoided that use of the term because it might be confusing to say that we select a "variable" from a `DataFrame` and assign it to a Python variable. But you might see this use of the term elsewhere, so I thought I would mention it.

Chapter 8

Distributions

In this chapter we'll see three ways to describe a distribution:

- A probability mass function (PMF), which represents a set of values and the number of times each one appears in a dataset.

- A cumulative distribution function (CDF), which contains the same information as a PMF in a form that makes it easier to visualize, make comparisons, and perform some computations.

- A kernel density estimate (KDE), which is like a smooth, continuous version of a histogram.

As examples, we'll use data from the General Social Survey (GSS) to look at distributions of age and income, and to explore the relationship between income and education. But we'll start with one of the most important ideas in statistics, the distribution.

8.1 Distributions

A distribution is a set of values and their corresponding probabilities. For example, if you roll a six-sided die, there are six possible outcomes – the numbers 1 through 6 – and they all have the same probability, 1/6. We can represent this distribution of outcomes with a table, like this:

Outcome	1	2	3	4	5	6
Probability	1/6	1/6	1/6	1/6	1/6	1/6

More generally, a distribution can have any number of values, the values can be any type, and the probabilities do not have to be equal. To represent distributions in Python, we'll use a library called `empiricaldist`, which stands for "empirical distribution", where "empirical" means it is based on data rather than a mathematical formula.

`empiricaldist` provides an object type called `Pmf`, which stands for "probability mass function". A `Pmf` object contains a set of possible outcomes and their probabilities. For example, here's a `Pmf` that represents the outcome of rolling a six-sided die:

```
from empiricaldist import Pmf

outcomes = [1,2,3,4,5,6]
die = Pmf(1/6, outcomes)
```

The first argument is the probability of the outcomes; the second argument is the list of outcomes. We can display the result like this.

```
die
```

	probs
1	0.166667
2	0.166667
3	0.166667
4	0.166667
5	0.166667
6	0.166667

A `Pmf` object is a specialized version of a Pandas `Series`, so it provides all of the methods of a `Series`, plus some additional methods we'll see soon.

8.2 The General Social Survey

We'll use `Pmf` objects to represent distributions of values from a new dataset, the General Social Survey (GSS). The GSS surveys a representative sample of adult residents of the U.S. and asks questions about demographics, personal history, and beliefs about social and political issues. It is widely used by politicians, policy makers, and researchers.

The GSS dataset contains hundreds of columns. I've selected just a few and save the extract in an HDF file, which is more compact than the original fixed-width file, and faster to read. Instructions for downloading the file are in the notebook for this chapter.

```
data_file = 'gss_extract_2022.hdf'
```

We'll use the Pandas `read_hdf` function to read the data file and load `gss`, which is a `DataFrame`.

8.3 Distribution of Education

```python
import pandas as pd

gss = pd.read_hdf(data_file, 'gss')
gss.shape
```

(72390, 9)

`gss` has one row for each respondent and one column for each question in the extract. Here are the first few rows.

```python
gss.head()
```

	year	id	age	educ	degree	sex	gunlaw	grass	realinc
0	1972	1	23	16	3	2	1	NaN	18951
1	1972	2	70	10	0	1	1	NaN	24366
2	1972	3	48	12	1	2	1	NaN	24366
3	1972	4	27	17	3	2	1	NaN	30458
4	1972	5	61	12	1	2	1	NaN	50763

I'll explain these columns as we go along, but if you want more information, you can read the online documentation at https://gssdataexplorer.norc.org. In the GSS documentation, you'll see that they use the term "variable" for a column that contains answers to survey questions.

8.3 Distribution of Education

To get started with this dataset, let's look at the `educ` column, which records the number of years of education for each respondent. We can select this column from the `DataFrame` like this:

```python
educ = gss['educ']
```

To see what the distribution of the responses looks like, we can use the `hist` method to plot a histogram.

```python
import matplotlib.pyplot as plt

educ.hist(grid=False)
plt.xlabel('Years of education')
plt.ylabel('Number of respondents')
plt.title('Histogram of education level');
```

Histogram of education level

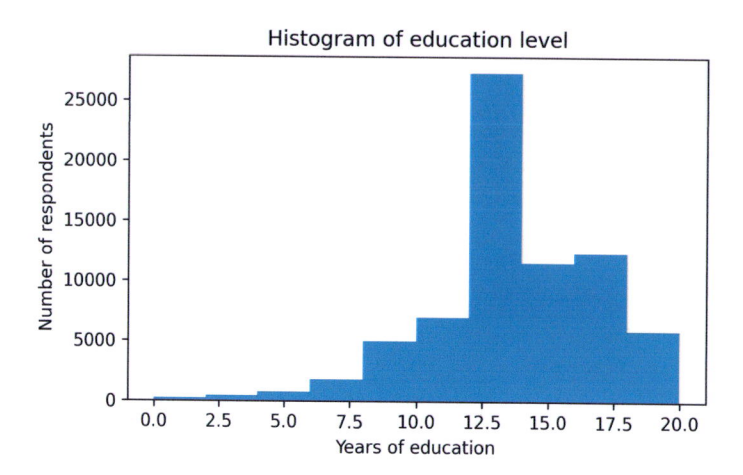

Based on the histogram, we can see the general shape of the distribution and the central tendency – it looks like the peak is near 12 years of education. But a histogram is not the best way to visualize this distribution because it obscures some important details.

An alternative is to use a `Pmf` object. The function `Pmf.from_seq` takes any kind of sequence – like a list, tuple, or Pandas `Series` – and computes the distribution of the values.

```
pmf_educ = Pmf.from_seq(educ, normalize=False)
type(pmf_educ)
```

empiricaldist.empiricaldist.Pmf

With the keyword argument `normalize=False`, the result contains counts rather than probabilities. Here are the first few values in `educ` and their counts.

```
pmf_educ.head()
```

	probs
educ	
0.000000	177
1.000000	49
2.000000	158

In this dataset, there are 177 respondents who report that they have no formal education, and 49 who have only one year.

8.3 Distribution of Education

Here are the last few values.

```
pmf_educ.tail()
```

	probs
educ	
18.000000	2945
19.000000	1112
20.000000	1803

There are 1803 respondents who report that they have 20 or more years of formal education, which probably means they attended college and graduate school. We can use the bracket operator to look up a value in `pmf_educ` and get the corresponding count.

```
pmf_educ[20]
```

1803

Often when we make a `Pmf`, we want to know the *fraction* of respondents with each value, rather than the counts. We can do that by setting `normalize=True`. Then we get a **normalized** `Pmf`, which means that the fractions add up to 1.

```
pmf_educ_norm = Pmf.from_seq(educ, normalize=True)
pmf_educ_norm.head()
```

	probs
educ	
0.000000	0.002454
1.000000	0.000679357
2.000000	0.00219058

Now if we use the bracket operator to look up a value, the result is a fraction rather than a count.

```
pmf_educ_norm[20]
```

0.0249975737241255

The result indicates that about 2.5% of the respondents have 20 years of education. But we can also interpret this result as a probability – if we choose a random respondent, the probability is 2.5% that they have 20 years of education.

When a `Pmf` contains probabilities, we can say that it represents a proper probability mass function, or PMF. With apologies for confusing notation, I'll use `Pmf` to mean a kind of Python object, and PMF to mean the concept of a probability mass function.

`Pmf` provides a `bar` method that plots the values and their probabilities as a bar chart.

```
pmf_educ_norm.bar(label='educ')

plt.xlabel('Years of education')
plt.xticks(range(0, 21, 4))
plt.ylabel('PMF')
plt.title('Distribution of years of education')
plt.legend();
```

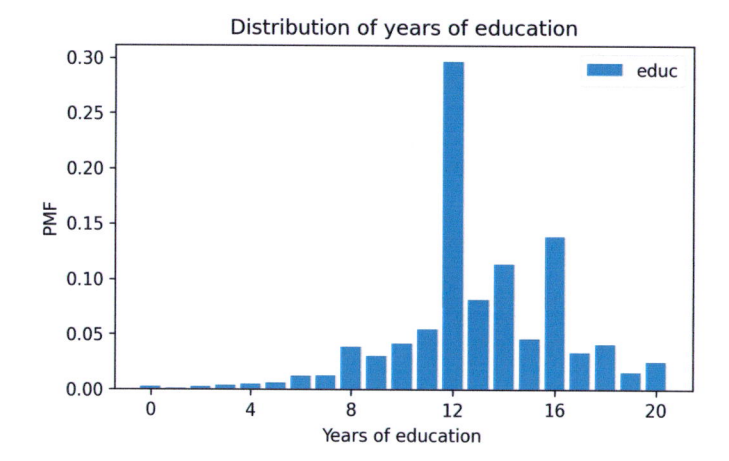

In this figure, we can see that the most common value is 12 years, but there are also peaks at 14 and 16, which correspond to two and four years of college. For this data, plotting the `Pmf` is probably a better choice than the histogram. The `Pmf` shows all unique values, so we can see where the peaks are.

Exercise: Let's look at the `year` column in the `DataFrame`, which represents the year each respondent was interviewed. Make an unnormalized `Pmf` for `year` and plot the result as a bar chart. Use the bracket operator to look up the number of respondents interviewed in 2022.

8.4 Cumulative Distribution Functions

If we compute the cumulative sum of a PMF, the result is a cumulative distribution function (CDF). To see what that means, and why it is useful, let's look at a simple example. Suppose we have a sequence of five values.

```
values = 1, 2, 2, 3, 5
```

8.4 Cumulative Distribution Functions

Here's the `Pmf` of these values.

```
pmf = Pmf.from_seq(values)
pmf
```

	probs
1	0.2
2	0.4
3	0.2
5	0.2

If you draw a random value from `values`, the `Pmf` tells you the chance of getting x, for any value of x.

- The probability of the value 1 is `0.2`,
- The probability of the value 2 is `0.4`, and
- The probabilities for 3 and 5 are `0.2` each.

The `Pmf` object has a method called `make_cdf` that computes the cumulative sum of the probabilities in the `Pmf` and returns a `Cdf` object.

```
cdf = pmf.make_cdf()
cdf
```

	probs
1	0.2
2	0.6
3	0.8
5	1

If you draw a random value from `values`, the `Cdf` tells you the chance of getting a value *less than or equal to* x, for any given x.

- The `Cdf` of 1 is `0.2` because one of the five values is less than or equal to 1,
- The `Cdf` of 2 is `0.6` because three of the five values are less than or equal to 2,
- The `Cdf` of 3 is `0.8` because four of the five values are less than or equal to 3,
- The `Cdf` of 5 is `1.0` because all of the values are less than or equal to 5.

If we make a `Cdf` from a proper `Pmf`, where the probabilities add up to 1, the result represents a proper CDF. As with `Pmf` and PMF, I'll use `Cdf` to refer to a Python object and CDF to refer to the concept.

8.5 CDF of Age

To see why CDFs are useful, let's consider the distribution of ages for respondents in the General Social Survey. The column we'll use is `age`.

According to the codebook, the range of the values is from 18 to 89, where 89 means "89 or older". The special codes 98 and 99 mean "Don't know" and "Didn't answer". We can use `replace` to replace the special codes with `NaN`.

```
age = gss['age']
```

`empiricaldist` provides a `Cdf.from_seq` function that takes any kind of sequence and computes the CDF of the values.

```
from empiricaldist import Cdf

cdf_age = Cdf.from_seq(age)
```

The result is a `Cdf` object, which provides a method called `plot` that plots the CDF as a line.

```
cdf_age.plot()

plt.xlabel('Age (years)')
plt.ylabel('CDF')
plt.title('Distribution of age');
```

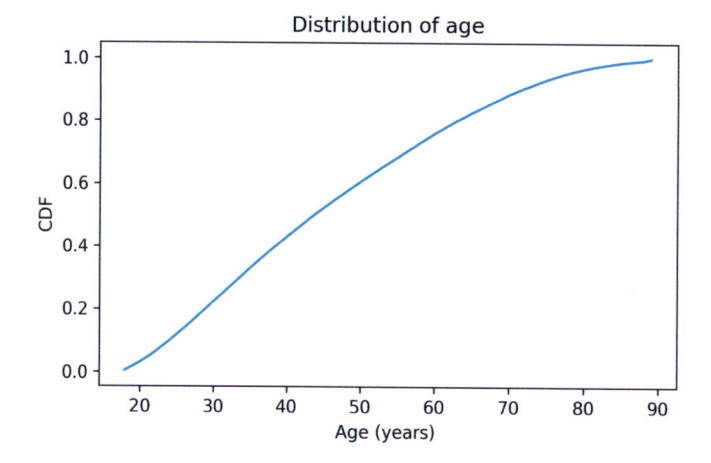

The x-axis is the ages, from 18 to 89. The y-axis is the cumulative probabilities, from 0 to 1.

8.5 CDF of Age

The `Cdf` object can be used as a function, so if you give it an age, it returns the corresponding probability in a NumPy array.

```
q = 51
p = cdf_age(q)
p
```

`array(0.62121445)`

q stands for "quantity", which is another name for a value in a distribution. p stands for probability, which is the result. In this example, the quantity is age 51, and the corresponding probability is about 0.62. That means that about 62% of the respondents are age 51 or younger. The arrow in the following figure shows how you could read this value from the CDF, at least approximately.

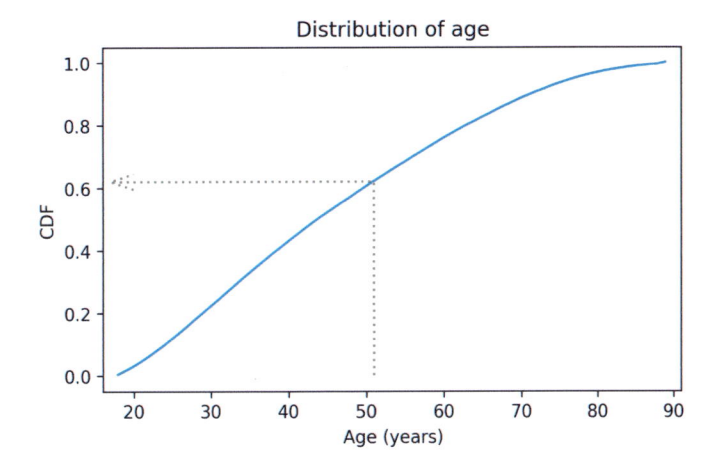

The CDF is an invertible function, which means that if you have a probability, p, you can look up the corresponding quantity, q. The `Cdf` object provides a method called `inverse` that computes the inverse of the cumulative distribution function.

```
p1 = 0.25
q1 = cdf_age.inverse(p1)
q1
```

`array(32.)`

In this example, we look up the probability 0.25 and the result is 32. That means that 25% of the respondents are age 32 or less. Another way to say the same thing is "age 32 is the 25th percentile of this distribution".

If we look up probability 0.75, it returns 60, so 75% of the respondents are 60 or younger.

```
p2 = 0.75
q2 = cdf_age.inverse(p2)
q2
```

```
array(60.)
```

In the following figure, the arrows show how you could read these values from the CDF.

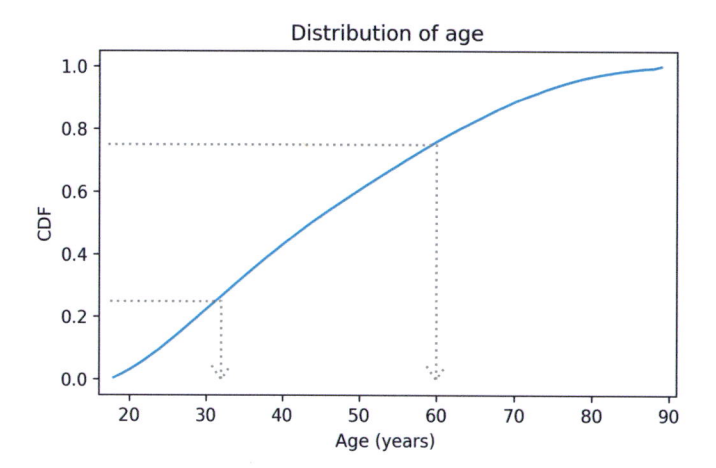

Distribution of age

The distance from the 25th to the 75th percentile is called the **interquartile range** or IQR. It measures the spread of the distribution, so it is similar to standard deviation or variance. Because it is based on percentiles, it doesn't get thrown off by outliers as much as standard deviation does. So IQR is more **robust** than variance, which means it works well even if there are errors in the data or extreme values.

Exercise: Using `cdf_age`, compute the fraction of respondents in the GSS dataset who are *older* than 65. Recall that the CDF computes the fraction who are less than or equal to a value, so the complement is the fraction who exceed a value.

Exercise: The distribution of income in almost every country is long-tailed, which means there are a small number of people with very high incomes. In the GSS dataset, the `realinc` column represents total household income, converted to 1986 dollars. We can get a sense of the shape of this distribution by plotting the CDF. Select `realinc` from the `gss` dataset, make a `Cdf` called `cdf_income`, and plot it. Remember to label the axes!

Because the tail of the distribution extends to the right, the mean is greater than the median. Use the `Cdf` object to compute the fraction of respondents whose income is at or below the mean.

8.6 Comparing Distributions

So far we've seen two ways to represent distributions, PMFs and CDFs. Now we'll use PMFs and CDFs to compare distributions, and we'll see the pros and cons of each. One way to compare distributions is to plot multiple PMFs on the same axes. For example, suppose we want to compare the distribution of age for male and female respondents. First we'll create a Boolean Series that's true for male respondents and another that's true for female respondents.

```
male = (gss['sex'] == 1)
female = (gss['sex'] == 2)
```

We can use these Series to select ages for male and female respondents.

```
male_age = age[male]
female_age = age[female]
```

And plot a PMF for each.

```
pmf_male_age = Pmf.from_seq(male_age)
pmf_male_age.plot(label='Male')

pmf_female_age = Pmf.from_seq(female_age)
pmf_female_age.plot(label='Female')

plt.xlabel('Age (years)')
plt.ylabel('PMF')
plt.title('Distribution of age by sex')
plt.legend();
```

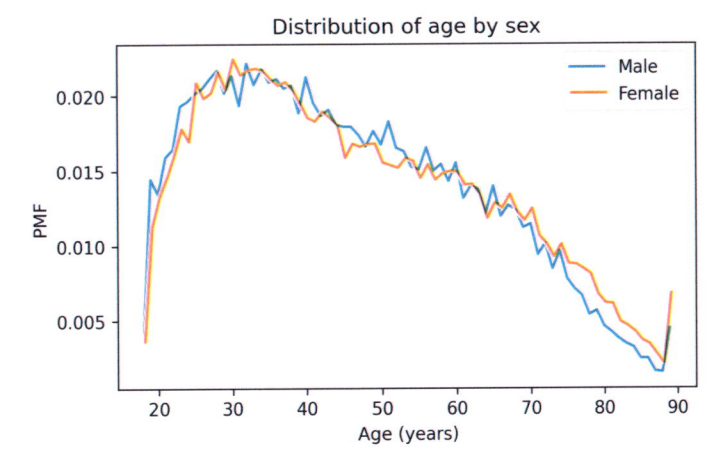

A plot as variable as this is often described as **noisy**. If we ignore the noise, it looks like the PMF is higher for men between ages 40 and 50, and higher for women between ages 70 and 80. But both of those differences might be due to randomness.

Now let's do the same thing with CDFs – everything is the same except we replace `Pmf` with `Cdf`.

```
cdf_male_age = Cdf.from_seq(male_age)
cdf_male_age.plot(label='Male')

cdf_female_age = Cdf.from_seq(female_age)
cdf_female_age.plot(label='Female')

plt.xlabel('Age (years)')
plt.ylabel('CDF')
plt.title('Distribution of age by sex')
plt.legend();
```

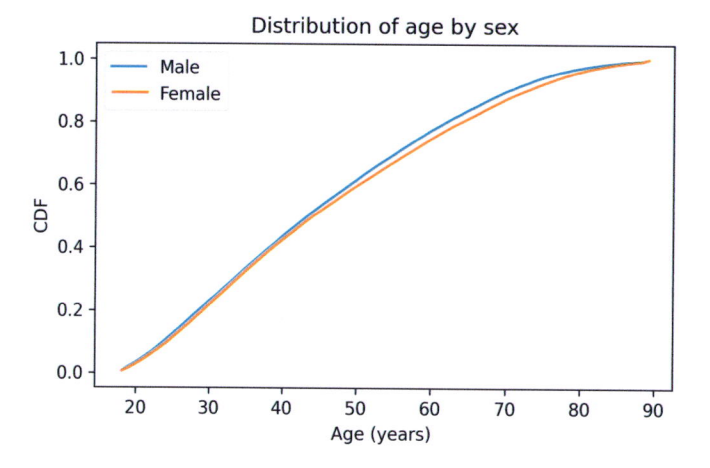

Because CDFs smooth out randomness, they provide a better view of real differences between distributions. In this case, the lines are close together until age 40 – after that, the CDF is higher for men than women.

So what does that mean? One way to interpret the difference is that the fraction of men below a given age is generally more than the fraction of women below the same age. For example, about 77% of men are 60 or less, compared to 75% of women.

```
cdf_male_age(60), cdf_female_age(60)
```

(array(0.7721998), array(0.7474241))

8.7 Comparing Incomes

Going the other way, we could also compare percentiles. For example, the median age woman is older than the median age man, by about one year.

```
cdf_male_age.inverse(0.5), cdf_female_age.inverse(0.5)
```

```
(array(44.), array(45.))
```

Exercise: What fraction of men are over 80? What fraction of women?

8.7 Comparing Incomes

As another example, let's look at household income and compare the distribution before and after 1995 (I chose 1995 because it's roughly the midpoint of the survey). We'll make two Boolean `Series` objects to select respondents interviewed before and after 1995.

```
pre95 = (gss['year'] < 1995)
post95 = (gss['year'] >= 1995)
```

Now we can plot the PMFs of `realinc`, which records household income converted to 1986 dollars.

```
realinc = gss['realinc']

Pmf.from_seq(realinc[pre95]).plot(label='Before 1995')
Pmf.from_seq(realinc[post95]).plot(label='After 1995')

plt.xlabel('Income (1986 USD)')
plt.ylabel('PMF')
plt.title('Distribution of income')
plt.legend();
```

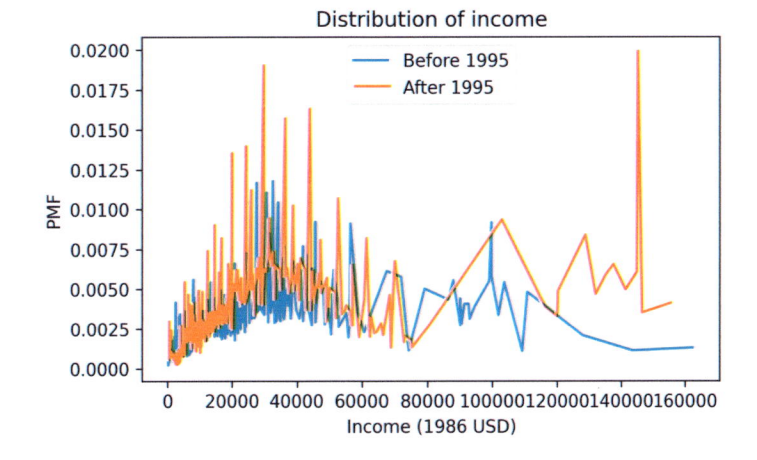

There are a lot of unique values in this distribution, and none of them appear very often. As a result, the PMF is so noisy and we can't really see the shape of the distribution. It's also hard to compare the distributions. It looks like there are more people with high incomes after 1995, but it's hard to tell. We can get a clearer picture with a CDF.

```
Cdf.from_seq(realinc[pre95]).plot(label='Before 1995')
Cdf.from_seq(realinc[post95]).plot(label='After 1995')

plt.xlabel('Income (1986 USD)')
plt.ylabel('CDF')
plt.title('Distribution of income')
plt.legend();
```

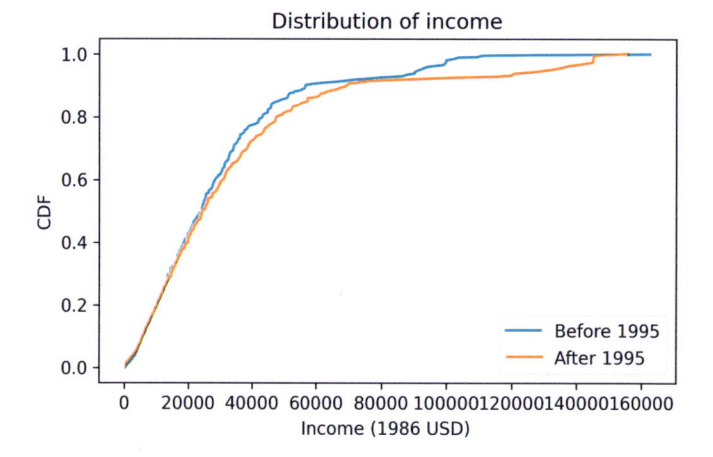

Below $30,000 the CDFs are almost identical; above that, we can see that the post-1995 distribution is shifted to the right. In other words, the fraction of people with high incomes is about the same, but the income of high earners has increased.

In general, I recommend CDFs for exploratory analysis. They give you a clear view of the distribution, without too much noise, and they are good for comparing distributions.

Exercise: Let's compare incomes for different levels of education in the GSS dataset. We'll use the `degree` column, which represents the highest degree each respondent has earned. In this column, the value 1 indicates a high school diploma, 2 indicates an Associate's degree, and 3 indicates a Bachelor's degree.

Compute and plot the distribution of income for each group. Remember to label the CDFs, display a legend, and label the axes. Write a few sentences that describe and interpret the results.

8.8 Modeling Distributions

Some distributions have names. For example, you might be familiar with the normal distribution, also called the Gaussian distribution or the bell curve. And you might have heard of others like the exponential distribution, binomial distribution, or maybe Poisson distribution. These "distributions with names" are called **theoretical** because they are based on mathematical functions, as contrasted with empirical distributions, which are based on data.

Many things we measure have distributions that are well approximated by theoretical distributions, so these distributions are sometimes good models for the real world. In this context, what I mean by a **model** is a simplified description of the world that is accurate enough for its intended purpose.

To check whether a theoretical distribution is a good model for a dataset, we can compare the CDF of the data to the CDF of a normal distribution with the same mean and standard deviation. I'll demonstrate with a sample from a normal distribution, then we'll try it with real data.

The following statement uses NumPy's `random` library to generate 1000 values from a normal distribution with mean 10 and standard deviation 1.

```
sample = np.random.normal(10, 1, size=1000)
```

Here's what the empirical distribution of the sample looks like.

```
cdf_sample = Cdf.from_seq(sample)
cdf_sample.plot(label='Random sample')

plt.xlabel('x')
plt.ylabel('CDF')
plt.legend();
```

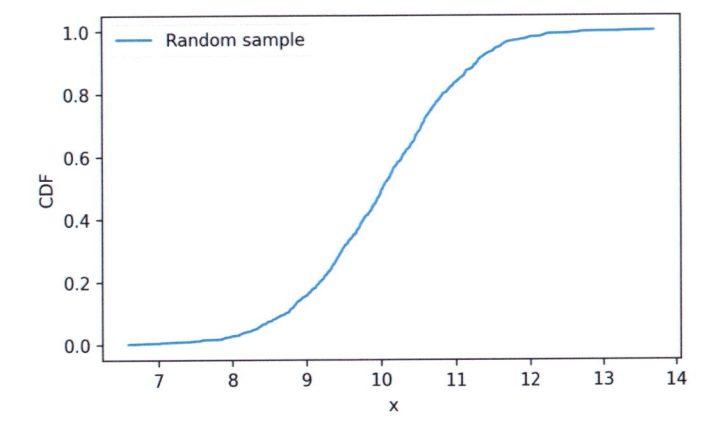

Now let's compute the CDF of a normal distribution with the actual values of the mean and standard deviation.

```
from scipy.stats import norm

qs = np.linspace(6, 14)
ps = norm(10, 1).cdf(qs)
```

First we import `norm` from `scipy.stats`, which is a collection of functions related to statistics. Then we use `linspace()` to create an array of equally-spaced values from -3 to 3 – those are the `qs` where we will evaluate the normal CDF. Next, `norm(10, 1)` creates an object that represents a normal distribution with mean 10 and standard deviation 1. Finally, `cdf` computes the CDF of the normal distribution, evaluated at each of the `qs`.

I'll plot the normal CDF with a gray line and then plot the CDF of the data again.

```
plt.plot(qs, ps, color='gray', label='Normal CDF')
cdf_sample.plot(label='Random sample')

plt.xlabel('x')
plt.ylabel('CDF')
plt.legend();
```

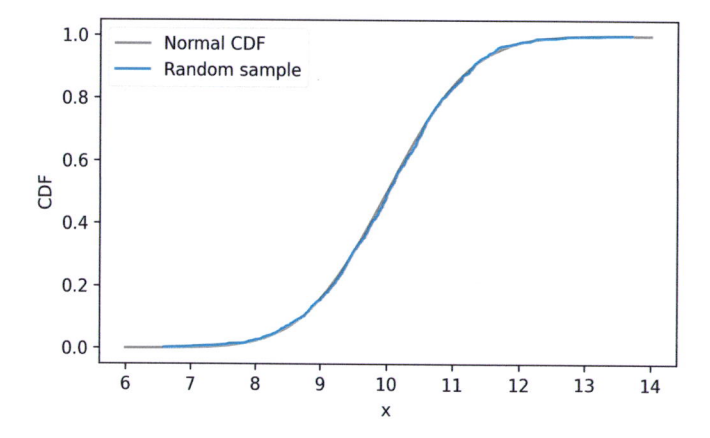

The CDF of the random sample agrees with the normal model – which is not surprising because the data were actually sampled from a normal distribution. When we collect data in the real world, we do not expect it to fit a normal distribution as well as this. In the next exercise, we'll try it and see.

Exercise: In many datasets, the distribution of income is approximately **lognormal**, which means that the logarithms of the incomes fit a normal distribution. Let's see whether that's true for the GSS data.

8.9 Kernel Density Estimation

- Extract `realinc` from `gss` and compute the logarithms of the incomes using `np.log10()`.

- Compute the mean and standard deviation of the log-transformed incomes.

- Use `norm` to make a normal distribution with the same mean and standard deviation as the log-transformed incomes.

- Plot the CDF of the normal distribution.

- Compute and plot the CDF of the log-transformed incomes.

How similar are the CDFs of the log-transformed incomes and the normal distribution?

8.9 Kernel Density Estimation

We have seen two ways to represent distributions, PMFs and CDFs. Now we'll learn another way: a probability density function, or PDF. The `norm` function, which we used to compute the normal CDF, can also compute the normal PDF.

```
xs = np.linspace(6, 14)
ys = norm(10, 1).pdf(xs)
```

Here's what it looks like.

```
plt.plot(xs, ys, color='gray', label='Normal PDF')

plt.xlabel('x')
plt.ylabel('PDF')
plt.title('Normal density function')
plt.legend();
```

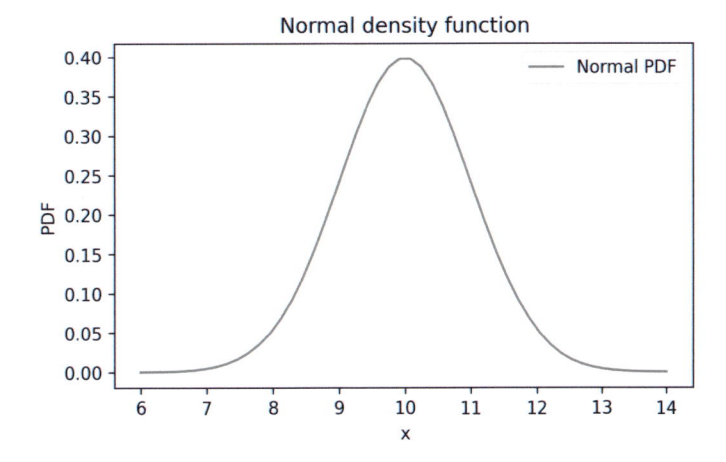

The normal PDF is the classic "bell curve". Now, it is tempting to compare the PMF of the data to the PDF of the normal distribution, but that doesn't work. Let's see what happens if we try:

```
plt.plot(xs, ys, color='gray', label='Normal PDF')

pmf_sample = Pmf.from_seq(sample)
pmf_sample.plot(label='Random sample')

plt.xlabel('x')
plt.ylabel('PDF')
plt.title('Normal density function')
plt.legend();
```

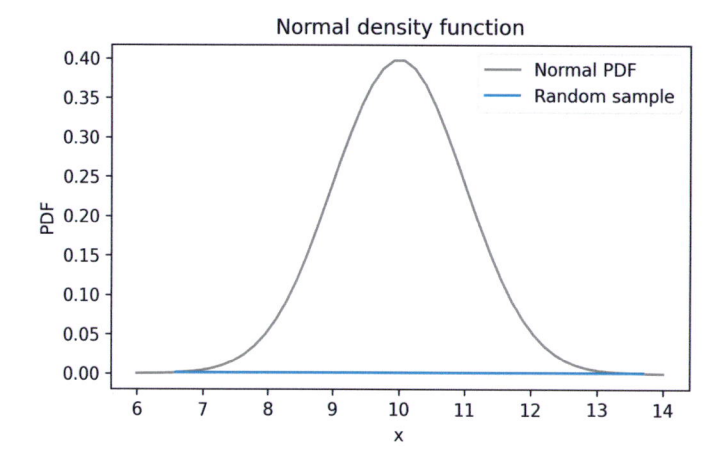

The PMF of the sample is a flat line across the bottom. In the random sample, every value is unique, so they all have the same probability, one in 1000.

However, we can use the points in the sample to estimate the PDF of the distribution they came from. This process is called **kernel density estimation**, or KDE. To generate a KDE plot, we'll use the Seaborn library, imported as `sns`. Seaborn provides `kdeplot`, which takes the sample, estimates the PDF, and plots it.

```
import seaborn as sns

sns.kdeplot(sample, label='Estimated sample PDF')

plt.xlabel('x')
plt.ylabel('PDF')
plt.title('Normal density function')
plt.legend();
```

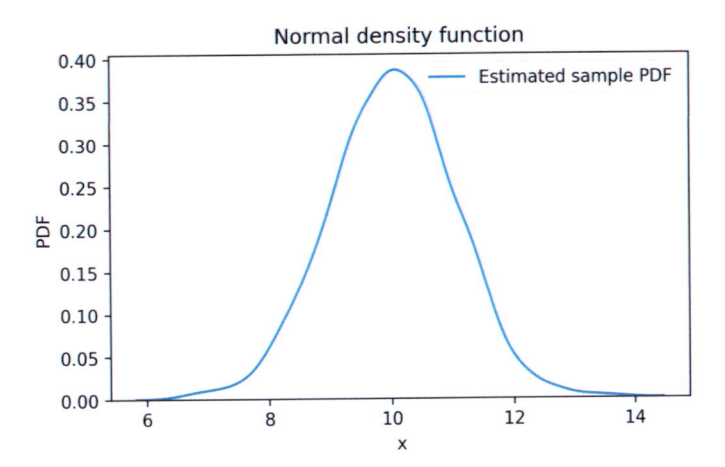

8.9 Kernel Density Estimation

[Figure: Normal density function showing Estimated sample PDF curve, x-axis from ~5 to ~14, PDF from 0.00 to 0.40]

Now we can compare the KDE plot and the normal PDF.

```
plt.plot(xs, ys, color='gray', label='Normal PDF')
sns.kdeplot(sample, label='Estimated sample PDF')

plt.xlabel('x')
plt.ylabel('PDF')
plt.title('Normal density function')
plt.legend();
```

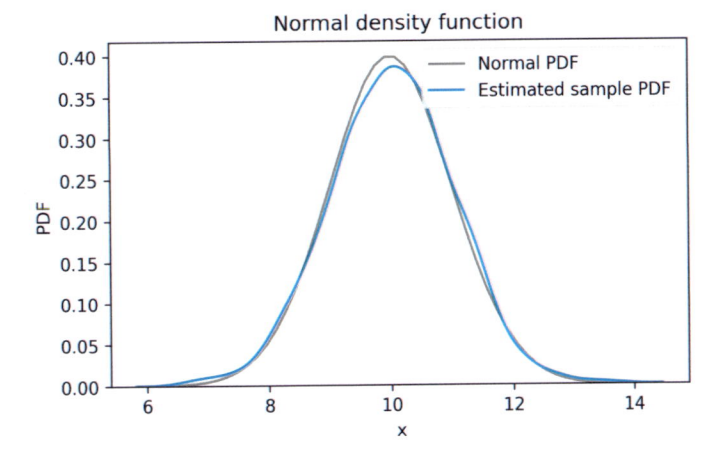

[Figure: Normal density function with Normal PDF (gray) and Estimated sample PDF (blue) overlaid]

The KDE plot matches the normal PDF well. We can see places where the data deviate from the model, but because we know the data really came from a normal distribution, we know those deviations are due to random sampling.

Comparing PDFs is a sensitive way to look for differences, but often it is too sensitive – it can be hard to tell whether apparent differences mean anything, or if they are just random, as in this case.

Exercise: In a previous exercise, we used CDFs to see if the distribution of income fits a lognormal distribution. We can make the same comparison using a PDF and KDE.

- Again, extract `realinc` from `gss` and compute its logarithm using `np.log10()`.

- Compute the mean and standard deviation of the log-transformed incomes.

- Use `norm` to make a normal distribution with the same mean and standard deviation as the log-transformed incomes.

- Plot the PDF of the normal distribution.

- Use `sns.kdeplot()` to estimate and plot the density of the log-transformed incomes.

8.10 Summary

In this chapter, we've seen three ways to visualize distributions: PMFs, CDFs, and KDE plots. In general, I use CDFs when I am exploring data – that way, I get the best view of what's going on without getting distracted by noise. Then, if I am presenting results to an audience unfamiliar with CDFs, I might use a PMF if the dataset contains a small number of unique values, or KDE if there are many unique values.

Chapter 9

Relationships

This chapter explores relationships between variables.

- We will visualize relationships using scatter plots, box plots, and violin plots,
- And we will quantify relationships using correlation and simple regression.

The most important lesson in this chapter is that you should always visualize the relationship between variables before you try to quantify it – otherwise, you are likely to be misled.

9.1 Exploring relationships

So far we have mostly considered one variable at a time. Now it's time to explore relationships between variables. As a first example, we'll look at the relationship between height and weight. We'll use data from the Behavioral Risk Factor Surveillance System (BRFSS), which is run by the Centers for Disease Control. Based on the BRFSS data from 2021, I have created an extract with one row for each survey respondent and one column for each of the variables I selected.

```
import pandas as pd

brfss = pd.read_hdf('brfss_2021.hdf', 'brfss')
brfss.shape
```

(438693, 10)

Here are the first few rows.

```
brfss.head()
```

	HTM4	WTKG3	_SEX	_AGEG5YR	_VEGESU1	_INCOMG1	_LLCPWT	_HTM4G10	AGE
0	150	32.66	2	11	2.14	3	744.746	140	72
1	168	NaN	2	10	1.28	NaN	299.137	160	67
2	165	77.11	2	11	0.71	2	587.863	160	72
3	163	88.45	2	9	1.65	5	1099.62	160	62
4	180	93.44	1	12	2.58	2	1711.83	170	77

The BRFSS includes hundreds of variables. For the examples in this chapter, we'll work with just these nine. The ones we'll start with are `HTM4`, which records each respondent's height in centimeters, and `WTKG3`, which records weight in kilograms.

```
height = brfss['HTM4']
weight = brfss['WTKG3']
```

To visualize the relationship between these variables, we'll make a **scatter plot**, which shows one marker for each pair of values. Scatter plots are common and readily understood, but they are surprisingly hard to get right. As a first attempt, we'll use `plot` with the style string `o`, which plots a circle for each data point.

```
import matplotlib.pyplot as plt

plt.plot(height, weight, 'o')

plt.xlabel('Height in cm')
plt.ylabel('Weight in kg')
plt.title('Scatter plot of weight versus height');
```

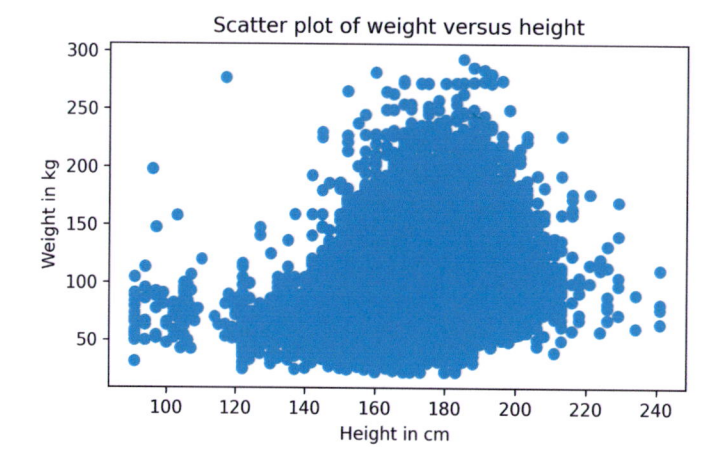

9.1 Exploring relationships

Each marker represents the height and weight of one person. Based on the shape of the result, it looks like taller people are heavier, but there are a few things about this plot that make it hard to interpret. Most importantly, it is **overplotted**, which means that there are markers piled on top of each other so you can't tell where there are a lot of data points and where there is just one. When that happens, the picture can be misleading.

One way to improve the plot is to use transparency, which we can do with the keyword argument `alpha`. The lower the value of alpha, the more transparent each data point is.
Here's what it looks like with `alpha=0.01`.

```
plt.plot(height, weight, 'o', alpha=0.01)

plt.xlabel('Height in cm')
plt.ylabel('Weight in kg')
plt.title('Scatter plot of weight versus height');
```

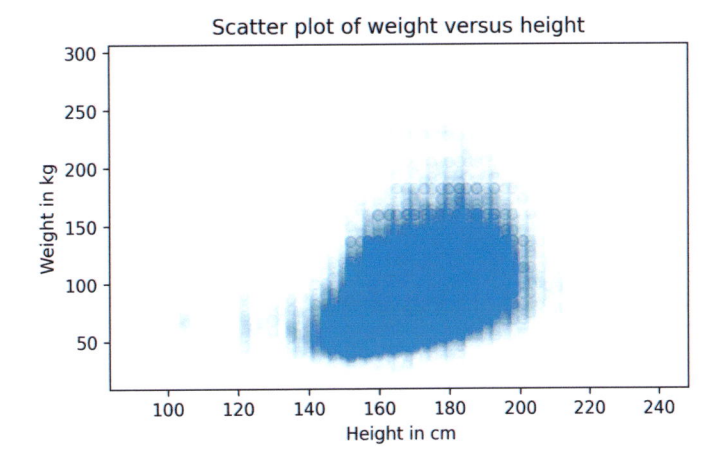

This is better, but there are so many data points, the scatter plot is still overplotted. The next step is to make the markers smaller. With `markersize=0.5` and a low value of alpha, the scatter plot is less saturated. Here's what it looks like.

```
plt.plot(height, weight, 'o', alpha=0.01, markersize=0.5)

plt.xlabel('Height in cm')
plt.ylabel('Weight in kg')
plt.title('Scatter plot of weight versus height');
```

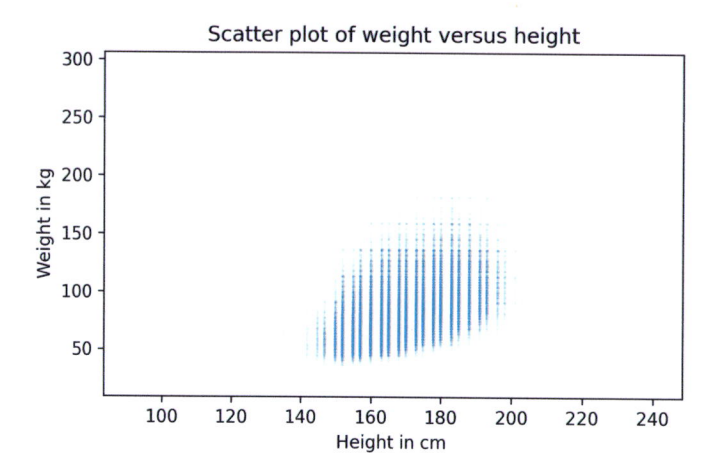

Scatter plot of weight versus height

Again, this is better, but now we can see that the points fall in discrete columns. That's because most heights were reported in inches and converted to centimeters. We can break up the columns by adding random noise to the values, which is called **jittering**. We'll can use NumPy to generate noise from a normal distribution with mean 0 and standard deviation 2.

```
import numpy as np

noise = np.random.normal(0, 2, size=len(brfss))
height_jitter = height + noise
```

Here's what the plot looks like with jittered heights.

```
plt.plot(height_jitter, weight, 'o', alpha=0.01, markersize=0.5)

plt.xlabel('Height in cm')
plt.ylabel('Weight in kg')
plt.title('Scatter plot of weight versus height');
```

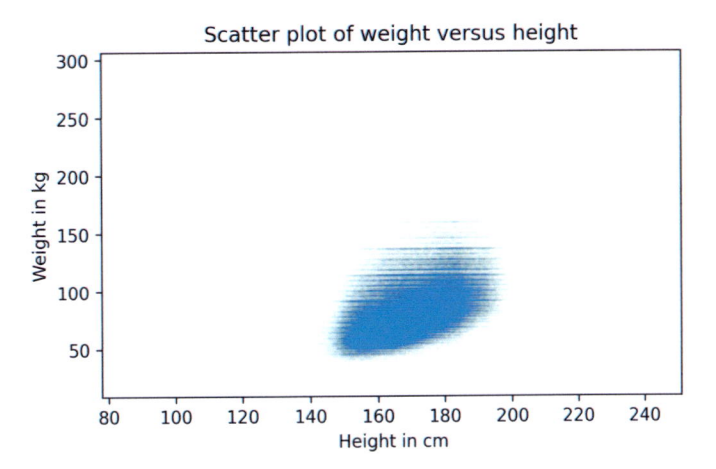

9.1 Exploring relationships

Scatter plot of weight versus height

The columns are gone, but now we can see that there are rows where people rounded off their weight. We can fix that by jittering weight, too.

```
noise = np.random.normal(0, 2, size=len(brfss))
weight_jitter = weight + noise
```

Here's what it looks like.

```
plt.plot(height_jitter, weight_jitter, 'o',
         alpha=0.01, markersize=0.5)

plt.xlabel('Height in cm')
plt.ylabel('Weight in kg')
plt.title('Scatter plot of weight versus height');
```

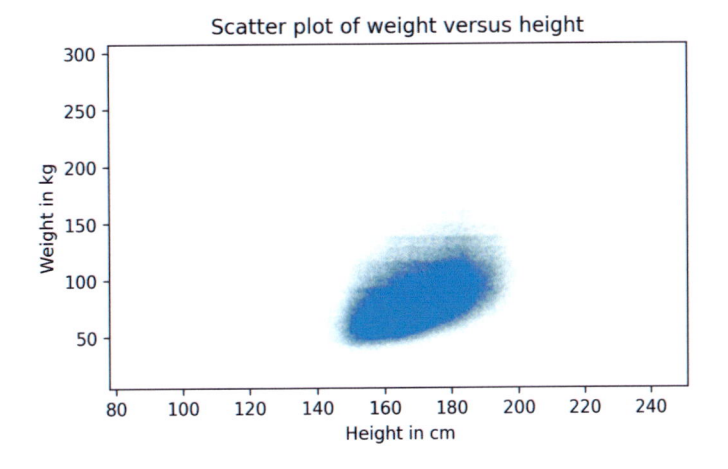

Finally, let's zoom in on the area where most of the data points are. The functions `xlim` and `ylim` set the lower and upper limits of the x-axis and y-axis; in this case, we plot heights from 140 to 200 centimeters and weights up to 160 kilograms. Here's what it looks like.

```
plt.plot(height_jitter, weight_jitter, 'o', alpha=0.01, markersize=0.5)

plt.xlim([140, 200])
plt.ylim([0, 160])
plt.xlabel('Height in cm')
plt.ylabel('Weight in kg')
plt.title('Scatter plot of weight versus height');
```

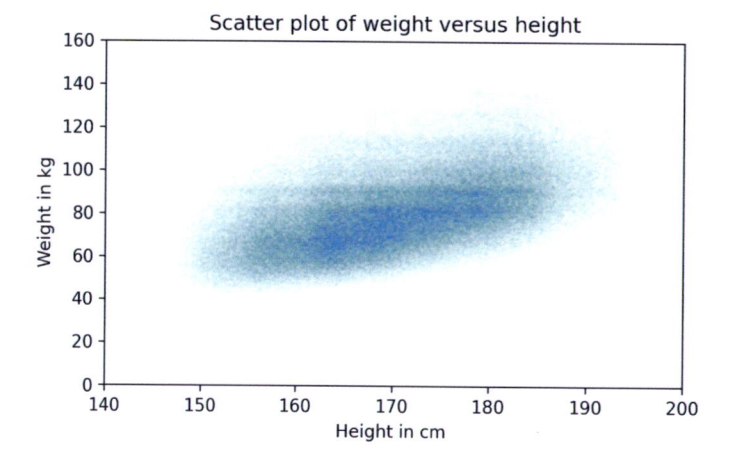

Now we have a reliable picture of the relationship between height and weight. Below you can see the misleading plot we started with and the more reliable one we ended with. They are clearly different, and they suggest different relationships between these variables.

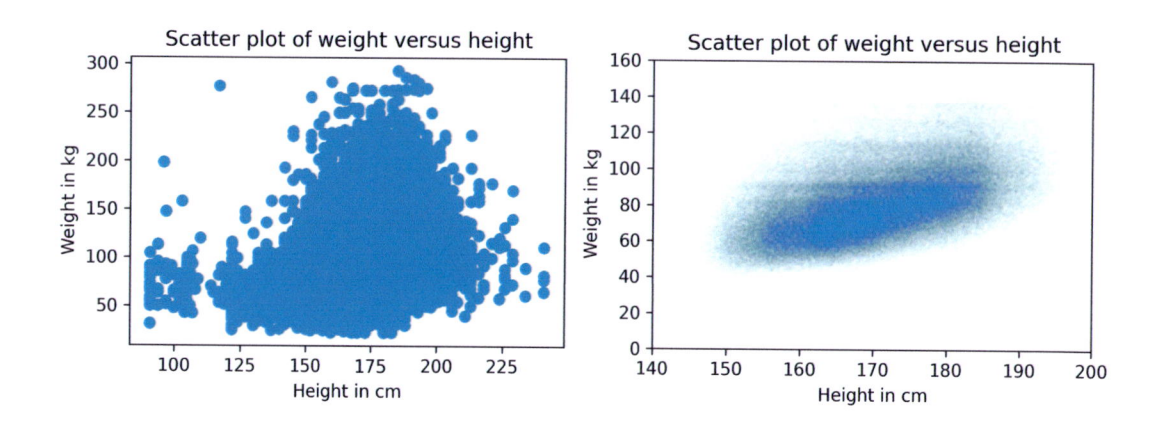

The point of this example is that it takes some effort to make an effective scatter plot.

9.2 Visualizing relationships

Exercise: Do people tend to gain weight as they get older? We can answer this question by visualizing the relationship between weight and age. But before we make a scatter plot, it is a good idea to visualize distributions one variable at a time. So let's look at the distribution of age.

The BRFSS dataset includes a column, `AGE`, which represents each respondent's age in years. To protect respondents' privacy, ages are rounded off into 5-year bins. The values in `AGE` are the midpoints of the bins.

- Extract the variable `'AGE'` from `brfss` and assign it to `age`.
- Plot the PMF of `age` as a bar chart, using `Pmf` from `empiricaldist`.

Exercise: Now let's look at the distribution of weight. The column that contains weight in kilograms is `WTKG3`. Because this column contains many unique values, displaying it as a PMF doesn't work very well. Instead, use `Cdf` from `empiricaldist` to plot the CDF of weight.

Exercise: Now make a scatter plot of `weight` versus `age`. Adjust `alpha` and `markersize` to avoid overplotting. Use `ylim` to limit the y-axis from 0 to 200 kilograms.

Exercise: In the previous exercise, the ages fall in columns because they've been rounded into 5-year bins. If we jitter them, the scatter plot will show the relationship more clearly.

- Add random noise to `age` with mean `0` and standard deviation `2.5`.
- Make a scatter plot and adjust `alpha` and `markersize` again.

9.2 Visualizing relationships

In the previous section we used scatter plots to visualize the relationship between weight and height. In this section, we'll explore the relationship between weight and *age*, and we'll see two new ways to visualize relationships: box plots and violin plots.

Let's start with a scatter plot.

```
age = brfss['AGE']
noise = np.random.normal(0, 1.0, size=len(brfss))
age_jitter = age + noise

plt.plot(age_jitter, weight_jitter, 'o', alpha=0.01, markersize=0.5)

plt.xlabel('Age in years')
plt.ylabel('Weight in kg')
plt.title('Weight versus age');
```

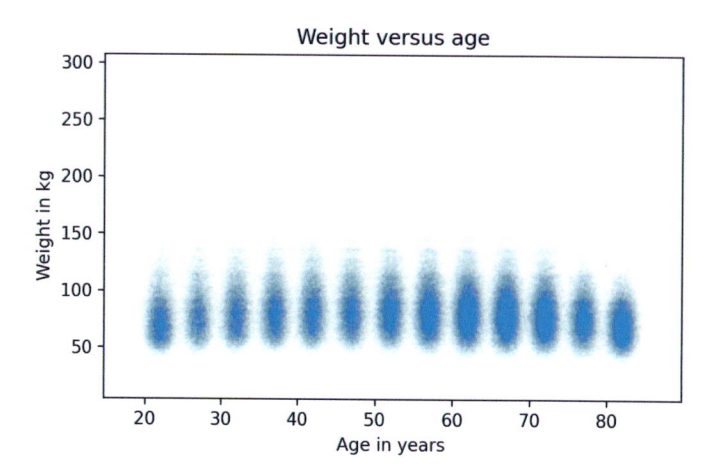

Weight versus age

The ages are jittered, but the standard deviation of the noise is small enough that there's still space between the columns. That makes it possible to see the shape of the distribution in each age group, as well as the differences between groups.

If we take this idea one step farther, we can use KDE to estimate the density function in each column and plot it. This way of visualizing the data is called a **violin plot**. Seaborn provides a function that makes violin plots, but before we can use it, we have to get rid of any rows with missing data. Here's how:

```
data = brfss.dropna(subset=['AGE', 'WTKG3'])
data.shape
```

(393080, 10)

`dropna` creates a new `DataFrame` that omits the rows in `brfss` where `AGE` or `WTKG3` are `NaN`. Now we can call `violinplot` like this:

```
import seaborn as sns

sns.violinplot(x='AGE', y='WTKG3', data=data, inner=None)

plt.xlabel('Age in years')
plt.ylabel('Weight in kg')
plt.title('Weight versus age');
```

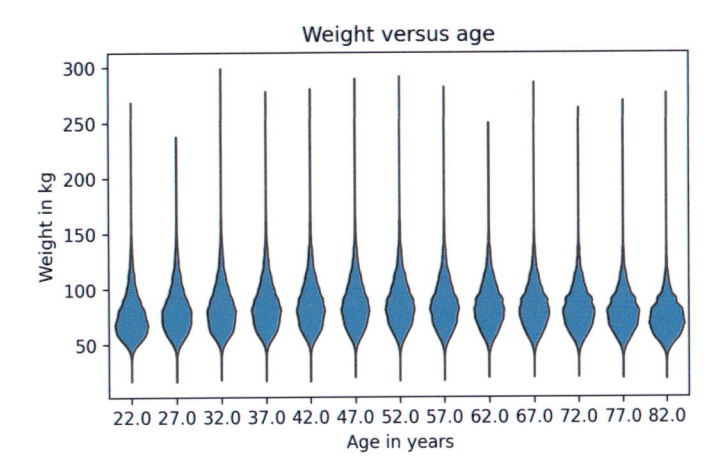

9.2 Visualizing relationships   121

The `x` and `y` arguments are the names of columns from `data`, which is the `DataFrame` we just created. The argument `inner=None` simplifies the plot. In the result each shape shows the distribution of weight in one age group. The width of each shape is proportional to the estimated density, so it's like two vertical KDEs plotted back to back.

Another, related way to look at data like this is called a **box plot**, which shows summary statistics of the values in each group. Seaborn provides a function that makes box plots – we can call it like this:

```
sns.boxplot(x='AGE', y='WTKG3', data=data, whis=10)

plt.xlabel('Age in years')
plt.ylabel('Weight in kg')
plt.title('Weight versus age');
```

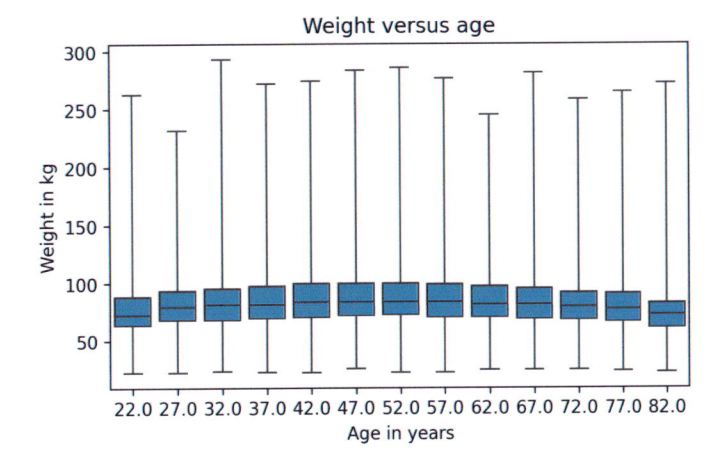

Each box represents the distribution of weight in an age group. The height of each box represents the interquartile range, which is the range from the 25th to the 75th percentile. The line in the middle of each box is the median.

The keyword argument `whis` determines the behavior of the whiskers that extend above and below the boxes. With `whis`=10, they extend far enough to show the minimum and maximum values.

In my opinion, this plot gives us the best view of the relationship between weight and age.

- Looking at the medians, we can see that people in their 40s are the heaviest; younger and older people are lighter.

- Looking at the sizes of the boxes, it seems like people in their 40s have the most variability in weight, too.

- Looking at the whiskers, we can see that the distribution of weight is skewed – that is, the heaviest people are farther from the median than the lightest people.

When a distribution is skewed toward higher values, it is sometimes useful to plot it on a logarithmic scale. We can do that with the Pyplot function `yscale`.

```
sns.boxplot(x='AGE', y='WTKG3', data=data, whis=10)

plt.yscale('log')
plt.xlabel('Age in years')
plt.ylabel('Weight in kg (log scale)')
plt.title('Weight versus age');
```

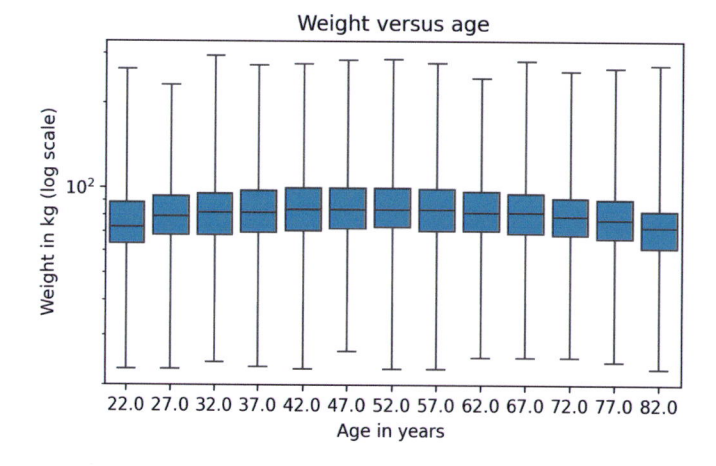

On a log scale, the distributions are symmetric, so the whiskers extend about the same distance in both directions, the boxes are close to the middle of the figure, and we can see the relationship between age and weight clearly.

In the following exercises, you can generate violin and box plots for other variables.

Exercise: Previously we looked at a scatter plot of height and weight, and saw that taller people tend to be heavier. Now let's take a closer look using a box plot. The `brfss` DataFrame contains a column named `_HTMG10` that represents height in centimeters, binned into 10 cm groups.

- Make a box plot that shows the distribution of weight in each height group.

- Plot the y-axis on a logarithmic scale.

Suggestion: If the labels on the x-axis collide, you can rotate them with `plt.xticks(rotation=45)`.

Exercise: As a second example, let's look at the relationship between income and height. In the BRFSS, income is represented as a categorical variable – that is, respondents are assigned to one of seven income categories. The column name is `_INCOMG1`. Before we connect income with anything else, let's look at the distribution by computing the PMF. Extract `_INCOMG1` from `brfss` and assign it to `income`. Then plot the PMF of `income` as a bar chart.

Exercise: Generate a violin plot that shows the distribution of height in each income group. Can you see a relationship between these variables?

9.3 Quantifying Correlation

In the previous section, we visualized relationships between pairs of variables. Now we'll quantify the strength of those relationships by computing their correlation.

When people say "correlation" casually, they might mean any relationship between two variables. In statistics, it usually means a **correlation coefficient**, which is a number between -1 and 1 that quantifies the strength of a linear relationship between variables. To demonstrate, we'll select three columns from the BRFSS dataset:

```
columns = ['HTM4', 'WTKG3', 'AGE']
subset = brfss[columns]
```

The result is a `DataFrame` with just those columns. With this subset of the data, we can use the `corr` method, like this:

```
subset.corr()
```

	HTM4	WTKG3	AGE
HTM4	1	0.469398	-0.122187
WTKG3	0.469398	1	-0.0679024
AGE	-0.122187	-0.0679024	1

The result is a **correlation matrix**. Reading across the first row, the correlation of `HTM4` with itself is 1. That's expected – the correlation of anything with itself is 1.

The next entry is more interesting: the correlation of height and weight is about 0.45. It's positive, which means taller people are heavier, and it's moderate in strength, which means it has some predictive value – if you know someone's height, you can make a somewhat better guess about their weight.

The correlation between height and age is about -0.09. It's negative, which means that older people tend to be shorter, but it's weak, which means that knowing someone's age would not help much if you were trying to guess their height.

Reading across the second row, we can see that the correlation of height and weight is the same as the correlation of weight and height – because correlation is commutative.

And we can see that the correlation of weight and age is only 0.001, which is very small. It is tempting to conclude that there is no relationship between age and weight, but we have already seen that there is. So why is the correlation so low? Remember that the relationship between weight and age looks like this.

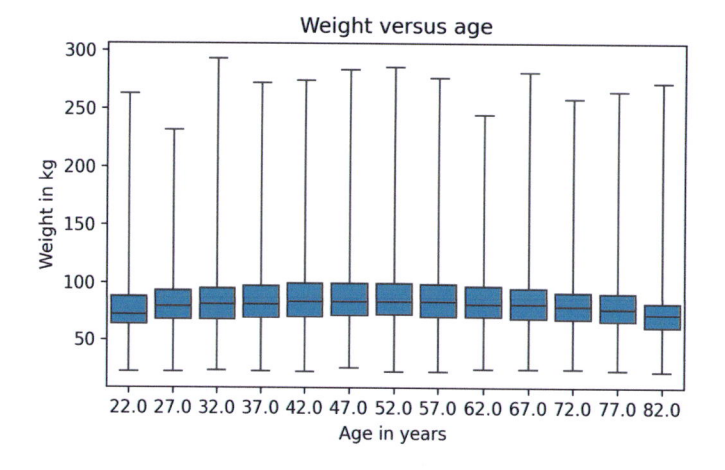

As age increases, weight goes up and then down, so the relationship is nonlinear. But correlation only measures linear relationships. When the relationship is nonlinear, correlation generally underestimates how strong it is.

To demonstrate this point more clearly, let's generate some fake data: `xs` contains equally-spaced points between -1 and 1; `ys` is `xs` squared plus some random noise.

```
xs = np.linspace(-1, 1)
ys = xs**2 + np.random.normal(0, 0.05, len(xs))
```

9.3 Quantifying Correlation

Here's the scatter plot of these values.

```
plt.plot(xs, ys, 'o', alpha=0.5)
plt.xlabel('x')
plt.ylabel('y')
plt.title('Scatter plot of a fake dataset');
```

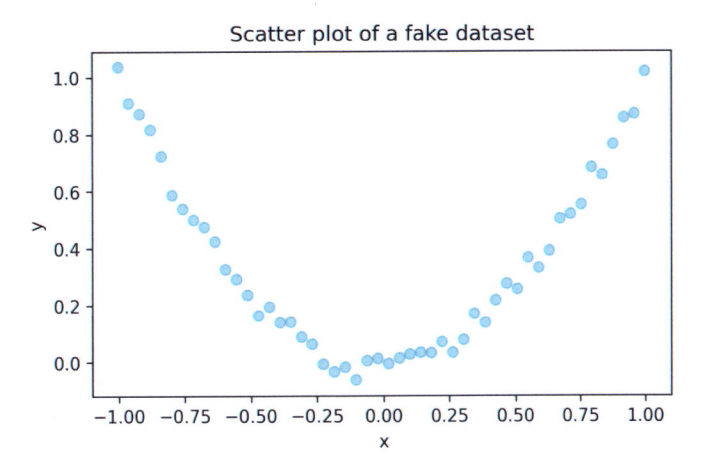

This is a strong relationship in the sense that you can make a much better guess about `y` if you are given `x`. But here's the correlation matrix:

```
np.corrcoef(xs, ys)
```

```
array([[1.        , 0.00993964],
       [0.00993964, 1.        ]])
```

Even though there is a strong nonlinear relationship, the computed correlation is close to zero. In general, if correlation is high – that is, close to 1 or -1 – you can conclude that there is a strong linear relationship. But if correlation is close to zero, that doesn't mean there is no relationship; there might be a nonlinear relationship. This is one reason correlation can be misleading.

And there's another reason to be careful with correlation – it doesn't mean what people take it to mean. Specifically, correlation says nothing about the slope of the line that fits the data. If we say that two variables are correlated, that means we can use one to predict the other. But that might not be what we care about.

For example, suppose we are concerned about the health effects of weight gain, so we plot weight versus age from 20 to 50 years old. I'll generate two fake datasets to demonstrate the point. In each dataset, `xs` represents age and `ys` represents weight.

```
np.random.seed(18)
xs1 = np.linspace(20, 50)
ys1 = 75 + 0.02 * xs1 + np.random.normal(0, 0.15, len(xs1))
```

```
np.random.seed(18)
xs2 = np.linspace(20, 50)
ys2 = 65 + 0.2 * xs2 + np.random.normal(0, 3, len(xs2))
```

Here's what the two scatter plots look like.

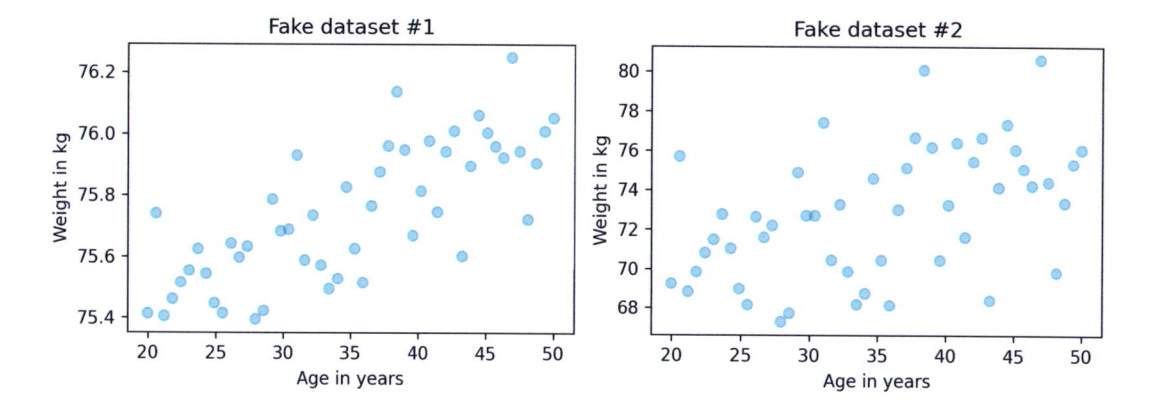

I constructed these examples so they look similar, but they have substantially different correlations.

```
rho1 = np.corrcoef(xs1, ys1)[0, 1]
rho1
```

0.7579660563439401

```
rho2 = np.corrcoef(xs2, ys2)[0, 1]
rho2
```

0.4782776976576317

In the first dataset, the correlation is strong, close to 0.75. In the second dataset, the correlation is moderate, close to 0.5. So we might think the first relationship is more important. But look more closely at the y-axis in both figures.

In the first example, the average weight gain over 30 years is less than 1 kilogram; in the second it is more than 5 kilograms! If we are concerned about the health effects of weight gain, the second relationship is probably more important, even though the correlation is lower. In this scenario, the statistic we really care about is the slope of the line that fits the data, not the

9.4 Simple Linear Regression

coefficient of correlation. In the next section, we'll use linear regression to compute that slope, but first let's practice with correlation.

Exercise: The purpose of the BRFSS is to explore health risk factors, so it includes questions about diet. The column `_VEGESU1` represents the number of servings of vegetables respondents reported eating per day. Before we compute correlations, let's look at the distribution of this variable. Extract `_VEGESU1` from `brfss` and assign it to `vegesu` – then plot the CDF of the values.

The original dataset includes a small number of values greater than 10, some of them unreasonably large. For this extract, I have cut off the values at 10.

Exercise: Now let's visualize the relationship between age and vegetables. Make a box plot that summarizes the distribution of vegetable servings in each age group. How would you describe the relationship, if any?

Exercise: Finally, let's look at correlations between age, income, and vegetable servings.

- From `brfss`, select the columns `'AGE'`, `_INCOMG1`, and `_VEGESU1`.

- Compute the correlation matrix for these variables.

Is the correlation between age and vegetable servings what you expected based on the box plot?

9.4 Simple Linear Regression

In the previous section we saw that correlation does not always measure what we really want to know. In this section, we look at an alternative: simple linear regression. Here "simple" means there are only two variables, as opposed to "multiple" regression, which can work with any number of variables.

In the previous section, I generated fake datasets showing two hypothetical relationships between weight and age. We computed correlations for both datasets, now let's compute lines of best fit. We can use `linregress` from the SciPy `stats` library, which takes two sequences as arguments. Here are the results for Fake Dataset #1.

```
from scipy.stats import linregress

res1 = linregress(xs1, ys1)
res1._asdict()
```

```
{'slope': 0.018821034903244386,
 'intercept': 75.08049023710964,
 'rvalue': 0.7579660563439402,
 'pvalue': 1.8470158725246148e-10,
 'stderr': 0.002337849260560818,
 'intercept_stderr': 0.08439154079040358}
```

The result is a `LinregressResult` object that contains five values: `slope` is the slope of the line of best fit for the data, `intercept` is the intercept, and `rvalue` is correlation. We'll ignore the other values for now.

For Fake Dataset #1, the estimated slope is about 0.019 kilograms per year or about 0.56 kilograms over the 30-year range.

```
res1.slope * 30
```

0.5646310470973316

Here are the results for Fake Dataset #2.

```
res2 = linregress(xs2, ys2)
res2._asdict()
```

{'slope': 0.17642069806488855,
 'intercept': 66.60980474219305,
 'rvalue': 0.47827769765763173,
 'pvalue': 0.0004430600283776241,
 'stderr': 0.04675698521121631,
 'intercept_stderr': 1.6878308158080697}

The estimated slope is almost 10 times higher, about 0.18 kilograms per year or about 5.3 kilograms per 30 years.

```
res2.slope * 30
```

5.292620941946657

We can use the results from `linregress` to plot the line of best fit and see how it relates to the data. First we get the minimum and maximum of the observed `xs`. Then we multiply by the slope and add the intercept.

```
low, high = xs1.min(), xs1.max()
fx = np.array([low, high])
fy = res1.intercept + res1.slope * fx
```

Here's what the result looks like for the first example.

```
plt.plot(xs1, ys1, 'o', alpha=0.5)
plt.plot(fx, fy, '-')

plt.xlabel('Age in years')
plt.ylabel('Weight in kg')
plt.title('Fake Dataset #1');
```

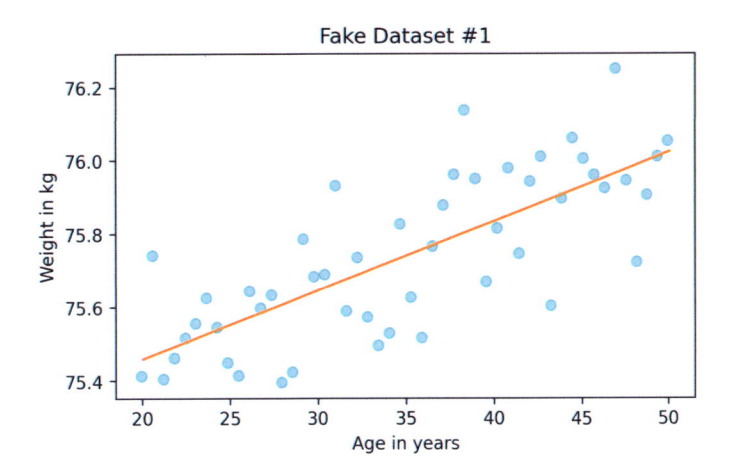

9.4 Simple Linear Regression

[Figure: Fake Dataset #1 — scatter plot of Weight in kg vs Age in years with regression line]

We can do the same thing for the second example.

```
low, high = xs2.min(), xs2.max()
fx = np.array([low, high])
fy = res2.intercept + res2.slope * fx
```

And here's what the result looks like.

```
plt.plot(xs2, ys2, 'o', alpha=0.5)
plt.plot(fx, fy, '-')

plt.xlabel('Age in years')
plt.ylabel('Weight in kg')
plt.title('Fake Dataset #2');
```

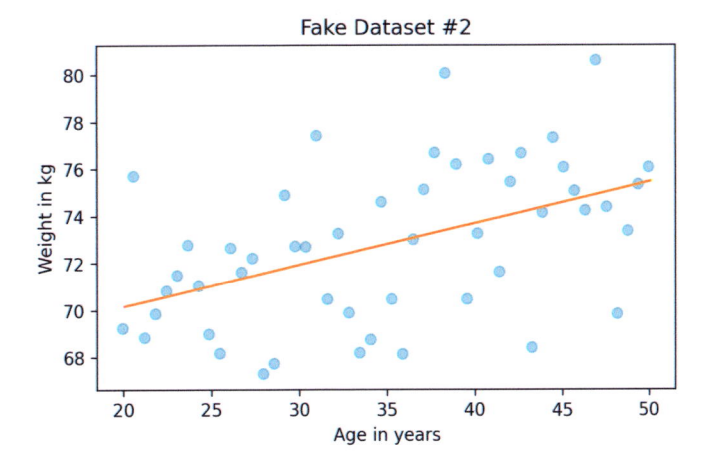

[Figure: Fake Dataset #2 — scatter plot of Weight in kg vs Age in years with regression line]

At first glance it might seem like the slope is steeper in the first figure, but don't be fooled. If you look closely at the vertical scales, the slope in the second figure is almost 10 times higher.

9.5 Regression of Height and Weight

Now let's look at an example of regression with real data. Here's the scatter plot of height and weight one more time.

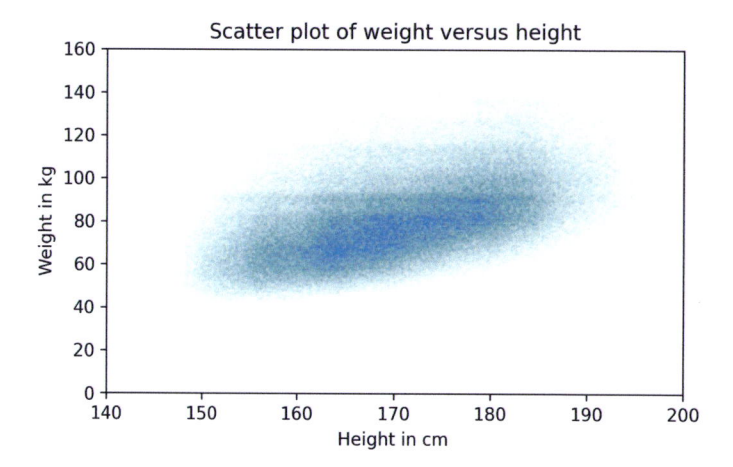

```
plt.plot(height_jitter, weight_jitter, 'o',
         alpha=0.01, markersize=0.5)

plt.xlim([140, 200])
plt.ylim([0, 160])
plt.xlabel('Height in cm')
plt.ylabel('Weight in kg')
plt.title('Scatter plot of weight versus height');
```

To compute the regression line, we'll use `linregress` again. But it can't handle `NaN` values, so we have to use `dropna` to remove rows that are missing the data we need.

```
data = brfss.dropna(subset=['WTKG3', 'HTM4'])
```

Now we can compute the linear regression.

```
res_hw = linregress(data['HTM4'], data['WTKG3'])
res_hw._asdict()
```

```
{'slope': 0.9366891536604244,
 'intercept': -76.44247680097321,
 'rvalue': 0.4693981914367916,
 'pvalue': 0.0,
 'stderr': 0.002806793650907722,
 'intercept_stderr': 0.47939863668166327}
```

9.5 Regression of Height and Weight

The slope is about 0.9 kilograms per centimeter, which means that we expect a person one centimeter taller to be almost a kilogram heavier. That's quite a lot. As before, we can compute the line of best fit:

```
low, high = data['HTM4'].min(), data['HTM4'].max()
fx = np.array([low, high])
fy = res_hw.intercept + res_hw.slope * fx
```

And here's what that looks like.

```
plt.plot(height_jitter, weight_jitter, 'o', alpha=0.01, markersize=0.5)
plt.plot(fx, fy, '-')

plt.xlim([140, 200])
plt.ylim([0, 160])
plt.xlabel('Height in cm')
plt.ylabel('Weight in kg')
plt.title('Scatter plot of weight versus height');
```

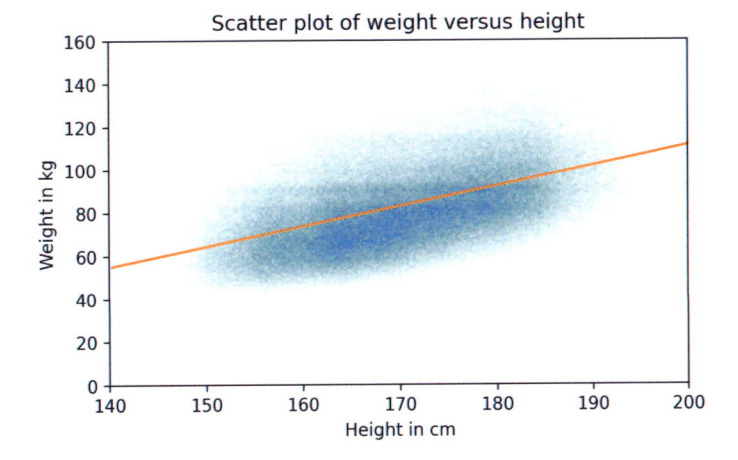

The slope of this line seems consistent with the scatter plot. As another example, here's the scatter plot of weight versus age, which we saw earlier.

```
plt.plot(age_jitter, weight_jitter, 'o',
         alpha=0.01, markersize=0.5)

plt.ylim([0, 160])
plt.xlabel('Age in years')
plt.ylabel('Weight in kg')
plt.title('Weight versus age');
```

Weight versus age

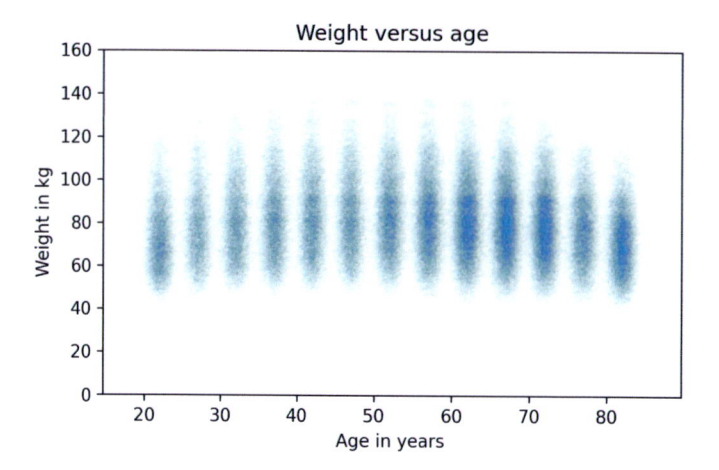

As we have seen before, the relationship is nonlinear. Let's see what we get if we compute a linear regression.

```
subset = brfss.dropna(subset=['WTKG3', 'AGE'])
res_aw = linregress(subset['AGE'], subset['WTKG3'])
res_aw._asdict()
```

{'slope': -0.08138685042569352,
 'intercept': 87.66340016901641,
 'rvalue': -0.06790235862083926,
 'pvalue': 0.0,
 'stderr': 0.0019073328587490353,
 'intercept_stderr': 0.11019675319089409}

The estimated slope is close to zero. Here's what the line of best fit looks like.

```
plt.plot(age_jitter, weight_jitter, 'o',
         alpha=0.01, markersize=0.5)

low, high = data['AGE'].min(), data['AGE'].max()
fx = np.array([low, high])
fy = res_aw.intercept + res_aw.slope * fx
plt.plot(fx, fy, '-')

plt.ylim([0, 160])
plt.xlabel('Age in years')
plt.ylabel('Weight in kg')
plt.title('Weight versus age');
```

9.5 Regression of Height and Weight

[Figure: Weight versus age scatter plot with regression line, x-axis: Age in years (20-80), y-axis: Weight in kg (0-160)]

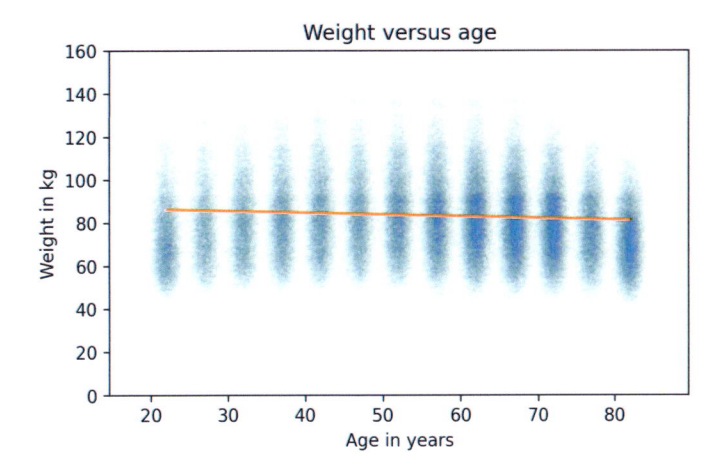

A straight line does not capture the relationship between these variables well. That's because linear regression has the same problem as correlation – it only measures the strength of a linear relationship.

In the next chapter, we'll see how to use multiple regression to quantify nonlinear relationships. But first, let's practice using simple regression.

Exercise: Who do you think eats more vegetables, people with low income, or people with high income? Let's find out. As we've seen previously, the column `_INCOMG1` represents income level and `_VEGESU1` represents the number of vegetable servings respondents reported eating per day. Make a scatter plot with vegetable servings versus income, that is, with vegetable servings on the y-axis and income group on the x-axis. You might want to use `ylim` to zoom in on the bottom half of the y-axis.

Exercise: Now estimate the slope of the relationship between vegetable consumption and income.

- Use `dropna` to select rows where `_INCOMG1` and `_VEGESU1` are not `NaN`.
- Extract `_INCOMG1` and `_VEGESU1` and compute the simple linear regression of these variables.
- Finally, plot the regression line on top of the scatter plot.

What is the slope of the regression line? What does this slope means in the context of the question we are exploring?

9.6 Summary

This chapter presents three ways to visualize the relationship between two variables: a scatter plot, violin plot, and box plot. A scatter plot is often a good choice when you are exploring a new data set, but it can take some attention to avoid overplotting. Violin plots and box plots are particularly useful when one of the variables has only a few unique values or the values have been rounded into bins.

We considered two ways to quantify the strength of a relationship: the coefficient of correlation and the slope of a regression line. These statistics capture different aspect of what we might mean by "strength". The coefficient of correlation indicates how well we can predict one variable, given the other. The slope of the regression line indicates how much difference we expect in one variable as we vary the other. One or the other might be more relevant, depending on the context.

Chapter 10

Regression

In the previous chapter we used simple linear regression to quantify the relationship between two variables. In this chapter we'll get farther into regression, including multiple regression and one of my all-time favorite tools, logistic regression. These tools will allow us to explore relationships among sets of variables. As an example, we will use data from the General Social Survey (GSS) to explore the relationship between education, sex, age, and income.

The GSS dataset contains hundreds of columns. We'll work with an extract that contains just the columns we need, as we did in Chapter 8. Instructions for downloading the extract are in the notebook for this chapter.

We can read the `DataFrame` like this and display the first few rows.

```
import pandas as pd

gss = pd.read_hdf('gss_extract_2022.hdf', 'gss')
gss.head()
```

	year	id	age	educ	degree	sex	gunlaw	grass	realinc
0	1972	1	23	16	3	2	1	NaN	18951
1	1972	2	70	10	0	1	1	NaN	24366
2	1972	3	48	12	1	2	1	NaN	24366
3	1972	4	27	17	3	2	1	NaN	30458
4	1972	5	61	12	1	2	1	NaN	50763

We'll start with a simple regression, estimating the parameters of real income as a function of years of education.

First we'll select the subset of the data where both variables are valid.

```
data = gss.dropna(subset=['realinc', 'educ'])
xs = data['educ']
ys = data['realinc']
```

Now we can use `linregress` to fit a line to the data.

```
from scipy.stats import linregress
res = linregress(xs, ys)
res._asdict()
```

```
{'slope': 3631.0761003894995,
 'intercept': -15007.453640508655,
 'rvalue': 0.37169252259280877,
 'pvalue': 0.0,
 'stderr': 35.625290800764,
 'intercept_stderr': 480.07467595184363}
```

The estimated slope is about 3450, which means that each additional year of education is associated with an additional $3450 of income.

10.1 Regression with StatsModels

SciPy doesn't do multiple regression, so we'll to switch to a new library, StatsModels. Here's the import statement.

```
import statsmodels.formula.api as smf
```

To fit a regression model, we'll use `ols`, which stands for "ordinary least squares", another name for regression.

```
results = smf.ols('realinc ~ educ', data=data).fit()
```

The first argument is a **formula string** that specifies that we want to regress income as a function of education. The second argument is the `DataFrame` containing the subset of valid data. The names in the formula string correspond to columns in the `DataFrame`.

The result from `ols` is an object that represents the model – it provides a function called `fit` that does the actual computation.

10.2 Multiple Regression

The result from `fit` is a `RegressionResultsWrapper`, which contains a `Series` called `params`, which contains the estimated intercept and the slope associated with `educ`.

```
results.params
```

```
Intercept   -15007.453641
educ          3631.076100
dtype: float64
```

The results from Statsmodels are the same as the results we got from SciPy, so that's good!

Exercise: Let's run another regression using SciPy and StatsModels, and confirm we get the same results. Compute the regression of `realinc` as a function of `age` using SciPy's `linregress` and then using StatsModels' `ols`. Confirm that the intercept and slope are the same. Remember to use `dropna` to select the rows with valid data in both columns.

10.2 Multiple Regression

In the previous section, we saw that income depends on education, and in the exercise we saw that it also depends on `age`. Now let's put them together in a single model.

```
results = smf.ols('realinc ~ educ + age', data=gss).fit()
results.params
```

```
Intercept   -17999.726908
educ          3665.108238
age             55.071802
dtype: float64
```

In this model, `realinc` is the variable we are trying to explain or predict, which is called the **dependent variable** because it depends on the the other variables – or at least we expect it to. The other variables, `educ` and `age`, are called **independent variables** or sometimes "predictors". The + sign indicates that we expect the contributions of the independent variables to be additive.

The result contains an intercept and two slopes, which estimate the average contribution of each predictor with the other predictor held constant.

- The estimated slope for `educ` is about 3665 – so if we compare two people with the same age, and one has an additional year of education, we expect their income to be higher by $3514.

- The estimated slope for `age` is about 55 – so if we compare two people with the same education, and one is a year older, we expect their income to be higher by $55.

In this model, the contribution of age is quite small, but as we'll see in the next section that might be misleading.

10.3 Grouping by Age

Let's look more closely at the relationship between income and age. We'll use a Pandas method we have not seen before, called `groupby`, to divide the `DataFrame` into age groups.

```
grouped = gss.groupby('age')
type(grouped)
```

pandas.core.groupby.generic.DataFrameGroupBy

The result is a `GroupBy` object that contains one group for each value of `age`. The `GroupBy` object behaves like a `DataFrame` in many ways. You can use brackets to select a column, like `realinc` in this example, and then invoke a method like `mean`.

```
mean_income_by_age = grouped['realinc'].mean()
```

The result is a Pandas `Series` that contains the mean income for each age group, which we can plot like this.

```
import matplotlib.pyplot as plt

plt.plot(mean_income_by_age, 'o', alpha=0.5)
plt.xlabel('Age (years)')
plt.ylabel('Income (1986 $)')
plt.title('Average income, grouped by age');
```

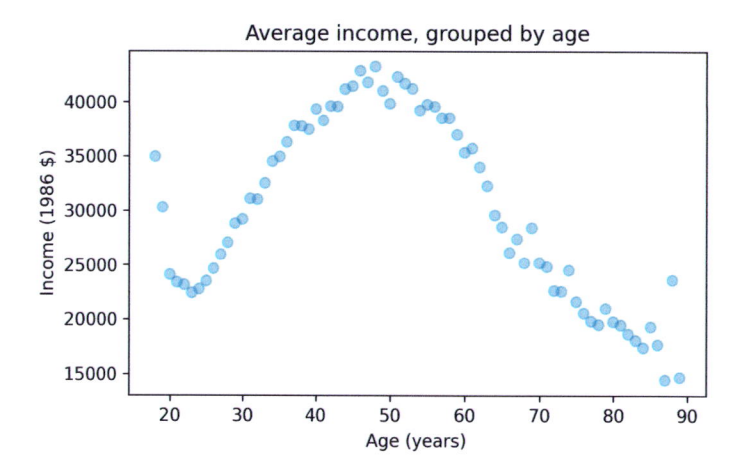

Average income increases from age 20 to age 50, then starts to fall. And that explains why the estimated slope is so small, because the relationship is nonlinear.

10.4 Visualizing regression results

To describe a nonlinear relationship, we'll create a new variable called `age2` that equals `age` squared – so it is called a **quadratic term**.

```
gss['age2'] = gss['age']**2
```

Now we can run a regression with both `age` and `age2` on the right side.

```
model = smf.ols('realinc ~ educ + age + age2', data=gss)
results = model.fit()
results.params
```

```
Intercept   -52599.674844
educ          3464.870685
age           1779.196367
age2           -17.445272
dtype: float64
```

In this model, the slope associated with `age` is substantial, about $1779 per year.

The slope associated with `age2` is about -$17. It might be unexpected that it is negative – we'll see why in the next section. But first, here are two exercises where you can practice using `groupby` and `ols`.

Exercise: Let's explore the relationship between income and education. First, group `gss` by `educ`. From the resulting `GroupBy` object, extract `realinc` and compute the mean. Then plot mean income in each education group. What can you say about the relationship between these variables? Does it look like a linear relationship?

Exercise: The graph in the previous exercise suggests that the relationship between income and education is nonlinear. So let's try fitting a nonlinear model.

- Add a column named `educ2` to the `gss` DataFrame – it should contain the values from `educ` squared.

- Run a regression that uses `educ`, `educ2`, `age`, and `age2` to predict `realinc`.

10.4 Visualizing regression results

In the previous section we ran a multiple regression model to characterize the relationships between income, age, and education. Because the model includes quadratic terms, the parameters are hard to interpret. For example, you might notice that the parameter for `educ` is negative, and that might be a surprise, because it suggests that higher education is associated with lower income. But the parameter for `educ2` is positive, and that makes a big difference. In this section we'll see a way to interpret the model visually and validate it against data.

Here's the model from the previous exercise.

```
gss['educ2'] = gss['educ']**2

model = smf.ols('realinc ~ educ + educ2 + age + age2', data=gss)
results = model.fit()
results.params
```

```
Intercept    -26336.766346
educ           -706.074107
educ2           165.962552
age            1728.454811
age2            -17.207513
dtype: float64
```

The `results` object provides a method called `predict` that uses the estimated parameters to generate predictions. It takes a `DataFrame` as a parameter and returns a `Series` with a prediction for each row in the `DataFrame`. To use it, we'll create a new `DataFrame` with `age` running from 18 to 89, and `age2` set to `age` squared.

```
import numpy as np

df = pd.DataFrame()
df['age'] = np.linspace(18, 89)
df['age2'] = df['age']**2
```

Next, we'll pick a level for `educ`, like 12 years, which is the most common value. When you assign a single value to a column in a `DataFrame`, Pandas makes a copy for each row.

```
df['educ'] = 12
df['educ2'] = df['educ']**2
```

Then we can use `results` to predict the average income for each age group, holding education constant.

```
pred12 = results.predict(df)
```

The result from `predict` is a `Series` with one prediction for each row. So we can plot it with age on the x-axis and the predicted income for each age group on the y-axis. And we'll plot the data for comparison.

10.4 Visualizing regression results

```
plt.plot(mean_income_by_age, 'o', alpha=0.5)
plt.plot(df['age'], pred12, label='High school', color='C4')

plt.xlabel('Age (years)')
plt.ylabel('Income (1986 $)')
plt.title('Income versus age, grouped by education level')
plt.legend();
```

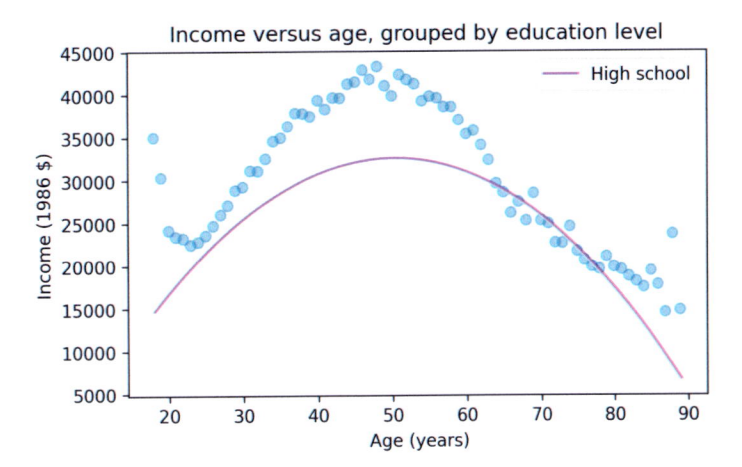

The dots show the average income in each age group. The line shows the predictions generated by the model, holding education constant. This plot shows the shape of the model, a downward-facing parabola.

We can do the same thing with other levels of education, like 14 years, which is the nominal time to earn an Associate's degree, and 16 years, which is the nominal time to earn a Bachelor's degree.

```
df['educ'] = 16
df['educ2'] = df['educ']**2
pred16 = results.predict(df)

df['educ'] = 14
df['educ2'] = df['educ']**2
pred14 = results.predict(df)
```

```
plt.plot(mean_income_by_age, 'o', alpha=0.5)
plt.plot(df['age'], pred16, ':', label='Bachelor')
plt.plot(df['age'], pred14, '--', label='Associate')
plt.plot(df['age'], pred12, label='High school', color='C4')

plt.xlabel('Age (years)')
plt.ylabel('Income (1986 $)')
plt.title('Income versus age, grouped by education level')
plt.legend();
```

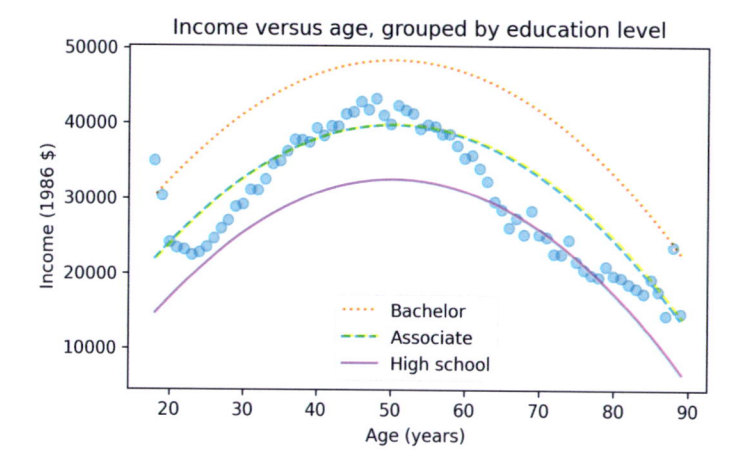

The lines show expected income as a function of age for three levels of education. This visualization helps validate the model, since we can compare the predictions with the data. And it helps us interpret the model since we can see the separate contributions of age and education.

Sometimes we can understand a model by looking at its parameters, but often it is better to look at its predictions. In the exercises, you'll have a chance to run a multiple regression, generate predictions, and visualize the results.

Exercise: At this point, we have a model that predicts income using age and education, and we've plotted predictions for different age groups, holding education constant. Now let's see what it predicts for different levels of education, holding age constant.

- Create an empty `DataFrame` named `df`.

- Using `np.linspace()`, add a column named `educ` to `df` with a range of values from 0 to 20.

- Add a column named `educ2` with the values from `educ` squared.

- Add a column named `age` with the constant value 30.

10.5 Categorical Variables

- Add a column named `age2` with the values from `age` squared.

- Use the `results` object and `df` to generate expected income as a function of education.

Exercise: Now let's visualize the results from the previous exercise.

- Group the GSS data by `educ` and compute the mean income in each education group.

- Plot mean income for each education group as a scatter plot.

- Plot the predictions from the previous exercise.

How do the predictions compare with the data?

10.5 Categorical Variables

Most of the variables we have used so far – like income, age, and education – are numerical. But variables like sex and race are **categorical** – that is, each respondent belongs to one of a specified set of categories. If there are only two categories, the variable is **binary**.

With StatsModels, it is easy to include a categorical variable as part of a regression model. Here's an example:

```
formula = 'realinc ~ educ + educ2 + age + age2 + C(sex)'
results = smf.ols(formula, data=gss).fit()
results.params
```

```
Intercept        -24635.767539
C(sex)[T.2.0]     -4891.439306
educ               -496.623120
educ2               156.898221
age                1720.274097
age2                -17.097853
dtype: float64
```

In the formula string, the letter `C` indicates that `sex` is a categorical variable. The regression treats the value `sex=1`, which is male, as the reference group, and reports the difference associated with the value `sex=2`, which is female. So the results indicate that income for women is about $4156 less than for men, after controlling for age and education. However, note that `realinc` represents household income. If the respondent is married, it includes both their own income and their spouse's. So we cannot interpret this result as an estimate of a gender gap in income.

10.6 Logistic Regression

In the previous section, we added a categorical variable on the right side of a regression formula – that is, we used it as a predictive variable.

But what if the categorical variable is on the left side of the regression formula – that is, it's the value we are trying to predict? In that case, we can use **logistic regression**.

As an example, one of the GSS questions asks "Would you favor or oppose a law which would require a person to obtain a police permit before he or she could buy a gun?" The responses are in a column called `gunlaw` – here are the values.

```
gss['gunlaw'].value_counts()
```

```
gunlaw
1.0    36367
2.0    11940
Name: count, dtype: int64
```

1 means yes and 2 means no, so most respondents are in favor.

Before we can use this variable in a logistic regression, we have to recode it so 1 means "yes" and 0 means "no". We can do that by replacing 2 with 0.

```
gss['gunlaw'] = gss['gunlaw'].replace([2], [0])
```

To run logistic regression, we'll use `logit`, which is named for the logit function, which is related to logistic regression.

```
formula = 'gunlaw ~ age + age2 + educ + educ2 + C(sex)'
results = smf.logit(formula, data=gss).fit()
```

```
Optimization terminated successfully.
         Current function value: 0.544026
         Iterations 5
```

Estimating the parameters for the logistic model is an iterative process, so the output contains information about the number of iterations. Other than that, everything is the same as what we have seen before.

10.6 Logistic Regression

Here are the estimated parameters.

```
results.params
```

```
Intercept      1.483746
C(sex)[T.2.0]  0.740717
age           -0.021274
age2           0.000216
educ          -0.098093
educ2          0.005557
dtype: float64
```

The parameters are in the form of **log odds** – I won't explain them in detail here, except to say that positive values make the outcome more likely and negative values make the outcome less likely. For example, the parameter associated with `sex`=2 is `0.74`, which indicates that women are more likely to support this form of gun control.

To see how much more likely, we can generate predictions, as we did with linear regression. As an example, we'll generate predictions for different ages and sexes, with education held constant. First we need a `DataFrame` with a range of values for `age` and a fixed value of `educ`.

```
df = pd.DataFrame()
df['age'] = np.linspace(18, 89)
df['educ'] = 12
```

Then we can compute `age2` and `educ2`.

```
df['age2'] = df['age']**2
df['educ2'] = df['educ']**2
```

We can generate predictions for men like this.

```
df['sex'] = 1
pred_male = results.predict(df)
```

And for women like this.

```
df['sex'] = 2
pred_female = results.predict(df)
```

Now, to visualize the results, we'll start by plotting the data. As we've done before, we'll divide the respondents into age groups and compute the mean in each group. The mean of a binary variable is the fraction of people in favor. Then we can plot the predictions.

```
grouped = gss.groupby('age')
favor_by_age = grouped['gunlaw'].mean()

plt.plot(favor_by_age, 'o', alpha=0.5)
plt.plot(df['age'], pred_female, label='Female')
plt.plot(df['age'], pred_male, '--', label='Male')

plt.xlabel('Age')
plt.ylabel('Probability of favoring gun law')
plt.title('Support for gun law versus age, grouped by sex')
plt.legend();
```

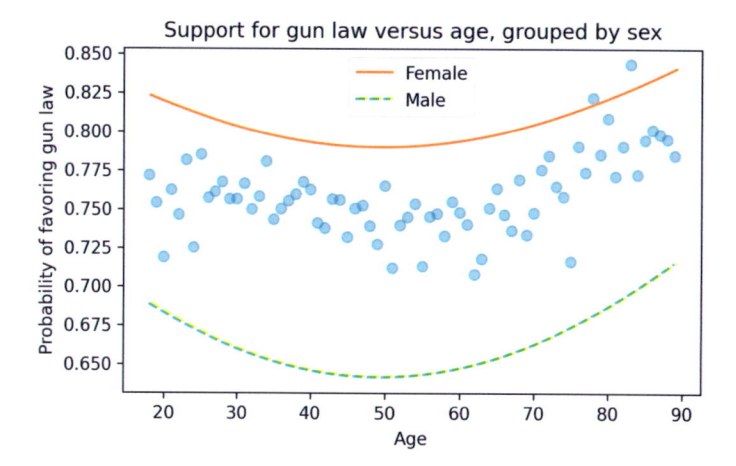

According to the model, people near age 50 are least likely to support gun control (at least as this question was posed). And women are more likely to support it than men, by about 15 percentage points.

Logistic regression is a powerful tool for exploring relationships between a binary variable and the factors that predict it. In the exercises, you'll explore the factors that predict support for legalizing marijuana.

Exercise: In the GSS dataset, the variable `grass` records responses to the question "Do you think the use of marijuana should be made legal or not?" Let's use logistic regression to explore relationships between this variable and age, sex, and education level.

1. First, use `replace` to recode the `grass` column so that 1 means yes and 0 means no. Use `value_counts` to check.

2. Next, use the StatsModels function `logit` to predict `grass` using the variables `age`, `age2`, `educ`, and `educ2`, along with `sex` as a categorical variable. Display the parameters. Are men or women more likely to support legalization?

3. To generate predictions, start with an empty DataFrame. Add a column called `age` that contains a sequence of values from 18 to 89. Add a column called `educ` and set it to 12 years. Then compute a column, `age2`, which is the square of `age`, and a column, `educ2`, which is the square of `educ`.

4. Use `predict` to generate predictions for men (`sex=1`) and women (`sex=2`).

5. Generate a plot that shows (a) the average level of support for legalizing marijuana in each age group, (b) the level of support the model predicts for men as a function of age, and (c) the level of support predicted for women as a function of age.

10.7 Summary

At this point, I'd like to summarize the topics we've covered so far, and make some connections that might clarify the big picture. A central theme of this book is **exploratory data analysis**, which is a process and set of tools for exploring a dataset, visualizing distributions, and discovering relationships between variables. The last four chapters demonstrate the steps of this process:

- Chapter 7 is about importing and cleaning data, and checking for errors and other special conditions. This might not be the most exciting part of the process, but time spent understanding data can save you from embarrassing errors.

- Chapter 8 is about exploring variables one at a time, visualizing distributions using PMFs, CDFs, and KDE, and choosing appropriate summary statistics.

- In Chapter 9 we explored relationships between variables two at a time, using scatter plots and other visualizations; and we quantified those relationships using correlation and simple regression.

- Finally, in this chapter, we explored multivariate relationships using multiple regression and logistic regression.

We moved through a lot of material quickly, but if you practice and apply these methods to other questions and datasets, you will learn more as you go. In the next chapter, we will move on to a new topic, resampling, which is a versatile tool for statistical inference.

Part III

Statistical Inference

Chapter 11

Resampling

This chapter introduces **resampling methods**, which are used to quantify the precision of an estimate. As a first example, we'll use results from a medical trial to estimate the efficacy of the vaccine.

11.1 Vaccine Testing

Suppose you read a report about a new vaccine and the manufacturer says it is 67% effective at preventing disease. You might wonder where that number comes from, what it means, and how confident we should be that it is correct. Results like this often come from a randomized controlled trial (RCT), which works like this:

- You recruit a large group of volunteers and divide them into two groups at random: the "treatment group" receives the vaccine; the "control group" does not.

- Then you follow both groups for a period of time and record the number of people in each group who are diagnosed with the disease.

As an example, suppose you recruit 43,783 participants and they are assigned to groups with approximately the same size.

```
n_control = 21885
n_treatment = 21911
```

During the observation period, 468 people are diagnosed with the disease: 352 in the control group and 116 in the treatment group.

```
k_control = 352
k_treatment = 116
```

We can use these results to compute the risk of getting the disease for each group, in cases per 1000 people

```
risk_control = k_control / n_control * 1000
risk_control
```

16.084075851039522

```
risk_treatment = k_treatment / n_treatment * 1000
risk_treatment
```

5.294144493633334

The risk is substantially lower in the treatment group – about 5 per 1000, compared to 16 – which suggests that the vaccine is effective. We can summarize these results by computing relative risk, which is the ratio of the two risks:

```
relative_risk = risk_treatment / risk_control
relative_risk
```

0.3291544097817203

The relative risk is about 0.33, which means that the risk of disease in the treatment group is 33% of the risk in the control group. Equivalently, we could report the complement of relative risk, which is **efficacy**:

```
efficacy = 1 - relative_risk
efficacy
```

0.6708455902182797

In this example the efficacy is 0.67, which means that the vaccine reduces the risk of disease by 67%. That's good news, but as skeptical data scientists, we should not assume that it is perfectly accurate. There are any number of things that might have gone wrong.

For example, if people in the treatment group know they have been vaccinated, they might take fewer precautions to prevent disease, and people in the control group might be more careful. That would affect the estimated efficacy, which is why a lot of trials are "blinded", meaning that the subjects don't know which group they are in.

The estimate would also be less accurate if people in either group don't follow the protocol. For example, someone in the treatment group might not complete treatment, or someone in the control group might receive treatment from another source. And there are many other possible sources of error, including honest mistakes and deliberate fraud.

In general it is hard to know whether estimates like this are accurate; nevertheless, there are things we can do to assess their quality. When estimates are reported in scientific journals, they almost always include one of two measurements of uncertainty: a standard error or a confidence interval. In the next section, I'll explain what they mean and show how to compute them.

11.2 Simulating One Group

In the example, there are 21,911 people in the treatment group and 116 of them got the disease, so the estimated risk is about 5 cases per 1000 people.

```
n_treatment, k_treatment, risk_treatment
```

(21911, 116, 5.294144493633334)

But it's easy to imagine that there might have been a few more cases, or fewer, just by chance. For example, if there had been 10 more cases, the estimated risk would be 5.8 per 1000, and if there had been 10 fewer, it would be 4.8.

```
(k_treatment + 10) / n_treatment * 1000
```

5.750536260325863

```
(k_treatment - 10) / n_treatment * 1000
```

4.837752726940806

That's a big enough difference that we should wonder how much variability there is in the estimate due to random variation. We'll answer that question in three steps:

- We'll write a function that uses a random number generator to simulate the trial.
- Then we'll run the function many times to see how much the estimate varies.
- And we'll summarize the results.

To simulate the trial, we'll use the `bernoulli` object from SciPy, which provides a function called `rvs` that simulates what we can think of as biased coin tosses. For example, suppose we flip 10 coins where the probability is 70% that each coin comes up heads. We can simulate that scenario like this.

```
from scipy.stats import bernoulli

bernoulli.rvs(p=0.7, size=10)
```

array([1, 1, 1, 0, 0, 1, 1, 1, 1, 1])

The result is an array where 1 represents heads and 0 represents tails.

We can use the following function to simulate a group of n patients, where the probability is p that each of them gets the disease.

```
def simulate_group(n, p):
    k = bernoulli.rvs(p, size=n).sum()
    risk = k / n * 1000
    return risk
```

This function uses `rvs` to generate an array of 1s and 0s, adds them up the number of cases, and returns the risk in cases per 1000 people. Here's how we call this function, passing as arguments the size of the treatment group and the estimated risk as a proportion:

```
p = k_treatment / n_treatment
simulate_group(n_treatment, p)
```

5.339783670302587

The result is a risk from a single simulated trial. If we run this function many times, it's like running the trial over and over.

```
t = [simulate_group(n_treatment, p)
     for i in range(1001)]
```

The result is a list of risks that shows how much we expect the results of the trial to vary due to randomness. We can use a KDE plot to visualize the distribution of these results.

```
import matplotlib.pyplot as plt
import seaborn as sns

sns.kdeplot(t, label='control')

plt.xlabel('Risk of disease (cases per 1000)')
plt.ylabel('Probability density')
plt.title('Risks from Simulations');
```

11.2 Simulating One Group

Risks from Simulations

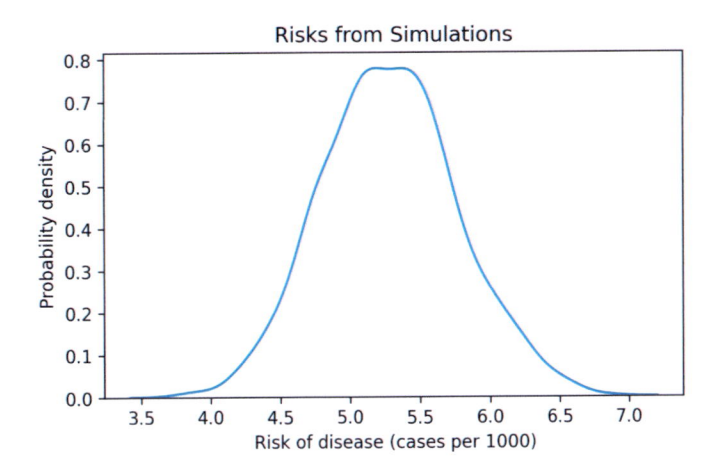

The mean of this distribution is about 5.3, which is close to the observed risk, as we should expect.

```
np.mean(t), risk_treatment
```

(5.284478654019068, 5.294144493633334)

The width of this distribution indicates how much variation there is in the estimate due to randomness. One way to quantify the width of the distribution is the standard deviation.

```
standard_error = np.std(t)
standard_error
```

0.48237692869481597

This result is called the **standard error**.

Another way to quantify the width of the distribution is an interval between two percentiles. For example, if we compute the 5th and 95th percentiles, the interval we get contains 90% of the simulated results.

```
confidence_interval = np.percentile(t, [5, 95])
confidence_interval
```

array([4.51827849, 6.11564967])

This result is called a **confidence interval**; specifically, this one is a "90% confidence interval", or 90% CI. If we assume that the observed risk is correct, and we run the same trial many times, we expect 90% of the results to fall in this interval.

Standard errors and confidence intervals quantify our uncertainty about the estimate due to random variation from one trial to another.

11.3 Simulating the Trial

In the previous section we simulated one group and estimated their risk. Now we'll simulate both groups and estimate the efficacy of the vaccine.

The following function takes four parameters: the sizes of the two groups and their actual risks.

```
def simulate_trial(n1, p1, n2, p2):
    risk1 = simulate_group(n1, p1)
    risk2 = simulate_group(n2, p2)
    efficacy = 1 - risk2 / risk1
    return efficacy
```

If we call this function once, it simulates both groups, computes the risks in each group, and uses the results to compute the efficacy of the treatment (assuming that the first group is the control).

```
p1 = k_control / n_control
p2 = k_treatment / n_treatment
simulate_trial(n_control, p1, n_treatment, p2)
```

0.7022507535102278

If we call it many times, the result is a list of efficacies from multiple simulated trials.

```
t2 = [simulate_trial(n_control, p1, n_treatment, p2)
      for i in range(1001)]
```

We can use a KDE plot to visualize the distribution of the results.

```
sns.kdeplot(t2)

plt.xlabel('Efficacy')
plt.ylabel('Probability density')
plt.title('Efficacies from Simulations');
```

11.3 Simulating the Trial

Efficacies from Simulations

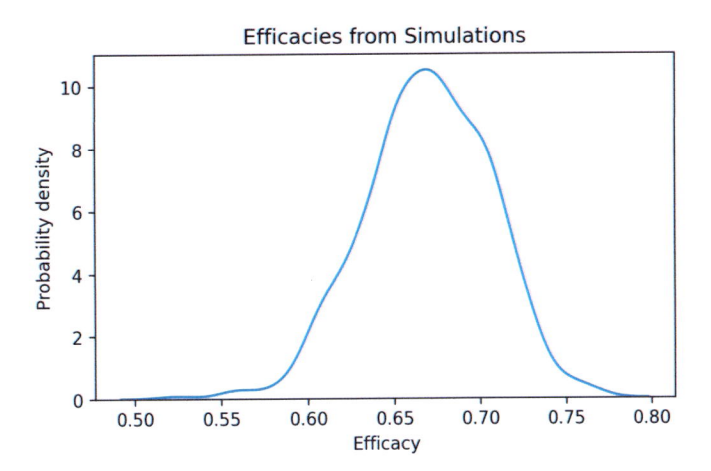

The mean of this distribution is close to the efficacy we computed with the results of the actual trial.

```
np.mean(t2), efficacy
```

(0.6697923695446464, 0.6708455902182797)

The standard deviation of this distribution is the standard error of the estimate.

```
np.std(t2)
```

0.03654909244711291

In a scientific paper, we could report the estimated efficacy and standard error as 0.67 (SE 0.035). As an alternative, we can use percentiles to compute a 90% confidence interval.

```
np.percentile(t2, [5, 95])
```

array([0.60861545, 0.7251222])

We could report these results as 0.67, 90% CI [0.61, 0.72].

The standard error and confidence interval represent nearly the same information. In general, I prefer to report a confidence interval because it is easier to interpret:

- Formally, the confidence interval means that if we run the same experiment again, we expect 90% of the results to fall between 61% and 72% (assuming that the estimated risks are correct).

- More casually, it means that it is plausible that the actually efficacy is as low as 61%, or as high as 72% (assuming there are no sources of error other than random variation).

11.4 Estimating Means

In the previous examples, we estimated risk, which is a proportion, and efficacy, which is a ratio of two proportions. As a third example, let's estimate a mean.

Suppose we want to estimate the average height of men in the United States. It would be impractical to measure everyone in the country, but if we choose a random sample of the population and measure the people in the sample, we can use the mean of the measurements to estimate the actual average in the population.

Ideally, the sample should be **representative**, which means that everyone in the population has an equal chance of appearing in the sample. In general, that's not easy to do. Depending on how you recruit people, your sample might have too many tall people or too many short people.

But let's suppose we have a representative sample of 103 adult male residents of the United States, the average height in the sample is 177 cm, and the standard deviation is 8.4 cm.

If someone asks for your best guess about the height of men in the U.S., you would report 177 cm. But how accurate do you think this estimate is? If you only measure 103 people from a population of about 100 million adult males, it seems like the actual average in the population might be substantially higher or lower.

Again, we can use random simulation to quantify the uncertainty of this estimate. As we did in the previous examples, we'll assume for purposes of simulation that the estimates are correct, and simulate the sampling process many times.

The following function takes as parameters the size of the sample, `n`, the presumed average height in the population, `mu`, and the presumed standard deviation, `sigma`.

```
def simulate_sample_mean(n, mu, sigma):
    sample = np.random.normal(mu, sigma, size=n)
    return sample.mean()
```

This function generates `n` random values from a normal distribution with the given mean and standard deviation, and returns their mean. We can run it like this, using the observed mean and standard deviation from the sample as the presumed mean and standard deviation of the population.

```
n_height = 103
mean_height = 177
std_height = 8.4

simulate_sample_mean(n_height, mean_height, std_height)
```

177.0925279328183

11.4 Estimating Means

If we run it many times, it simulates the sampling and measurement process and returns a list of results from many simulated experiments.

```
t3 = [simulate_sample_mean(n_height, mean_height, std_height)
      for i in range(1001)]
```

We can use a KDE plot to visualize the distribution of these values.

```
sns.kdeplot(t3)

plt.xlabel('Average height (cm)')
plt.ylabel('Probability density')
plt.title('Sampling Distribution of the Mean');
```

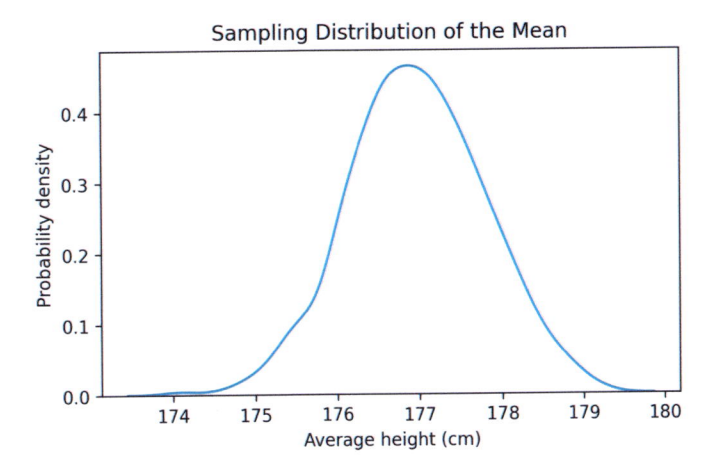

This result is called a **sampling distribution** because it represents the variation in the results due to the random sampling process. If we recruit 103 people and compute the mean of their heights, the result might be as low as 176 cm, or as high as 180 cm, due to chance.

The average of the sampling distribution is close to the presumed mean of the population.

```
np.mean(t3), mean_height
```

(176.97693409905207, 177)

The standard deviation of the sampling distribution is the standard error of the estimate.

```
standard_error = np.std(t3)
standard_error
```

0.8255649832811274

The interval between the 5th and 95th percentiles is a 90% confidence interval.

```
ci90 = np.percentile(t3, [5, 95])
ci90
```

```
array([175.57572755, 178.34974372])
```

If I reported this result in a paper, I would say that the estimated height of adult male residents of the U.S. is 177 cm, 90% CI [176, 178] cm.

Informally, that means that the estimate could plausibly be off by about a centimeter either way, due to random sampling. But we should remember that there are other possible sources of error, so we might be off by more than that.

11.5 The Resampling Framework

The examples in this chapter fit into the framework shown in this diagram:

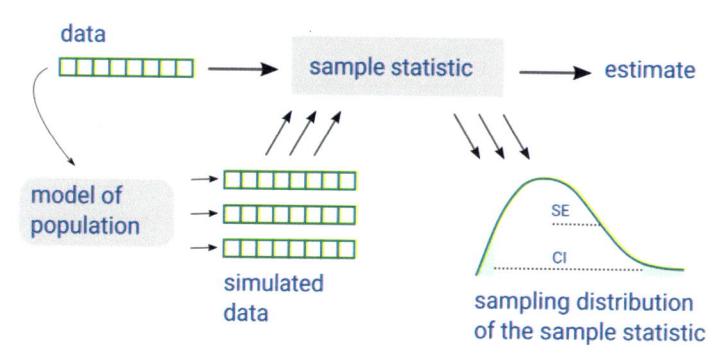

Using data from an experiment, we compute a sample statistic. In the vaccine example, we computed risks for each group and efficacy. In the height example, we computed the average height in the sample.

Then we build a model of the sampling process. In the vaccine example, the model assumes that everyone in each group has the same probability of getting sick, and we use the data to choose the probability. In the height example, the model assumes that heights are drawn from a normal distribution, and we use the data to choose the parameters `mu` and `sigma`.

We use the model to simulate the experiment many times. Each simulation generates a dataset which we use to compute the sample statistic.

Finally, we collect the sample statistics from the simulations, plot the sampling distribution, and compute standard error and a confidence interval.

I emphasize the role of the model in this framework because for a given experiment there might be several possible models, each including some elements of the real world and ignoring others.

11.5 The Resampling Framework

For example, our model of the vaccine experiment assumes that everyone in each group has the same risk, but that's probably not true. Here's another version of `simulate_group` that includes variation in risk within each group.

```
def simulate_variable_group(n, p):
    ps = np.random.uniform(0, 2*p, size=n)
    k = bernoulli.rvs(ps).sum()
    return k / n * 1000
```

This version of the function assumes that each person has a different probability of getting sick, drawn from a uniform distribution between 0 and 2*p. Of course, that's just a guess about how the probabilities might be distributed, but we can use it to get a sense of what effect this distribution has on the results.

The rest of the function is the same as the previous version: it uses `bernoulli` to simulate `n` patients, where each element of `ps` is the probability that one patient gets the disease. Here's how we call this function, simulating the treatment group.

```
p = k_treatment / n_treatment
simulate_variable_group(n_treatment, p)
```

4.290082606909771

The return value is the number of cases per 1000.

Exercise: Use this function to run 1001 simulations of the treatment group. Compute the mean of the results and confirm that it is close to the observed `risk_treatment`. To quantify the spread of the sampling distribution, compute the standard error. How does it compare to the standard error we computed with the original model, where everyone in the group has the same risk?

Exercise: The following is a version of `simulate_trial` that uses `simulate_variable_group`, from the previous exercise, to simulate the vaccine trial using the modified model, which includes variation in risk within the groups.

Use this function to simulate 1001 trials. Compute the mean of the sampling distribution and confirm that it is close to the observed `efficacy`. Compute the standard error and compare it to the standard error we computed for the original model.

```
def simulate_variable_trial(n1, p1, n2, p2):
    risk1 = simulate_variable_group(n1, p1)
    risk2 = simulate_variable_group(n2, p2)
    efficacy = 1 - risk2 / risk1
    return efficacy
```

Exercise: One nice thing about the resampling framework is that it is easy to compute the sampling distribution for other statistics. For example, suppose we want to estimate the coefficient of variation (standard deviation as a fraction of the mean) for adult male height. Here's how we can compute it.

```
cv = std_height / mean_height
cv
```

0.04745762711864407

In this example, the standard deviation is about 4.5% of the mean. The following is a version of `simulate_sample` that generates a random sample of heights and returns the coefficient of variation, rather than the mean.

```
def simulate_sample_cv(n, mu, sigma):
    sample = np.random.normal(mu, sigma, size=n)
    return sample.std() / sample.mean()
```

Use this function to simulate 1001 samples with size `n=103`, using `mean_height` for `mu` and `std_height` for `sigma`. Plot the sampling distribution of the coefficient of variation, and compute a 90% confidence interval.

11.6 Summary

Let's review the examples in this chapter:

1. We started with results from a vaccine trial. We estimated the effectiveness of the vaccine and used simulation to draw a random sample from the sampling distribution of effectiveness. We used that sample to compute a standard error and a 90% confidence interval, which measure the variability we would expect if we ran the experiment again (assuming that the observed efficacy is correct).

2. As a second example, we estimated the height of adult males in the U.S. and used simulation based on a normal model to compute the sampling distribution of the mean, standard error, and a confidence interval.

3. We implemented a second model of the vaccine trial, based on the assumption that there is variation in risk within the groups. The results from the two models are similar, which suggests that the simple model is good enough for practical purposes.

4. One of the advantages of resampling, compared to mathematical analysis, is that it is easy to compute the sampling distribution of almost any statistic. As an exercise, you computed the sampling distribution of the coefficient of variation.

Chapter 12

Bootstrap Sampling

In the previous chapter we used resampling to compute sampling distributions, which quantify the variability in an estimate due to random sampling.

In this chapter, we'll use data from the General Social Survey (GSS) to estimate average income and the 10th percentile of income. We'll see that the resampling method we used in the previous chapter works for the average but not for the 10th percentile. To solve this problem, we'll use another kind of resampling, called bootstrapping.

Then we'll use bootstrapping to compute sampling distributions for correlations and the parameters of linear regression. Finally, I'll point out a problem with bootstrap resampling when there are not enough different values in a dataset, and a way to solve it with KDE resampling.

12.1 Estimating Average Income

As a first example, we'll use data from the General Social Survey to estimate average family income. We'll work with an extract that contains just the columns we need, as we did in Chapter 8. Instructions for downloading the extract are in the notebook for this chapter.

We can load the data like this and display the first few rows.

```
import pandas as pd

gss = pd.read_hdf('gss_extract_2022.hdf', 'gss')
gss.head()
```

	year	id	age	educ	degree	sex	gunlaw	grass	realinc
0	1972	1	23	16	3	2	1	NaN	18951
1	1972	2	70	10	0	1	1	NaN	24366
2	1972	3	48	12	1	2	1	NaN	24366
3	1972	4	27	17	3	2	1	NaN	30458
4	1972	5	61	12	1	2	1	NaN	50763

The column `realinc` records family income, converted to 1986 dollars. The following figure uses the Seaborn function `kdeplot` to show the distribution of family income. The argument `cut=0` cuts off the curve so it doesn't extend beyond the observed minimum and maximum values.

```
import seaborn as sns
import matplotlib.pyplot as plt

sns.kdeplot(gss['realinc'] / 1000, label='GSS data', cut=0)

plt.xlabel('Family income ($1000s)')
plt.ylabel('PDF')
plt.title('Distribution of income')
plt.legend();
```

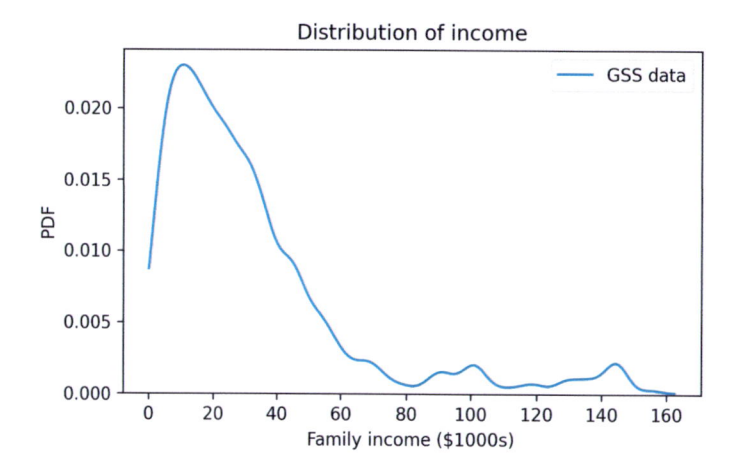

The distribution of income is skewed to the right; most household incomes are less than $60,000, but a few are substantially higher. Here are the mean and standard deviation of the reported incomes.

```
mean_realinc = gss['realinc'].mean()
std_realinc = gss['realinc'].std()
print(mean_realinc, std_realinc)
```

12.1 Estimating Average Income

```
32537.399981032493 30883.22609399141
```

The average family income in this sample is $32,537. But if we ran the GSS survey again, the average might be higher or lower. To see how much it might vary, we can use this function from the previous chapter to simulate the sampling process.

```
import numpy as np

def simulate_sample_mean(n, mu, sigma):
    sample = np.random.normal(mu, sigma, size=n)
    return sample.mean()
```

`simulate_sample_mean` takes as parameters the sample size and the mean and standard deviation. It generates a sample from a normal distribution and returns the mean.

Before we call this function, we have to count the number of valid responses.

```
n_realinc = gss['realinc'].count()
n_realinc
```

```
64912
```

Now, if we call `simulate_sample_mean` once, we get a single value from the sampling distribution of the mean.

```
simulate_sample_mean(n_realinc, mean_realinc, std_realinc)
```

```
32573.420195135117
```

If we call it many times, we get a random sample from the sampling distribution.

```
t1 = [simulate_sample_mean(n_realinc, mean_realinc, std_realinc)
      for i in range(1001)]
```

Here's what the sampling distribution looks like.

```
sns.kdeplot(t1)

plt.xlabel('Family income (1986 $)')
plt.ylabel('PDF')
plt.title('Sampling distribution of mean income');
```

Sampling distribution of mean income

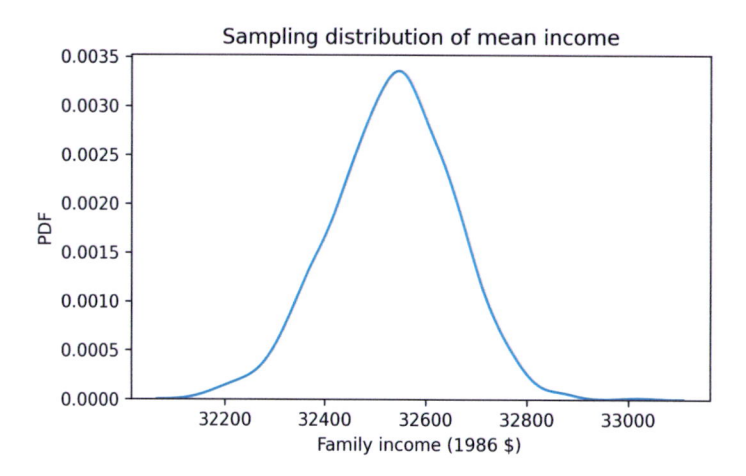

This distribution shows how much we would expect the observed mean to vary if we ran the GSS survey again. We'll use the following function to summarize the sampling distribution.

```
def summarize(t, digits=2, label=''):
    est = np.mean(t).round(digits)
    SE = np.std(t).round(digits)
    CI90 = np.percentile(t, [5, 95]).round(digits)
    data = [est, SE, CI90]
    columns = ['Estimate', 'SE', 'CI90']
    table = pd.DataFrame([data], index=[label], columns=columns)
    return table
```

```
summary1 = summarize(t1, digits=1)
summary1
```

	Estimate	SE	CI90
	32533.8	120.7	[32331.4 32724.2]

The result shows the mean of the sampling distribution, the standard error, and a 90% confidence interval. The mean of the sampling distribution is close to the mean of the data, as we expect. The standard error quantifies the width of the sampling distribution, which is about $121. Informally, that's how much we would expect the sample mean to change if we ran the survey again. And if we ran the survey many times and computed the average income each time, we would expect 90% of the results to fall in the range from 32,331 to 32,724.

In this section, we used a normal distribution to simulate the sampling process. The normal distribution is not a particularly good model for the distribution of income, but it works well enough for this example, and the results are reasonable. In the next section we'll see an example where the normal distribution is not good enough and the results are not reasonable. Then we'll see how to fix the problem.

12.2 Estimating Percentiles

Suppose that, instead of estimating the average income, we want to estimate the 10th percentile. Computing percentiles of income is often relevant to discussions of income inequality.

To compute the 10th percentile of the data, we can use the Pandas method `quantile`, which is similar to the NumPy function `percentile`, except that it drops `NaN` values. Also, the parameter of `quantile` is a probability between 0 and 1, rather than a percentage between 0 and 100.

```
gss['realinc'].quantile(0.1)
```

5730.0

The 10th percentile of the sample is $5730, but if we collected another sample, the result might be higher or lower. To see how much it would vary, we can use the following function to simulate the sampling process: `simulate_sample_percentile` generates a sample from a normal distribution and returns the 10th percentile.

```
def simulate_sample_percentile(n, mu, sigma):
    sample = np.random.normal(mu, sigma, size=n)
    return np.percentile(sample, 10)
```

If we call it many times, the result is a sample from the sampling distribution of the 10th percentile.

```
t2 = [simulate_sample_percentile(n_realinc, mean_realinc, std_realinc)
      for i in range(1001)]
```

Here's what that sampling distribution looks like.

```
sns.kdeplot(t2)

plt.xlabel('Family income (1986 $)')
plt.ylabel('PDF')
plt.title('Sampling distribution of the 10th percentile');
```

Sampling distribution of the 10th percentile

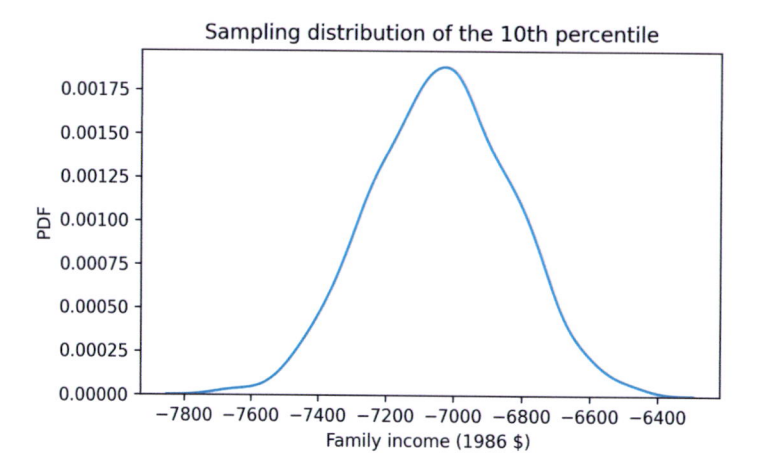

We can see that something has gone wrong. All of the values in the sampling distribution are negative, even though no one in the sample reported a negative income. To see what happened, let's look at the distribution of reported incomes again compared to the normal distribution with the same mean and standard deviation.

```
from scipy.stats import norm

xs = np.linspace(-50, 150)
ys = norm(mean_realinc/1000, std_realinc/1000).pdf(xs)
```

```
sns.kdeplot(gss['realinc'] / 1000, label='GSS data', cut=0)
plt.plot(xs, ys, color='0.7', label='normal model')

plt.xlabel('Family income ($1000s)')
plt.ylabel('PDF')
plt.title('Distribution of income')
plt.legend();
```

12.3 Bootstrapping

Distribution of income

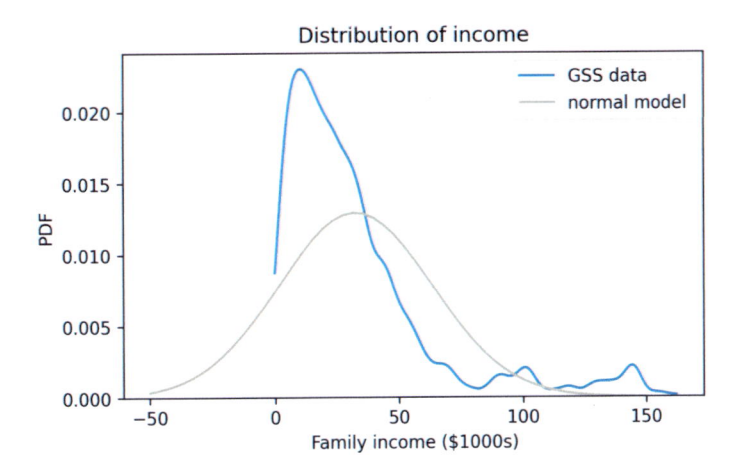

The problem is that the normal model extends past the lower bound of the observed values, so it doesn't produce sensible results. Fortunately there is a simple alternative that is more robust: bootstrapping.

12.3 Bootstrapping

Bootstrapping is a kind of resampling, based on the framework we saw in the previous chapter:

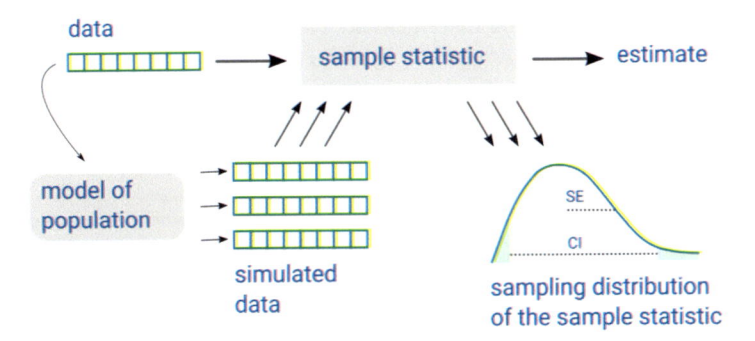

The idea is that we treat the original sample as if it were the entire population, and simulate the sampling process by choosing random rows with replacement. `DataFrame` provides a method called `sample` we can use to select a random sample of the rows.

```
bootstrapped = gss.sample(n=n_realinc, replace=True)
bootstrapped.shape
```

(64912, 9)

The argument `n=n_realinc` means that the bootstrapped sample has the same size as the original. `replace=True` means that sampling is done with replacement – that is, the same row can be chosen more than once. To see how many times each row appears in the bootstrapped sample, we can use `value_counts` and the `id` column, which contains a unique identifier for each respondent.

```
repeats = bootstrapped['id'].value_counts()
repeats.head()
```

```
id
90     55
373    49
322    47
190    46
975    46
Name: count, dtype: int64
```

Several of the rows appear more than 40 times. Since some rows appear many times, other rows don't appear at all. To see how many, we can use `set` subtraction to count the values of `id` that appear in the original dataset but not the bootstrapped sample.

```
unused = set(gss['id']) - set(bootstrapped['id'])
len(unused)
```

```
228
```

Now we can use bootstrapping to generate a sampling distribution. For example, the following function takes a `DataFrame`, generates a bootstrapped sample, and returns the average income.

```
def bootstrap_mean(df, varname):
    bootstrapped = df.sample(n=len(df), replace=True)
    return bootstrapped[varname].mean()
```

If we run it many times, we get a sample from the sampling distribution of the mean.

```
t3 = [bootstrap_mean(gss, 'realinc')
      for i in range(1001)]
```

Here's a summary of the results, compared to the results based on the normal model.

```
summary3 = summarize(t3)
table = pd.concat([summary1, summary3])
table.index = ['normal model', 'bootstrapping']
table
```

	Estimate	SE	CI90
normal model	32533.8	120.7	[32331.4 32724.2]
bootstrapping	32541	120.44	[32345.43 32735.15]

12.4 Working with Bigger Data

The results from bootstrap sampling are consistent with the results based on the normal model. Now let's see what happens when we estimate the 10th percentile. The following function generates a bootstrapped sample and returns the 10th percentile.

```
def bootstrap_income_percentile(df):
    bootstrapped = df.sample(n=len(df), replace=True)
    return bootstrapped['realinc'].quantile(0.1)
```

We can use it to generate a sample from the sampling distribution of the 10th percentile.

```
t4 = [bootstrap_income_percentile(gss)
      for i in range(1001)]
```

Here are the results from bootstrapping compared to the results from the normal model.

```
summary2 = summarize(t2)
summary4 = summarize(t4)
table = pd.concat([summary2, summary4])
table.index = ['normal model', 'bootstrapping']
table
```

	Estimate	SE	CI90
normal model	-7036.41	206.15	[-7377.72 -6709.54]
bootstrapping	5687.12	91.42	[5512.5 5827.5]

The results from bootstrapping are more sensible – the mean of the sampling distribution and the bounds of the confidence interval are positive and consistent with the 10th percentile of the data.

In general, bootstrapping is robust – that is, it works well with many different distributions and many different statistics. However, at the end of the chapter, we'll see one example where it fails.

12.4 Working with Bigger Data

As sample size increases, errors due to random sampling get smaller. To demonstrate this effect, we'll use data from the Behavioral Risk Factor Surveillance System (BRFSS) to estimate the average height for men in the United States.

First, let's read the 2021 data, which I have stored in an HDF file. Instructions for downloading it are in the notebook for this chapter.

```
import pandas as pd

brfss = pd.read_hdf('brfss_2021.hdf', 'brfss')
brfss.shape
```

(438693, 10)

This dataset contains 438,693 rows, one for each respondent, and 10 columns, one for each variable in the extract. Here are the first few rows.

```
brfss.head()
```

	HTM4	WTKG3	_SEX	_AGEG5YR	_VEGESU1	_INCOMG1	_LLCPWT	_HTM4G10	AGE
0	150	32.66	2	11	2.14	3	744.746	140	72
1	168	NaN	2	10	1.28	NaN	299.137	160	67
2	165	77.11	2	11	0.71	2	587.863	160	72
3	163	88.45	2	9	1.65	5	1099.62	160	62
4	180	93.44	1	12	2.58	2	1711.83	170	77

The HTM4 column contains the respondents' heights in centimeters.

```
height = brfss['HTM4']
```

To select male respondents, we'll use the SEX column to make a Boolean Series.

```
male = (brfss['_SEX'] == 1)
male.sum()
```

203760

We can use count to count the number of male respondents with valid height data.

```
n_height = height[male].count()
n_height
```

193701

12.4 Working with Bigger Data

Here is the mean and standard deviation of these values.

```
mean_height = height[male].mean()
std_height = height[male].std()
mean_height, std_height
```

(178.14807357731763, 7.987083970017878)

The average height for men in the U.S. is about 178 cm. To see how precise this estimate is, we can use bootstrapping to generate values from the sampling distribution. To reduce computation time, I set the number of iterations to 201.

```
t5 = [bootstrap_mean(brfss[male], 'HTM4')
      for i in range(201)]

summarize(t5, digits=3)
```

Estimate	SE	CI90
178.148	0.018	[178.121 178.176]

Because the sample size is so large, the standard error is small and the confidence interval is narrow. This result suggests that our estimate is very precise, which is true in the sense that the error due to random sampling is small.

But there are other sources of error. For example, the heights and weights in this dataset are self-reported, so they are vulnerable to **social desirability bias**, which is the tendency of people to represent themselves in a positive light.

It's also possible that there are errors in recording the data. In a previous year of the BRFSS, there are a suspicious number of heights recorded as 60 or 61 centimeters. I suspect that many of them are six feet tall, or six feet and one inch, and something went wrong in recording the data.

And that brings us to the point of this example:

> With large sample sizes, variability due to random sampling is small, but with real-world data, that often means that other sources of error are bigger. So we can't be sure that the estimate is accurate.

In fact, there is another source of error in this example that we have not taken into account: oversampling.

12.5 Weighted Bootstrapping

By design, the BRFSS oversamples some demographic groups – that is, people in some groups are more likely than others to appear in the sample. If people in these groups are taller than others on average, or shorter, our estimated mean would not be accurate.

We encountered this issue in Chapter 7, where we used data from the National Survey of Family Growth (NSFG) to compute the average birth weight for babies in the United States. In that example, we corrected for oversampling by computing a weighted mean.

In this example, we'll use a different method, **weighted bootstrapping**, to estimate the mean and compute a confidence interval. The BRFSS dataset includes a column, _LLCPWT, that contains sampling weights. The sampling weight for each respondent is the number of people in the population they represent. People in oversampled groups have lower sampling weights; people in undersampled groups have higher sampling weights. Here's what the range of values looks like.

```
brfss['_LLCPWT'].describe()
```

```
count    438693.000000
mean        560.851529
std        1136.781547
min           0.545800
25%          95.573000
50%         248.677287
75%         592.546811
max       49028.547000
Name: _LLCPWT, dtype: float64
```

The lowest sampling weight is about 0.5; the largest is about 49,000 – so that's a very wide range! We can take these weights into account by passing them as an argument to `sample`. That way, the probability that any row is selected is proportional to its sampling weight.

```
n = len(brfss)
bootstrapped = brfss.sample(n=n, replace=True, weights='_LLCPWT')
```

As we saw with unweighted bootstrapping, the same row can appear more than once. To see how many times, we can use `value_counts` and the `SEQNO` column, which contains a unique identifier for each respondent.

12.5 Weighted Bootstrapping

```
repeats = bootstrapped['SEQNO'].value_counts()
repeats.head()
```

```
SEQNO
2021000019    144
2021001348    132
2021000044    129
2021003808    127
2021000091    124
Name: count, dtype: int64
```

Some rows appear more than 100 times. Most likely, these are the rows for people from undersampled groups, who have the highest sampling weights.

To see how many rows don't appear at all, we can use `set` subtraction to count the values of `SEQNO` that appear in the original dataset but not the sample.

```
unused = set(brfss['SEQNO']) - set(bootstrapped['SEQNO'])
len(unused)
```

14616

There are thousands of rows that don't appear in this sample, but they are not dropped altogether – when we repeat this process, they will appear in other samples.

Now we can use weighted bootstrapping to generate values from the sampling distribution of the mean. The following function uses `sample` and the `_LLCPWT` column to generate a bootstrapped sample, then returns the average height.

```
def weighted_bootstrap_mean(df):
    n = len(df)
    sample = df.sample(n=n, replace=True, weights='_LLCPWT')
    return sample['HTM4'].mean()
```

I'll test this function with a `DataFrame` that contains only male respondents. If we run it once, we get a single value from the sampling distribution of the weighted mean.

```
male_df = brfss[male]
weighted_bootstrap_mean(male_df)
```

177.569630553049

If we run it many times, we get a random sample from the sampling distribution.

```
t6 = [weighted_bootstrap_mean(male_df)
      for i in range(201)]

summarize(t6, digits=3)
```

Estimate	SE	CI90
177.541	0.018	[177.513 177.573]

The mean of the sampling distribution estimates the average height for men in the U.S., corrected for oversampling. If we compare it to the unweighted mean we computed, it is a little lower.

```
print(np.mean(t6), mean_height)
```

177.54149968876962 178.14807357731763

So it seems like people in the oversampled groups are taller than others, on average, by enough to bring the unweighted mean up by about half a centimeter.

The difference between the weighted and unweighted averages is bigger than the width of the confidence interval. So in this example the error if we fail to correct for oversampling is bigger than variability due to random sampling.

12.6 Correlation and Regression

Bootstrap resampling can be used to estimate other statistics and their sampling distributions. For example, in Chapter 9 we computed the correlation between height and weight, which is about 0.47.

```
var1, var2 = 'HTM4', 'WTKG3'
corr = brfss[var1].corr(brfss[var2])
corr
```

0.4693981914367917

That correlation does not take into account oversampling. We can correct it with this function, which generates a weighted bootstrapped sample and uses it to compute the correlation of the columns specified by var1 and var2.

```
def weighted_bootstrap_corr(df, var1, var2):
    n = len(df)
    sample = df.sample(n=n, replace=True, weights='_LLCPWT')
    corr = sample[var1].corr(sample[var2])
    return corr
```

12.7 Limitations of Bootstrapping

Exercise: Use this function to draw 101 values from the sampling distribution of the correlation between height and weight. What is the mean of these values? Is it substantially different from the correlation we computed without correcting for oversampling? Compute the standard error and 90% confidence interval for the estimated correlation.

Exercise: In Chapter 9 we also computed the slope of the regression line for weight as a function of height. Here's the result.

```
from scipy.stats import linregress

subset = brfss.dropna(subset=['WTKG3', 'HTM4'])
res = linregress(subset['HTM4'], subset['WTKG3'])
res.slope
```

0.9366891536604244

The estimated slope is 0.94 kg/cm, which means that we expect someone 1 cm taller than average to be about 0.94 kg heavier than average.

Write a function called `weighted_bootstrap_slope` that takes a `DataFrame`, generates a weighted bootstrapped sample, runs `linregress` with height and weight, and returns the slope of the regression line.

Run it 101 times and collect the results. Use the sampling distribution to compute the mean of the slope estimates, standard error, and a 90% confidence interval.

12.7 Limitations of Bootstrapping

One limitation of bootstrapping is that it can be computationally expensive. With small datasets, it is usually fast enough that we can generate a thousand values from the sampling distribution, which means that we can compute standard errors and confidence intervals precisely. With larger datasets, we can cut the computation time by generating fewer values. With 100-200 values, the standard errors we get are usually precise enough, but the bounds of the confidence intervals might be noisier.

The other limitation, which can be more problematic, is that bootstrap sampling does not work well with datasets that contain a small number of different values. To demonstrate, I'll select data from the GSS for one year, 2018:

```
one_year = gss['year']==2018
gss2018 = gss[one_year]
```

And use bootstrapping to generate values from the sampling distribution of the 10th percentile.

```
t9 = [bootstrap_income_percentile(gss2018)
      for i in range(1001)]
```

Here are the results.

```
summary9 = summarize(t9)
summary9
```

Estimate	SE	CI90
5155.46	223.92	[5107.5 5107.5]

The estimate and the standard error look plausible at first glance, but the width of the confidence interval is 0, which suggests that something has gone wrong! The problem is that `realinc` is not really a numerical variable – it is a categorical variable in disguise. Using `value_counts`, we can see that there are only 26 distinct values in this column.

```
len(gss2018['realinc'].value_counts())
```

26

The reason is that the GSS does not ask respondents to report their incomes. Instead, it gives them a list of ranges and asks them to pick the range their income falls in. Then GSS analysts compute the midpoint of each range and convert to 1986 dollars by adjusting for inflation. As a result, there are only 26 distinct values for each year of the survey. When we generate a bootstrapped sample and compute the 10th percentile, we get a small subset of them. Here are the values that appear in our sample.

```
pd.Series(t9).value_counts().sort_index()
```

```
5107.5    955
5221.0      1
5448.0      1
5561.5      1
5675.0      1
5902.0      2
6015.5      1
6129.0      2
6242.5     37
Name: count, dtype: int64
```

There are only a few different values, and one of them appears more than 95% of the time. When we compute a 90% confidence interval, this value is both the 5th and the 95th percentile.

Bootstrapping works well for most distributions and most statistics, but the one thing it can't handle is lack of diversity in the data. Fortunately, this problem can be solved. The cause of the problem is that the data have been discretized excessively, so the solution is to smooth it. Jittering is one option. Another is to use kernel density estimation (KDE).

12.8 Resampling with KDE

We have used KDE several times to estimate and plot a probability density based on a sample. We can also use it to smooth data that have been discretized.

For this example, we'll compute the logarithms of the income values.

```
log_realinc = np.log10(gss2018['realinc'].dropna())
```

We've seen that the distribution of income is skewed so the tail extends farther to the right than the left. The logarithms of income have a more symmetric distribution that makes them work better with KDE. Here's what the estimated density looks like.

```
sns.kdeplot(log_realinc)

plt.xlabel('Income (log10 1986 dollars)')
plt.ylabel('Probability density')
plt.title('Estimated distribution of income');
```

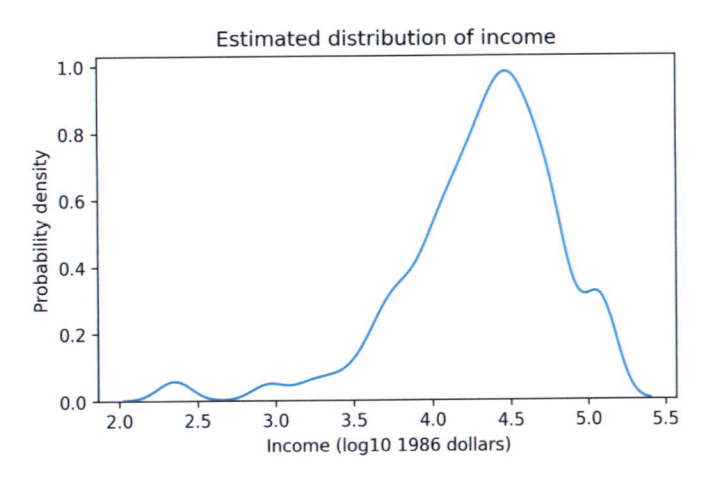

To draw samples from this distribution, we'll use a Scipy function called `gaussian_kde`, which takes the data and returns an object that represents the estimated density.

```
from scipy.stats import gaussian_kde

kde = gaussian_kde(log_realinc)
```

The resulting object provides a method called `resample` that draws random values from the estimated density. As we've done in previous examples, we'll generate a resampled dataset with the same size as the original – which is stored as `kde.n`.

```
sample = kde.resample(kde.n)
```

Now we can compute the 10th percentile and convert from a logarithm to a dollar value.

```
10 ** np.percentile(sample, 10)
```

5235.936465561343

The result is a random value from the sampling distribution of the 10th percentile. The following function encapsulates these steps.

```
def resample_kde_percentile(kde):
    sample = kde.resample(kde.n)
    return 10 ** np.percentile(sample, 10)
```

Now we can generate a sample from the sampling distribution.

```
t10 = [resample_kde_percentile(kde)
       for i in range(1000)]

summary10 = summarize(t10)
```

The following table compares the result to the previous result with bootstrapping.

```
table = pd.concat([summary9, summary10])
table.index = ['bootstrapping', 'KDE resampling']
table
```

	Estimate	SE	CI90
bootstrapping	5155.46	223.92	[5107.5 5107.5]
KDE resampling	5097.59	246.25	[4692.62 5485.93]

The means and standard errors are about the same with either method. But the confidence interval we get from KDE resampling is sensible.

12.9 Summary

There are ten examples in this chapter, so let's review them:

1. First we used resampling based on a normal model to estimate average family income in the GSS and compute a confidence interval.

2. Then we used the same method to estimate the 10th percentile of income, and we found that all of the values in the sampling distribution are negative. The problem is that the normal model does not fit the distribution of income.

3. To solve this problem, we switched to bootstrap sampling. First we estimated average family income and confirmed that the results are consistent with the results based on the normal model.

4. Then we used bootstrapping to estimate the 10th percentile of income. The results are much more plausible.

5. Next we used data from the BRFSS to estimate the average height of men in the U.S. Since this dataset is large, the confidence interval is very small. That means that the estimate is precise, in the sense that variability due to random sampling is small, but we don't know whether it is accurate, because there are other sources of error.

6. One of those sources of error is oversampling – that is, some people are more likely to appear in the sample than others. In the BFRSS, each respondent has a sampling weight that indicates how many people in the population they represent. We used these weights to do weighted bootstrapping, and found that the error due to oversampling is larger than the variability due to random sampling.

7. In one exercise you used weighted bootstrapping to estimate the correlation of height and weight and compute a confidence interval.

8. In another exercise you estimated the slope of a regression line and computed a confidence interval.

9. Then I demonstrated a problem with bootstrap sampling when the dataset has only a few different values,

10. And presented a solution using KDE to smooth the data and draw samples from an estimated distribution.

In the exercise below, you can work on one more example. It is a little more involved than the previous exercises, but I will walk you through it.

Exercise: In Chapter 10 we used logistic regression to model support for legalizing marijuana as a function of age, sex, and education level. Going back to that example, let's explore changes in support over time and generate predictions for the next decade.

To prepare the data for logistic regression, we have to recode the `grass` column so 1 means in favor of legalization and 0 means not in favor.

```
gss['grass'] = gss['grass'].replace(2, 0)
gss['grass'].value_counts()
```

```
grass
0.0    25997
1.0    12672
Name: count, dtype: int64
```

As explanatory variables we'll use `year` and `year` squared, which I'll store in a column called `year2`. Subtracting 1990 from `year` before squaring keeps the values of `year2` relatively small, which makes logistic regression work better.

```
gss['year2'] = (gss['year'] - 1990) ** 2.0
```

Now we can run the model like this:

```
import statsmodels.formula.api as smf

formula = 'grass ~ year + year2'
results = smf.logit(formula, data=gss).fit()
```

```
Optimization terminated successfully.
         Current function value: 0.585064
         Iterations 5
```

To generate predictions, I'll create a `DataFrame` with a range of values of `year` up to 2030, and corresponding values of `year2`.

```
years = np.linspace(1972, 2030)
df_pred = pd.DataFrame()
df_pred['year'] = years
df_pred['year2'] = (years - 1990) **2

pred = results.predict(df_pred)
```

I'll use `groupby` to compute the fraction of respondents in favor of legalization during each year.

12.9 Summary

```
grass_by_year = gss.groupby('year')['grass'].mean()
```

The following function plots the data and decorates the axes.

```
def plot_data():
    grass_by_year.plot(style='o', alpha=0.5, label='data')
    plt.xlabel('Year')
    plt.ylabel('Fraction in favor')
    plt.title('Support for legalization of marijuana')
    plt.legend(loc='upper left');
```

Here's what the predictions look like, plotted along with the data.

```
plt.plot(years, pred, label='logistic model', color='gray', alpha=0.4)
plot_data()
```

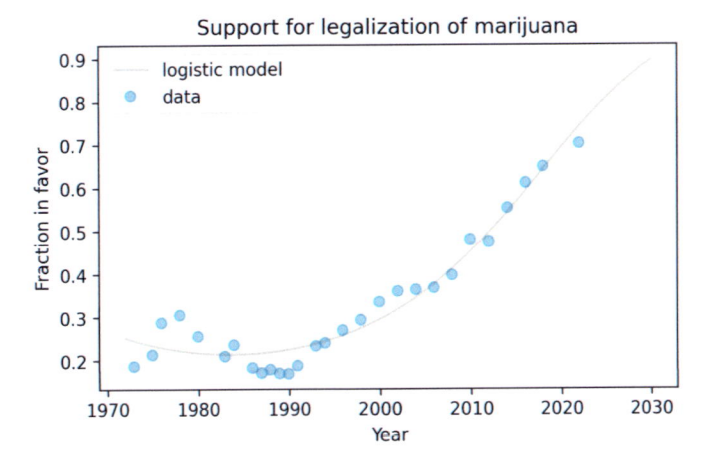

The model fits past data reasonably well and makes plausible predictions for the next decade, although we can never be sure that trends like this will continue.

This way of representing the results could be misleading because it does not show our uncertainty about the predictions. Random sampling is just one source of uncertainty among many, and for this kind of prediction it is certainly not the biggest. But it is the easiest to quantify, so let's do it, if only as an exercise.

Write a function called `bootstrap_regression_line` that takes a `DataFrame` as a parameter, uses `sample` to resample the rows, runs the logistic regression model, generates predictions for the rows in `df_pred`, and returns the predictions.

Call this function 101 times and save the results as a list of `Series` objects. To visualize the results, you have two options:

1. Loop through the list and plot each prediction using a gray line with a low value of `alpha`. The overlapping lines will form a region showing the range of uncertainty over time.

2. Pass the list of `Series` to `np.percentile` with the argument `axis=0` to compute the 5th and 95th percentile in each column. Plot these percentiles as two lines, or use `plt.fill_between` to plot a shaded region between them.

Chapter 13

Hypothesis Testing

This chapter introduces statistical hypothesis testing, which is such a contentious topic in the history of statistics, it's hard to provide a simple definition. Instead, I'll start with an example, present the problem hypothesis testing is intended to solve, and then show a solution.

The solution I'll show is different from what you might find in a statistics book. Instead of mathematical analysis, we will use computational simulations. This approach has two advantages and one disadvantage:

- Advantage: The standard statistics curriculum includes many different tests, and many people find it hard to remember which one to use. In my opinion, simulation makes it clearer that there is only one testing framework.

- Advantage: Simulations make modeling decision explicit. All statistical methods are based on models, but when we use mathematical methods, it is easy to forget the assumptions they are based on. With computation, the assumptions are more visible, and it is easier to try different models.

- Disadvantage: Simulation uses a lot of computation. Some of the examples in this notebook take several seconds to run; for some of them, there are analytic methods that are much faster.

The examples in this chapter include results from a clinical trial related to peanut allergies, and survey data from the National Survey of Family Growth (NSFG) and the Behavioral Risk Factor Surveillance System (BRFSS).

13.1 Testing Medical Treatments

The LEAP study was a randomized trial that tested the effect of eating peanut snacks on the development of peanut allergies. The subjects were infants who were at high risk of developing peanut allergies because they had been diagnosed with other food allergies. Over a period of several years, half of the subjects were periodically given a snack containing peanuts; the other half were given no peanuts at all.

The conclusion of the study, reported in 2015 is:

> Of the children who avoided peanut, 17% developed peanut allergy by the age of 5 years. Remarkably, only 3% of the children who were randomized to eating the peanut snack developed allergy by age 5. Therefore, in high-risk infants, sustained consumption of peanut beginning in the first 11 months of life was highly effective in preventing the development of peanut allergy.

Detailed results of the study are reported in the *New England Journal of Medicine*. In that article, Figure 1 shows the number of subjects in the treatment and control groups, which happened to be equal.

```
n_control = 314
n_treatment = 314
```

And from Figure 2 we can extract the number of subjects who developed peanut allergies in each group. Specifically, we'll use the numbers from the "intention to treat analysis for both cohorts".

```
k_control = 54
k_treatment = 10
```

Using these numbers, we can compute the risk in each group as a percentage.

```
risk_control = k_control / n_control * 100
risk_control
```

17.197452229299362

```
risk_treatment = k_treatment / n_treatment * 100
risk_treatment
```

3.1847133757961785

These are consistent with the percentages reported in the paper.

13.1 Testing Medical Treatments

To quantify the difference between the groups, we'll use relative risk, which is the ratio of the risks in the two groups.

```
relative_risk_actual = risk_treatment / risk_control
relative_risk_actual
```

0.1851851851851852

The risk in the treatment group is about 18% of the risk in the control group, which means the treatment might prevent 82% of cases.

These results seem impressive, but as skeptical data scientists we should wonder whether it is possible that we are getting fooled by randomness. Maybe the apparent difference between the groups is due to chance, not the effectiveness of the treatment. To see whether this is likely, we will simulate the experiment using a model where the treatment has no effect, and see how often we see such a big difference between the groups.

Let's imagine a world where the treatment is completely ineffective, so the risk is actually the same in both groups, and the difference we saw is due to chance. If that's true, we can estimate the hypothetical risk by combining the two groups.

```
n_all = n_control + n_treatment
k_all = k_control + k_treatment
risk_all = k_all / n_all
risk_all
```

0.10191082802547771

If the risk is the same for both groups, it is close to 10%. Now we can use this hypothetical risk to simulate the experiment. The following function takes as parameters the size of the group, n, and the risk, p. It simulates the experiment and returns the number of cases as a percentage of the group, which is the observed risk.

```
from scipy.stats import bernoulli

def simulate_group_percent(n, p):
    k = bernoulli.rvs(p, size=n).sum()
    risk = k / n * 100
    return risk
```

If we call this function many times, the result is a list of observed risks, one for each simulated experiment. Here's the list for the treatment group.

```
t1 = [simulate_group_percent(n_treatment, risk_all)
      for i in range(1001)]
```

And the control group.

```
t2 = [simulate_group_percent(n_control, risk_all)
      for i in range(1001)]
```

If we divide these lists elementwise, the result is a list of relative risks, one for each simulated experiment.

```
relative_risks = np.divide(t2, t1)
```

We can use a KDE plot to visualize the distribution of these results.

```
import matplotlib.pyplot as plt
import seaborn as sns

sns.kdeplot(relative_risks)

plt.xlabel('Relative risk')
plt.ylabel('Probability density')
plt.title('Relative risks from simulation');
```

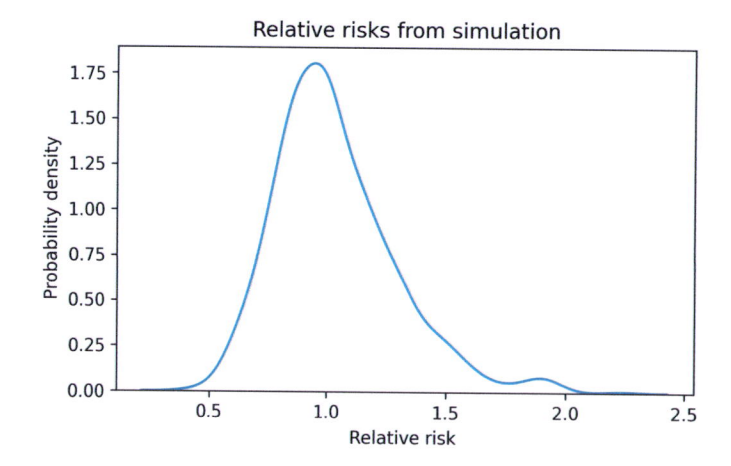

Remember that these simulations are based on the assumption that the risk is the same for both groups, so we expect the relative risk to be near 1 most of the time. And it is.

In some simulated experiments, the relative risk is as low as 0.5 or as high as 2, which means it is plausible we could see results like that by chance, even if there is no difference between groups.

But the relative risk in the actual experiment was 0.18, and we never see a result as small as that in the simulated experiments. We can conclude that the relative risk we saw is unlikely if the risk is actually the same in both groups.

13.2 Computing p-values

Now suppose that in addition to the treatment and control groups, the experiment included a placebo group that was given a snack that contained no peanuts. Suppose this group was the same size as the others, and 42 of the subjects developed peanut allergies.

To be clear, there was no third group, and I made up these numbers, but let's see how this hypothetical example works out. Here's the risk in the placebo group.

```
n_placebo = 314
k_placebo = 42

risk_placebo = k_placebo / n_placebo * 100
risk_placebo
```

13.375796178343949

And here's the relative risk compared to the control group.

```
relative_risk_placebo = risk_placebo / risk_control
relative_risk_placebo
```

0.7777777777777778

The relative risk is less than 1, which means the risk in the placebo group is a bit lower than in the control group. So we might wonder whether the placebo was actually effective. To answer that question, at least partially, we can go back to the results from the simulated experiments.

Under the assumption that there is actually no difference between the groups, it would not be unusual to see a relative risk as low as 0.78 by chance. In fact, we can compute the probability of seeing a relative risk as low or lower than `relative_risk_placebo`, even if the two groups are the same, like this:

```
p_value = (relative_risks <= relative_risk_placebo).mean()
p_value
```

0.12887112887112886

This probability is called a **p-value**. In this case, it is about 13%, which means that even if the two groups are the same, we expect to see a relative risk as low as 0.78 about 13% of the time. So, for this imagined experiment, we can't rule out the possibility that the apparent difference is due to chance.

13.3 Are First Babies More Likely To Be Late?

In the previous example, we computed relative risk, which is a ratio of two proportions. As a second example, let's consider a difference between two means.

When my wife and I were expecting our first child, we heard that first babies are more likely to be born late. But we also heard that first babies are more likely to be born early. So which is it? As a data scientist with too much time on my hands, I decided to find out. I used data from the National Survey of Family Growth (NSFG), the same survey we used in Chapter 7. At the end of that chapter, we stored a subset of the data in an HDF file. Now we can read it back.

```
import pandas as pd

nsfg = pd.read_hdf('nsfg.hdf', 'nsfg')
nsfg.head()
```

	CASEID	PREGORDR	HOWPREG_N	HOWPREG_P	MOSCURRP	NOWPRGDK	PREGEND1
0	70627	1	NaN	NaN	NaN	NaN	6
1	70627	2	NaN	NaN	NaN	NaN	1
2	70627	3	NaN	NaN	NaN	NaN	6
3	70628	1	NaN	NaN	NaN	NaN	6
4	70628	2	NaN	NaN	NaN	NaN	6

We'll use the `OUTCOME` column to select pregnancies that ended with a live birth.

```
live = (nsfg['OUTCOME'] == 1)
live.sum()
```

6693

And we'll use `PRGLNGTH` to select babies that were born full term, that is, during or after the 37th week of pregnancy.

```
fullterm = (nsfg['PRGLNGTH'] >= 37) & (nsfg['PRGLNGTH'] < 48)
```

This dataset includes data from 2724 first babies.

```
first = live & fullterm & (nsfg['BIRTHORD'] == 1)
n_first = first.sum()
n_first
```

2724

13.3 Are First Babies More Likely To Be Late?

And 3115 other (not first) babies.

```
other = live & fullterm & (nsfg['BIRTHORD'] > 1)
n_other = other.sum()
n_other
```

3115

Now we can select pregnancy lengths for the first babies and others.

```
length = nsfg['PRGLNGTH']
length_first = length[first]
length_other = length[other]
```

Here are the mean pregnancy lengths for the two groups, in weeks.

```
length_first.mean(), length_other.mean()
```

(39.39647577092511, 39.19775280898877)

In this dataset, first babies are born a little later on average. The difference is about 0.2 weeks, or 33 hours.

```
diff_actual = length_first.mean() - length_other.mean()
diff_actual, diff_actual * 7 * 24
```

(0.19872296193634043, 33.38545760530519)

Relative to an average length of 39 weeks, that's not a very big difference. We might wonder if a difference as big as this would be likely, even if the two groups are the same. To answer that question, let's imagine a world where there is no difference in pregnancy length between first babies and others. How should we model a world like that? As always with modeling decisions, there are many options. A simple one is to combine the two groups and compute the mean and standard deviation of pregnancy length, like this.

```
length_live_full = length[live&fullterm]
mean = length_live_full.mean()
std = length_live_full.std()
mean, std
```

(39.29046069532454, 1.1864094701037655)

Now we can use `simulate_sample_mean` from Chapter 11 to draw a random sample from a normal distribution with the given parameters and return the mean.

```
def simulate_sample_mean(n, mu, sigma):
    sample = np.random.normal(mu, sigma, size=n)
    return sample.mean()
```

If we run it 1001 times, it runs the sampling and measurement process and returns a list of results from 1001 simulated experiments. Here are the results with sample size `n_first`:

```
t_first = [simulate_sample_mean(n_first, mean, std)
           for i in range(1001)]
```

And with sample size `n_other`.

```
t_other = [simulate_sample_mean(n_other, mean, std)
           for i in range(1001)]
```

If we subtract the simulated means elementwise, the result is a list of observed differences from simulated experiments where the distribution is the same for both groups.

```
diffs = np.subtract(t_first, t_other)
```

We can use a KDE plot to visualize the distribution of these values.

```
sns.kdeplot(diffs)

plt.xlabel('Difference in pregnancy length (weeks)')
plt.ylabel('Probability density')
plt.title('Distribution of differences');
```

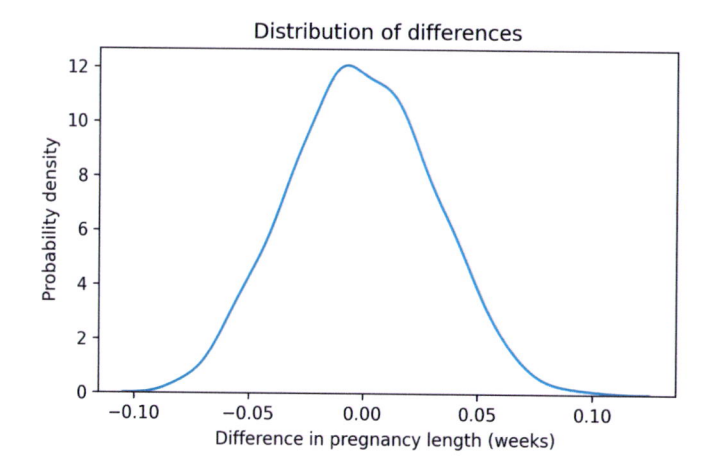

13.4 The Hypothesis Testing Framework

The center of this distribution is near zero, which makes sense if the distribution in both group is the same. Just by chance, we sometimes see differences as big as 0.1 weeks, but in 1001 simulations, we never see a difference as big as the observed difference in the data, which is almost 0.2 weeks.

Based on this result, we can pretty much rule out the possibility that the difference we saw is due to random sampling. But we should remember that there are other possible sources of error. For one, pregnancy lengths in the NSFG are self-reported. When the respondents are interviewed, their recollection of first babies might be less accurate than their recollection of more recent babies. Or the estimation of pregnancy length might be less accurate with less experienced mothers.

A correspondent of mine – who knows more than me about giving birth – suggested yet another possibility. If a first baby is born by Caesarean section, it is more likely that subsequent deliveries will be scheduled, and less likely that they will go much past 39 weeks. So that could bring the average down for non-first babies.

In summary, the results in this section suggest that the observed difference is unlikely to be due to chance, but there are other possible explanations.

13.4 The Hypothesis Testing Framework

The examples we've done so far fit into the framework shown in this diagram:

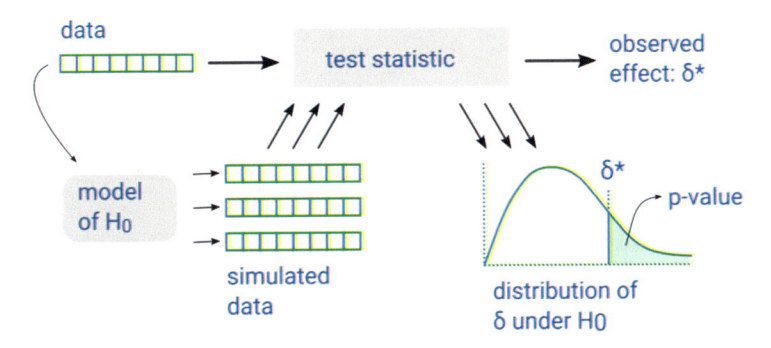

Using data from an experiment, we compute the observed **test statistic**, denoted δ^* in the diagram, which quantifies the size of the observed effect. In the peanut allergy example, the test statistic is relative risk. In the pregnancy length example, it is the difference in the means.

Then we build a model of a world where the effect does not exist. This model is called the **null hypothesis** and denoted H_0. In the peanut allergy example, the model assumes that the risk is the same in both groups. In the pregnancy example, it assumes that the lengths are drawn from the same normal distribution.

Next we use the model to simulate the experiment many times. Each simulation generates a dataset which we use to compute a test statistic, δ. Finally, we collect the test statistics from the simulations and compute a p-value, which is the probability under the null hypothesis of seeing a test statistic as big as the observed effect, $\delta*$.

If the p-value is small, we can usually rule out the possibility that the observed effect is due to random variation. But often there are other explanations we can't rule out, including measurement error and unrepresentative sampling.

I emphasize the role of the model in this framework because for a given experiment there might be several possible models, each including some elements of the real world and ignoring others. For example, we used a normal distribution to model variation in pregnancy length. If we don't want to make this assumption, an alternative is to simulate the null hypothesis by shuffling the pregnancy lengths.

The following function takes two sequences representing the pregnancy lengths for the two groups. It appends them into a single sequence, shuffles it, and then splits it again into groups with the same size as the originals. The return value is the difference in means between the groups.

```
def simulate_two_groups(data1, data2):
    n, m = len(data1), len(data2)
    data = np.append(data1, data2)
    np.random.shuffle(data)
    group1 = data[:n]
    group2 = data[n:]
    return group1.mean() - group2.mean()
```

If we call this function once, we get a random difference in means from a simulated world where the distribution of pregnancy lengths is the same in both groups.

```
simulate_two_groups(length_first, length_other)
```

0.008109710250479907

Exercise: Use this function to run 1001 simulations of the null hypothesis and save the results as `diff2`. Make a KDE plot to compare the distribution of `diff2` to the results from the normal model, `diff`.

Compute the probability of seeing a difference as big as `diff_actual`. Is this p-value consistent with the results we got with the normal model?

Exercise: Are first babies more likely to be *light*? To find out, we can use the birth weight data from the NSFG. The variables we need use special codes to represent missing data, so let's replace them with `NaN`.

```
nsfg['BIRTHWGT_LB1'] = nsfg['BIRTHWGT_LB1'].replace([0, 98, 99], np.nan)
nsfg['BIRTHWGT_OZ1'] = nsfg['BIRTHWGT_OZ1'].replace([0, 98, 99], np.nan)
```

13.5 Testing Correlation

And combine pounds and ounces into a single variable.

```
birthwgt = nsfg['BIRTHWGT_LB1'] + nsfg['BIRTHWGT_OZ1'] / 16
```

We can use `first` and `other` to select birth weights for first babies and others, dropping the `NaN` values.

```
birthwgt_first = birthwgt[first].dropna()
birthwgt_other = birthwgt[other].dropna()
```

In this dataset, it looks like first babies are a little lighter, on average.

```
print(birthwgt_first.mean(), birthwgt_other.mean())
```

7.3370276162790695 7.507115749525616

But as usual, we should wonder whether we are being fooled by randomness. To find out, compute the actual difference between the means. Then use `simulate_two_groups` to simulate a world where birth weights for both groups are drawn from the same distribution. Under the null hypothesis, how often does the difference in means exceed the actual difference in the dataset? What conclusion can you draw from this result?

13.5 Testing Correlation

The method we used in the previous section is called a **permutation test** because we shuffled the pregnancy lengths before splitting them into groups ("permute" is another word for shuffle). In this section we'll use a permutation test to check whether an observed correlation might be due to chance.

Let's look again at the correlations we computed in Chapter 9, using data from the Behavioral Risk Factor Surveillance System (BRFSS). The following cell reads the data.

```
import pandas as pd

brfss = pd.read_hdf('brfss.hdf', 'brfss')
brfss.shape
```

(418268, 9)

The correlations we computed were between height, weight and age.

```
columns = ['HTM4', 'WTKG3', 'AGE']
subset = brfss[columns]
corr_actual = subset.corr()
corr_actual
```

	HTM4	WTKG3	AGE
HTM4	1	0.477151	-0.13598
WTKG3	0.477151	1	-0.0649505
AGE	-0.13598	-0.0649505	1

The correlation between height and weight is about 0.48, which is moderately strong – if you know someone's height, you can make a better guess about their weight. The other correlations are weaker – for example, knowing someone's age would not substantially improve your guesses about their height or weight.

Because these correlations are so small, we might wonder whether they are due to chance. To answer this question, we can use permutation to simulate a world where there is actually no correlation between two variables.

But first we have to take a detour to figure out how to shuffle a Pandas `Series`. As an example, I'll extract the height data.

```
series = brfss['HTM4']
series.head()
```

```
0    157.0
1    163.0
2    165.0
3    165.0
4    152.0
Name: HTM4, dtype: float64
```

The idiomatic way to shuffle a `Series` is to use `sample` with the argument `frac=1`, which means that the fraction of the elements we want is `1`, that is, all of them.

13.5 Testing Correlation

By default, `sample` chooses elements without replacement, so the result contains all of the elements in a random order.

```
shuffled = series.sample(frac=1)
shuffled.head()
```

```
130148    157.0
396516    175.0
367273    155.0
59956     170.0
269497      NaN
Name: HTM4, dtype: float64
```

If we check the first few elements, it seems like a random sample, so that's good. But let's see what happens if we use the shuffled `Series` to compute a correlation.

```
corr = shuffled.corr(brfss['WTKG3'])
corr
```

0.477151462838814

That result looks familiar: it is the correlation of the unshuffled columns. The problem is that when we shuffle a `Series`, the index gets shuffled along with it. When we compute a correlation, Pandas uses the index to line up the elements from the first `Series` with the elements of the second `Series`. For many operations, that's the behavior we want, but in this case it defeats the purpose of shuffling!

The solution is to use `reset_index`, which gives the `Series` a new index, with the argument `drop=True`, which drops the old one. So we have to shuffle `series` like this.

```
shuffled = series.sample(frac=1).reset_index(drop=True)
```

Now we can compute a correlation with the shuffled `Series`.

```
corr = shuffled.corr(brfss['WTKG3'])
corr
```

0.0008229516424471632

The result is small, as we expect it to be when the elements are aligned at random. Rather than repeat this awful idiom, let's put it in a function and never speak of it again.

```
def shuffle(series):
    return series.sample(frac=1).reset_index(drop=True)
```

The following function takes a `DataFrame` and two column names, makes a shuffled copy of one column, and computes its correlation with the other.

```
def simulate_correlation(df, var1, var2):
    corr = shuffle(df[var1]).corr(df[var2])
    return corr
```

We only have to shuffle one of the columns – it doesn't get any more random if we shuffle both. Now we can use this function to generate a sample of correlations with shuffled columns.

```
corrs = [simulate_correlation(brfss, 'HTM4', 'WTKG3')
         for i in range(201)]
```

Here's the distribution of the correlations.

```
sns.kdeplot(corrs)

plt.xlabel('Correlation')
plt.ylabel('Probability density')
plt.title('Correlation from simulations with permutation');
```

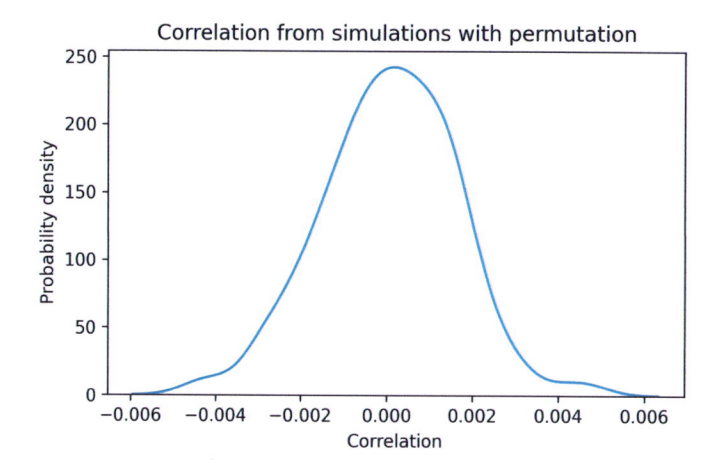

The center of the distribution is near 0, and the largest values (positive or negative) are around 0.005. If we compute the same distribution with different columns, the results are pretty much the same. With samples this big, the correlation between shuffled columns is generally small.

How do these values compare to the observed correlations?

- The correlation of height and weight is about 0.48, so it's extremely unlikely we would see a correlation as big as that by chance.

13.6 Testing Regression Models

- The correlation of height and age is smaller, around -0.14, but even that value would be unlikely by chance.

- And the correlation of weight and age is even smaller, about -0.06, but that's still 10 times bigger than the biggest correlation in the simulations.

We can conclude that these correlations are probably not due to chance. And that's useful in the sense that it rules out one possible explanation. But this example also demonstrates a limitation of this kind of hypothesis testing. With large sample sizes, variability due to randomness tends to be small, so it seldom explains the effects we see in real data.

And hypothesis testing can be a distraction from more important questions. In Chapter 9, we saw that the relationship between weight and age is nonlinear. But the coefficient of correlation only measures linear relationships, so it does not capture the real strength of the relationship. So testing a correlation might not be the most useful thing to do in the first place. We can do better by testing a regression model.

13.6 Testing Regression Models

In the previous sections we used permutation to simulate a world where there is no correlation between two variables. In this section we'll apply the same method to regression models. As an example, we'll use NSFG data to explore the relationship between a mother's age and her baby's birth weight.

In previous sections we computed birth weight and a Boolean variable that identifies first babies. Now we'll store them as columns in `nsfg`, so we can use them with StatsModels.

```
nsfg['BIRTHWGT'] = birthwgt
nsfg['FIRST'] = first
```

Next we'll select the subset of the rows that represent live, full-term births, and make a copy so we can modify the subset without affecting the original.

```
data = nsfg[live & fullterm].copy()
n = len(subset)
n
```

418268

To visualize the relationship between mother's age and birth weight, we'll use a box plot with mother's age grouped into 3-year bins. We'll use `np.arange` to make the bin boundaries, and `pd.cut` to put the values from `AGECON` into bins.

```
bins = np.arange(15, 40, 3)
data['AGEGRP'] = pd.cut(data['AGECON'], bins)
```

The label for each bin is the midpoint of the range. Now here's the box plot.

```
sns.boxplot(x='AGEGRP', y='BIRTHWGT', data=data, whis=10)

plt.xlabel("Mother's age (years)")
plt.ylabel('Birthweight (pounds)')
plt.xticks(rotation=30);
```

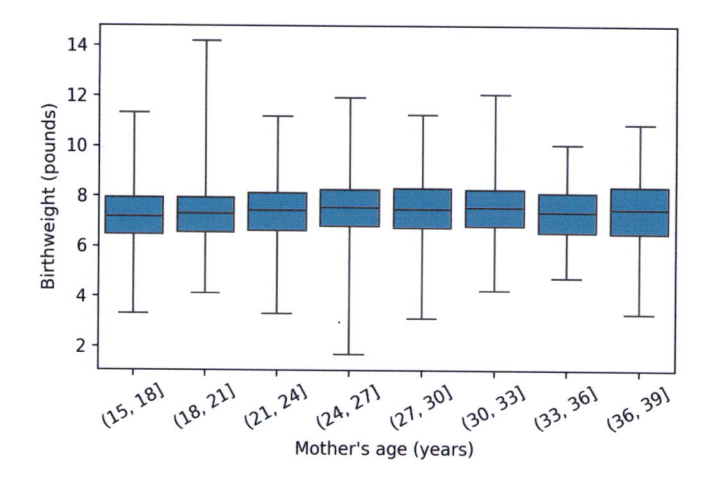

It looks like the average birth weight is highest if the mother is 24-30 years old, and slightly lower if she is younger or older. So the relationship might be nonlinear. Nevertheless, let's start with a linear model and work our way up. Here's a simple regression of birth weight as a function of the mother's age at conception.

```
import statsmodels.formula.api as smf

results = smf.ols('BIRTHWGT ~ AGECON', data=data).fit()
results.params
```

```
Intercept    7.025486
AGECON       0.016407
dtype: float64
```

The slope of the regression line is 0.016 pounds per year, which means that if one mother is a year older than another, we expect her baby to be about 0.016 pounds heavier (about a quarter of an ounce).

This parameter is small, so we might wonder whether the apparent effect is due to chance. To answer that question, we'll use permutation to simulate a world where there is no relationship between mother's age and birth weight.

The following function takes a `DataFrame`, shuffles the `AGECON` column, computes a linear regression model, and returns the estimated slope.

```
def simulate_slope(data):
    data['SHUFFLED'] = shuffle(data['AGECON'])
    formula = 'BIRTHWGT ~ SHUFFLED'
    results = smf.ols(formula, data=data).fit()
    return results.params['SHUFFLED']
```

If we call it many times, we get a sample from the distribution of slopes under the null hypothesis.

```
slopes_null = [simulate_slope(data) for i in range(201)]
```

After 201 attempts, the largest slope is about 0.010, which is smaller than the observed slope, about 0.016. We conclude that the observed effect is bigger than we would expect to see by chance.

```
print(np.max(slopes_null), results.params['AGECON'])
```

0.009536120931481635 0.01640747818656365

13.7 Controlling for Age

In a previous exercise, you computed the difference in birth weight between first babies and others, which is about 0.17 pounds, and you checked whether we are likely to see a difference as big as that by chance. If things went according to plan, you found that it is very unlikely.

But that doesn't necessarily mean that there is anything special about first babies that makes them lighter than others. Rather, knowing a baby's birth order might provide information about some other factor that is related to birth weight.

The mother's age could be that factor. First babies are likely to have younger mothers than other babies, and younger mothers tend to have lighter babies. The difference we see in first babies might be explained by their mothers' ages. So let's see what happens if we control for age. Here's a simple regression of birth weight as a function of the Boolean variable `FIRST`.

```
formula = 'BIRTHWGT ~ FIRST'
results = smf.ols(formula, data=data).fit()
results.params
```

Intercept   7.507116
FIRST[T.True]   -0.170088
dtype: float64

The parameter associated with FIRST is -0.17 pounds, which is the same as the difference in means we computed. But now we can add AGECON as a control variable.

```
formula = 'BIRTHWGT ~ FIRST + AGECON'
results = smf.ols(formula, data=data).fit()
results.params
```

```
Intercept          7.163240
FIRST[T.True]     -0.121771
AGECON             0.013145
dtype: float64
```

The age effect accounts for some of the difference between first babies and others. After controlling for age, the remaining difference is about 0.12 pounds.

Since the age effect is nonlinear, we can can control for age more effectively by adding AGECON2.

```
data['AGECON2'] = data['AGECON'] ** 2
```

```
formula = 'BIRTHWGT ~ FIRST + AGECON + AGECON2'
results = smf.ols(formula, data=data).fit()
results.params
```

```
Intercept          6.128590
FIRST[T.True]     -0.099338
AGECON             0.096781
AGECON2           -0.001615
dtype: float64
```

```
slope_actual = results.params['FIRST[T.True]']
slope_actual
```

-0.09933806121560428

When we use a quadratic model to control for the age effect, the remaining difference between first babies and others is smaller again, about 0.099 pounds.

One of the warning signs of a spurious relationship between two variables is that the effect gradually disappears as you add control variables. So we should wonder whether the remaining effect might be due to chance. To find out, we'll use the following function, which simulates a world where there is no difference in weight between first babies and others. It takes a DataFrame as a parameter, shuffles the FIRST column, runs the regression model with AGECON and AGECON2, and returns the estimated difference.

13.7 Controlling for Age

```
def simulate_slope2(data):
    data['SHUFFLED'] = shuffle(data['FIRST'])
    formula = 'BIRTHWGT ~ AGECON + AGECON2 + C(SHUFFLED)'
    results = smf.ols(formula, data=data).fit()
    return results.params['C(SHUFFLED)[T.True]']
```

If we run it many times, we get a sample from the distribution of the test statistic under the null hypothesis.

```
slopes_null = [simulate_slope2(data) for i in range(201)]
```

The range of values is wide enough that it occasionally exceeds the observed effect size.

```
print(min(slopes_null), max(slopes_null))
```

-0.09842209405975708 0.11993351438646496

The p-value is about 2%.

```
p_value = (np.abs(slopes_null) > np.abs(slope_actual)).mean()
p_value
```

0.01990049751243781

This result indicates that an observed difference of 0.1 pounds is possible, but not likely, if the actual difference between the groups is zero.

So how should we interpret a result like this? In the tradition of statistical hypothesis testing, it is common to use 5% as the threshold between results that are considered "statistically significant" or not. By that standard, the weight difference between first babies and others is statistically significant.

However, there are several problems with this practice:

- First, the choice of the threshold should depend on the context. For a life-and-death decision, we might choose a more stringent threshold. For a topic of idle curiosity, like this one, we could be more relaxed.

- But it might not be useful to apply a threshold at all. An alternative (which is common in practice) is to report the p-value and let it speak for itself. It provides no additional value to declare that the result is significant or not.

- Finally, the use of the word "significant" is dangerously misleading, because it implies that the result is important in practice. But a small p-value only means that an observed effect would be unlikely to happen by chance. It doesn't mean it is important.

This last point is particularly problematic with large datasets, because very small effects can be statistically significant. We saw an example with the BRFSS dataset, where the correlations we tested were *all* statistically significant, even the ones that are too small to matter in practice.

13.8 Summary

Let's review the examples in this chapter:

1. We started with data from LEAP, which studied the effect of eating peanuts on the development of peanut allergies. The test statistic was relative risk, and the null hypothesis was that the treatment was ineffective.

2. Then we looked at the difference in pregnancy length for first babies and others. We used the difference in means as the test statistic, and two models of the null hypothesis: one based on a normal model and the other based on permutation of the data. As an exercise, you tested the difference in weight between first babies and others.

3. Next we used permutation to test correlations, using height, weight, and age data from the BRFSS. This example shows that with large sample sizes, observed effects are often "statistically significant", even if they are too small to matter in practice.

4. We used regression models to explore the effect of maternal age on birth weight. To see whether the effect might be due to chance, we used the slope of the regression line as the test statistic, and permutation to model the null hypothesis.

5. Finally, we explored the possibility that the first baby effect is actually an indirect maternal age effect. After controlling for the mother's age, we tested whether the remaining difference between first babies and others might happen by chance. We used permutation to model the null hypothesis and the estimated slope as a test statistic.

As a final exercise, below, you can use the same methods to explore the effect of paternal age on birth weight.

Exercise: A paternal age effect is a relationship between the age of a father and a variety of outcomes for his children. There is some evidence that young fathers and old fathers have lighter babies, on average, than fathers in the middle range of ages. Let's see if that's true for the babies in the NSFG dataset. The `HPAGELB` column encodes the father's age.

```
data['YO_DAD'] = data['HPAGELB'].isin([1, 6])
```

13.8 Summary

We can use the result in a regression model to compute the difference in birth weight for young and old fathers compared to the others.

```
formula = 'BIRTHWGT ~ YO_DAD'
results = smf.ols(formula, data=data).fit()
results.params
```

```
Intercept        7.447477
YO_DAD[T.True]  -0.140045
dtype: float64
```

The difference is negative, which is consistent with the theory, and about 0.14 pounds, which is comparable in size to the (apparent) first baby effect. But there is a strong correlation between father's age and mother's age. So what seems like a paternal effect might actually be an indirect maternal effect. To find out, let's see what happens if we control for the mother's age. Run this model again with `AGECON` and `AGECON2` as predictors. Does the observed effect of paternal age get smaller?

To see if the remaining effect could be due to randomness, write a function that shuffles `YO_DAD`, runs the regression model, and returns the parameter associated with the shuffled column. How often does this parameter exceed the observed value? What conclusion can we draw from the results?

Part IV

Case Study: Political Alignment

Chapter 14

Political Alignment and Polarization

This chapter and the next make up a case study that uses data from the General Social Survey (GSS) to explore political beliefs and political alignment (conservative, moderate, or liberal) in the United States. In this chapter, we will:

1. Compare the distributions of political alignment from 1974 and 2022.

2. Plot the mean and standard deviation of responses over time as a way of quantifying shifts in political alignment and polarization.

3. Use local regression to plot a smooth line through noisy data.

4. Use cross tabulation to compute the fraction of respondents in each category over time.

5. Plot the results using a custom color palette.

As an exercise, you will look at changes in political party affiliation over the same period. In the next chapter, we'll use the same dataset to explore the relationship between political alignment and other attitudes and beliefs.

We'll use an extract of the data that I have cleaned and resampled to correct for stratified sampling. Instructions for downloading the file are in the notebook for this chapter. It contains three resamplings – we'll use the first, gss0, to get started.

```
datafile = 'gss_pacs_resampled.hdf'
gss = pd.read_hdf(datafile, key='gss0')
gss.shape
```

(72390, 207)

… 210 … Chapter 14 Political Alignment and Polarization

14.1 Political Alignment

The people surveyed for the GSS were asked about their "political alignment", which is where they place themselves on a spectrum from liberal to conservative. They were asked:

> We hear a lot of talk these days about liberals and conservatives. I'm going to show you a seven-point scale on which the political views that people might hold are arranged from extremely liberal–point 1–to extremely conservative–point 7. Where would you place yourself on this scale?

Here is the scale they were shown:

Code	Response
1	Extremely liberal
2	Liberal
3	Slightly liberal
4	Moderate
5	Slightly conservative
6	Conservative
7	Extremely conservative

The variable `polviews` contains the responses.

```
polviews = gss['polviews']
```

To see how the responses have changed over time, we'll inspect them at the beginning and end of the observation period. First we'll make a Boolean Series that's `True` for responses from 1974, and select the responses from 1974.

```
year74 = (gss['year'] == 1974)
polviews74 = polviews[year74]
```

And we can do the same for 2022.

```
year22 = (gss['year'] == 2022)
polviews22 = polviews[year22]
```

14.1 Political Alignment

We'll use the following function to count the number of times each response occurs.

```
def values(series):
    '''Count the values and sort.

    series: pd.Series

    returns: series mapping from values to frequencies
    '''
    return series.value_counts(dropna=False).sort_index()
```

Here are the responses from 1974.

```
values(polviews74)
```

```
polviews
1.0     31
2.0    201
3.0    211
4.0    538
5.0    223
6.0    181
7.0     30
NaN     69
Name: count, dtype: int64
```

And here are the responses from 2022.

```
values(polviews22)
```

```
polviews
1.0     184
2.0     433
3.0     391
4.0    1207
5.0     472
6.0     548
7.0     194
NaN     115
Name: count, dtype: int64
```

Looking at these counts, we can get an idea of what the distributions look like, but in the next section we'll get a clearer picture by plotting them.

14.2 Visualizing Distributions

To visualize these distributions, we'll use a Probability Mass Function (PMF), which is similar to a histogram, but there are two differences:

- In a histogram, values are often put in bins, with more than one value in each bin. In a PMF each value gets its own bin.

- A histogram computes a count, that is, how many times each value appears; a PMF computes a probability, that is, what fraction of the time each value appears.

We'll use the `Pmf` class from `empiricaldist` to compute a PMF.

```
from empiricaldist import Pmf

pmf74 = Pmf.from_seq(polviews74)
pmf74
```

polviews	probs
1	0.0219081
2	0.142049
3	0.149117
4	0.380212
5	0.157597
6	0.127915
7	0.0212014

The following cell imports the function we'll use to decorate the axes in plots.

```
from utils import decorate
```

Here's the distribution from 1974:

```
pmf74.bar(label='1974', color='C0', alpha=0.7)

decorate(
    xlabel='Political view on a 7-point scale',
    ylabel='Fraction of respondents',
    title='Distribution of political views',
)
```

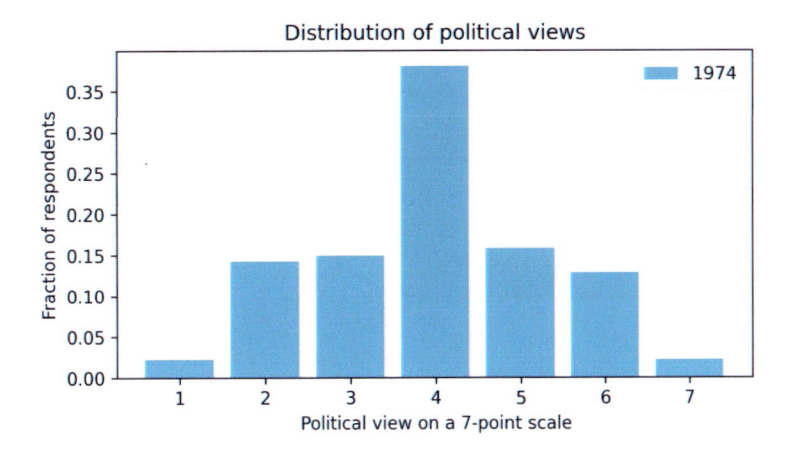

14.2 Visualizing Distributions

[Bar chart: Distribution of political views, 1974, showing fractions roughly 0.02, 0.14, 0.15, 0.38, 0.16, 0.13, 0.02 for points 1–7]

And from 2022:

```
pmf22 = Pmf.from_seq(polviews22)
pmf22.bar(label='2022', color='C1', alpha=0.7)

decorate(
    xlabel='Political view on a 7-point scale',
    ylabel='Fraction of respondents',
    title='Distribution of political views',
)
```

[Bar chart: Distribution of political views, 2022, showing fractions roughly 0.05, 0.13, 0.12, 0.35, 0.14, 0.16, 0.06 for points 1–7]

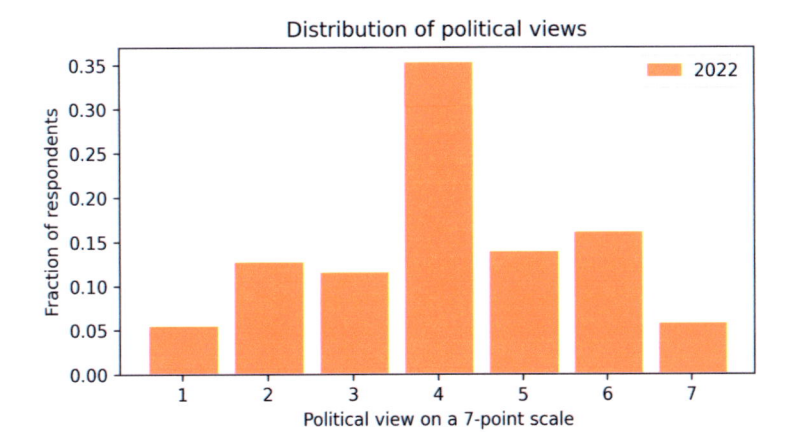

In both cases, the most common response is 4, which is the code for 'moderate'. Few respondents describe themselves as 'extremely' liberal or conservative. So maybe we're not so polarized after all.

To make it easier to compare the distributions, I'll plot them side by side.

```
df = pd.DataFrame({'pmf74': pmf74, 'pmf22': pmf22})
df.plot(kind='bar')

decorate(
    xlabel='Political view on a 7-point scale',
    ylabel='Fraction of respondents',
    title='Distribution of political views',
)
```

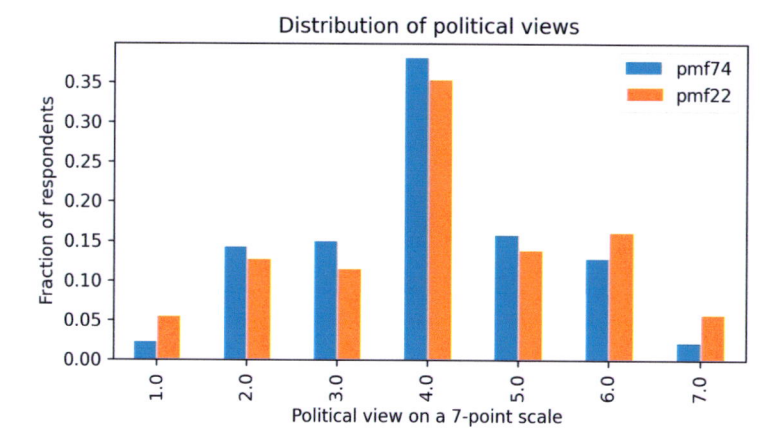

Now we can see the changes in the distribution more clearly – the fraction of people at the extremes (1, 6, and 7) has increased, and the fraction of people near the middle (2, 3, 4, and 5) has decreased.

Exercise: To summarize these changes, we can compare the mean and standard deviation of `polviews` in 1974 and 2022. The mean of the responses measures the balance of people in the population with liberal or conservative leanings. If the mean increases over time, that might indicate a shift in the population toward conservatism. The standard deviation measures the dispersion of views in the population – if it increases over time, that might indicate an increase in polarization.

Compute the mean and standard deviation of `polviews74` and `polviews22`. What do they indicate about changes over this interval?

14.3 Plotting a Time Series

At this point we have looked at the endpoints, 1974 and 2022, but we don't know what happened in between. To see how the distribution changed over time, we can use `groupby` to group the respondents by year.

14.3 Plotting a Time Series

```
gss_by_year = gss.groupby('year')
type(gss_by_year)
```

pandas.core.groupby.generic.DataFrameGroupBy

The result is a `DataFrameGroupBy` object that represents a collection of groups.

Now we can use the bracket operator to select the `polviews` column.

```
polviews_by_year = gss_by_year['polviews']
type(polviews_by_year)
```

pandas.core.groupby.generic.SeriesGroupBy

A column from a `DataFrameGroupBy` is a `SeriesGroupBy`. If we invoke `mean` on it, the result is a series that contains the mean of `polviews` for each year of the survey.

```
mean_series = polviews_by_year.mean()
```

And here's what it looks like.

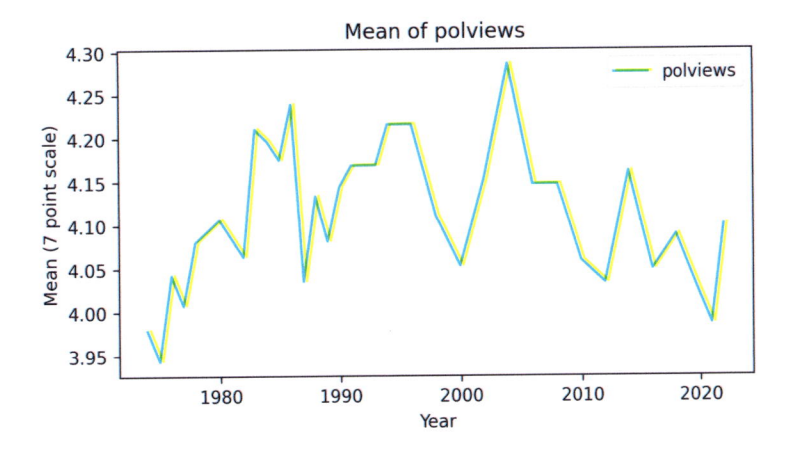

```
mean_series.plot(color='C2', label='polviews')
decorate(xlabel='Year',
        ylabel='Mean (7 point scale)',
        title='Mean of polviews')
```

The mean increased between 1974 and 2000, decreased since then, and ended up almost where it started.

The difference between the highest and lowest points is only 0.34 points on a 7-point scale, so none of these changes are drastic.

```
mean_series.max() - mean_series.min()
```

0.34240143126104083

Exercise: The standard deviation quantifies the spread of the distribution, which is one way to measure polarization. Plot standard deviation of `polviews` for each year of the survey from 1972 to 2022. Does it show evidence of increasing polarization?

14.4 Smoothing the Curve

In the previous section we plotted mean and standard deviation of `polviews` over time. In both plots, the values are highly variable from year to year. We can use **local regression** to compute a smooth line through these data points.

The following function takes a Pandas `Series` and uses an algorithm called LOWESS to compute a smooth line. LOWESS stands for "locally weighted scatterplot smoothing".

```
from statsmodels.nonparametric.smoothers_lowess import lowess

def make_lowess(series):
    '''Use LOWESS to compute a smooth line.

    series: pd.Series

    returns: pd.Series
    '''
    y = series.values
    x = series.index.values

    smooth = lowess(y, x)
    index, data = np.transpose(smooth)

    return pd.Series(data, index=index)
```

14.4 Smoothing the Curve

We'll use the following function to plot data points and the smoothed line.

```
def plot_series_lowess(series, color):
    '''Plots a series of data points and a smooth line.

    series: pd.Series
    color: string or tuple
    '''
    series.plot(linewidth=0, marker='o', color=color, alpha=0.5)
    smooth = make_lowess(series)
    smooth.plot(label='', color=color)
```

The following figure shows the mean of `polviews` and a smooth line.

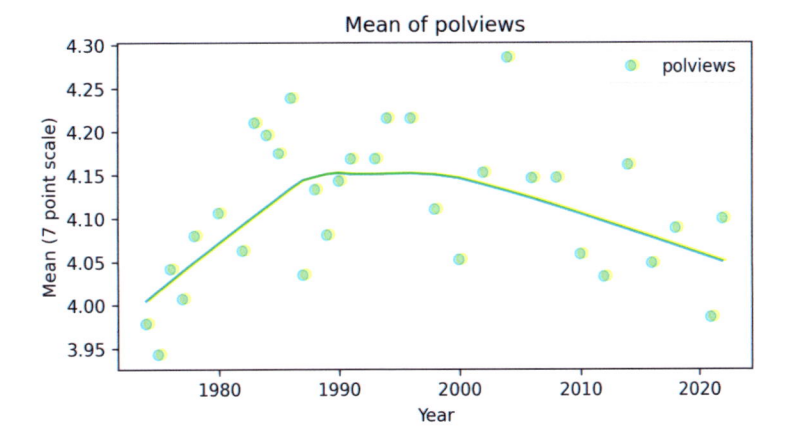

```
mean_series = gss_by_year['polviews'].mean()
plot_series_lowess(mean_series, 'C2')
decorate(xlabel='Year',
         ylabel='Mean (7 point scale)',
         title='Mean of polviews')
```

One reason the PMFs for 1974 and 2022 did not look very different is that the mean went up (more conservative) and then down again (more liberal). Generally, it looks like the U.S. has been trending toward liberal for the last 20 years, or more, at least in the sense of how people describe themselves.

Exercise: Use `plot_series_lowess` to plot the standard deviation of `polviews` with a smooth line.

14.5 Cross Tabulation

In the previous sections, we treated `polviews` as a numerical quantity, so we were able to compute means and standard deviations. But the responses are really categorical, which means that each value represents a discrete category, like 'liberal' or 'conservative'. In this section, we'll treat `polviews` as a categorical variable, compute the number of respondents in each category during each year, and plot changes over time.

Pandas provides a function called `crosstab` that computes a **cross tabulation** Here's how we can use to compute the number of respondents in each category during each year.

```
year = gss['year']
column = gss['polviews']

xtab = pd.crosstab(year, column)
```

The result is a `DataFrame` with one row for each year and one column for each category. Here are the first few rows.

```
xtab.head()
```

polviews	1	2	3	4	5	6	7
year							
1974	31	201	211	538	223	181	30
1975	56	184	207	540	204	162	45
1976	31	198	175	564	209	206	34
1977	37	181	214	594	243	164	42
1978	21	140	255	559	265	187	25

It contains one row for each value of `year` and one column for each value of `polviews`. Reading the first row, we see that in 1974, 31 people gave response 1, 201 people gave response 2, and so on.

The number of respondents varies from year to year. To make meaningful comparisons over time, we need to normalize the results, which means computing for each year the *fraction* of respondents in each category, rather than the count. `crosstab` takes an optional argument that normalizes each row.

```
xtab_norm = pd.crosstab(year, column, normalize='index')
```

Here's what that looks like for the 7-point scale.

```
xtab_norm.head()
```

14.5 Cross Tabulation

polviews year	1	2	3	4	5	6	7
1974	0.0219081	0.142049	0.149117	0.380212	0.157597	0.127915	0.0212014
1975	0.0400572	0.131617	0.148069	0.386266	0.145923	0.11588	0.0321888
1976	0.0218772	0.139732	0.1235	0.398024	0.147495	0.145378	0.0239944
1977	0.0250847	0.122712	0.145085	0.402712	0.164746	0.111186	0.0284746
1978	0.0144628	0.0964187	0.17562	0.384986	0.182507	0.128788	0.0172176

Looking at the numbers in the table, it's hard to see what's going on. In the next section, we'll plot the results.

To make the results easier to interpret, I'm going to replace the numeric codes 1-7 with strings. First I'll make a dictionary that maps from numbers to strings:

```
polviews_map = {
    1: 'Extremely liberal',
    2: 'Liberal',
    3: 'Slightly liberal',
    4: 'Moderate',
    5: 'Slightly conservative',
    6: 'Conservative',
    7: 'Extremely conservative',
}
```

Then we can use the `replace` function like this:

```
polviews7 = gss['polviews'].replace(polviews_map)
```

We can use `values` to confirm that the values in `polviews7` are strings.

```
values(polviews7)
```

```
polviews
Conservative               9612
Extremely conservative     2145
Extremely liberal          2095
Liberal                    7309
Moderate                  24157
Slightly conservative      9816
Slightly liberal           7799
NaN                        9457
Name: count, dtype: int64
```

If we make the cross tabulation again, we can see that the column names are strings.

```
xtab_norm = pd.crosstab(year, polviews7, normalize='index')
xtab_norm.columns
```

```
Index(['Conservative', 'Extremely conservative', 'Extremely liberal',
       'Liberal', 'Moderate', 'Slightly conservative', 'Slightly liberal'],
      dtype='object', name='polviews')
```

We are almost ready to plot the results, but first we need some colors.

14.6 Color Palettes

To represent political views, we'll use a color palette from blue to purple to red. Seaborn provides a variety of color palettes – we'll start with this one, which includes shades of blue and red. To represent moderates, we'll replace the middle color with purple.

```
palette = sns.color_palette('RdBu_r', 7)
palette[3] = 'purple'
sns.palplot(palette)
```

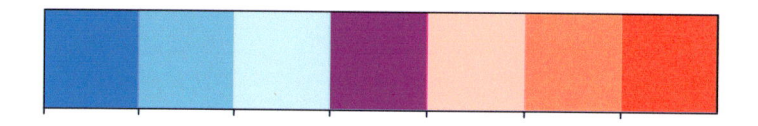

We'll make a dictionary that maps from the responses to the corresponding colors.

```
color_map = {}

for i, group in polviews_map.items():
    color_map[group] = palette[i-1]
```

Now we're ready to plot.

14.7 Plotting a Cross Tabulation

To see how the fraction of people with each political alignment has changed over time, we'll use `plot_series_lowess` to plot the columns from `xtab_norm`.

14.7 Plotting a Cross Tabulation

Here are the seven categories plotted as a function of time. The `bbox_to_anchor` argument passed to `plt.legend` puts the legend outside the axes of the figure.

```
groups = list(polviews_map.values())

for group in groups:
    series = xtab_norm[group]
    plot_series_lowess(series, color_map[group])

decorate(
    xlabel='Year',
    ylabel='Proportion',
    title='Fraction of respondents with each political view',
)

plt.legend(bbox_to_anchor=(1.02, 1.02));
```

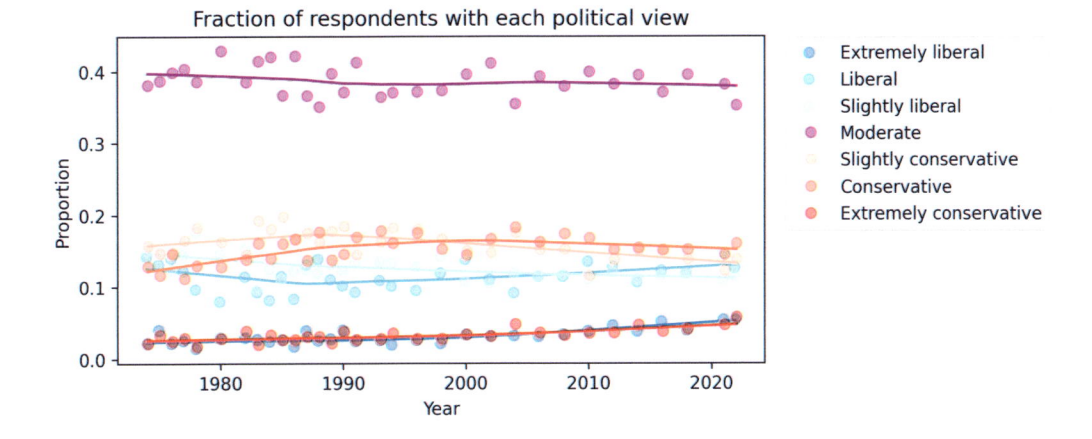

This way of looking at the results suggests that changes in political alignment during this period have generally been slow and small.

The fraction of self-described moderates has decreased slightly. The fraction of conservatives increased, but seems to be decreasing now – and the fraction of liberals seems to be increasing. The fraction of people at the extremes has increased, but it is hard to see clearly in this figure.

We can get a better view by plotting just the extremes.

```
selected_groups = ['Extremely liberal', 'Extremely conservative']

for group in selected_groups:
    series = xtab_norm[group]
    plot_series_lowess(series, color_map[group])

decorate(
    xlabel='Year',
    ylabel='Proportion',
    ylim=[0, 0.065],
    title='Fraction of respondents with extreme political views',
)
```

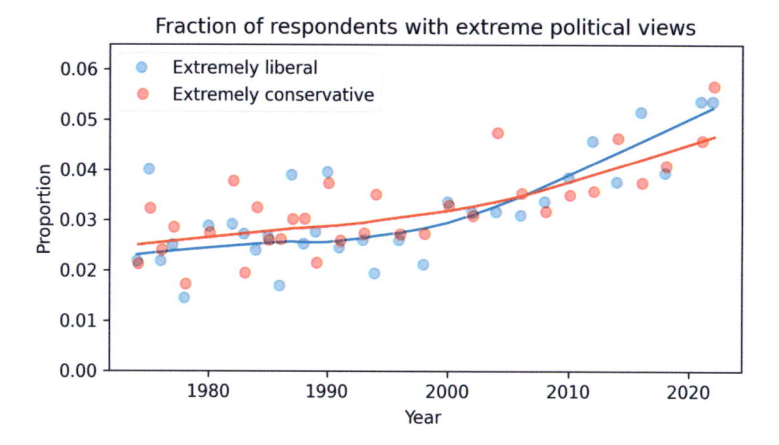

I used `ylim` to set the limits of the y-axis so it starts at zero, to avoid making the changes seem bigger than they are. This figure shows that the fraction of people who describe themselves as 'extreme' has increased from about 2.5% to about 5%. In relative terms, that's a big increase. But in absolute terms these tails of the distribution are still small.

Exercise: Let's do a similar analysis with `partyid`, which encodes responses to the question:

> Generally speaking, do you usually think of yourself as a Republican, Democrat, Independent, or what?

The valid responses are:

Code	Response
0	Strong democrat
1	Not str democrat
2	Ind, near dem
3	Independent
4	Ind, near rep
5	Not str republican
6	Strong republican
7	Other party

In the notebook for this chapter, there are some suggestions to get you started.

Here are the steps I suggest:

1) If you have not already saved this notebook, you should do that first. If you are running on Colab, select 'Save a copy in Drive' from the File menu.

2) Now, before you modify this notebook, make *another* copy and give it an appropriate name.

3) Search and replace `polviews` with `partyid` (use 'Edit->Find and replace').

4) Run the notebook from the beginning and see what other changes you have to make.

What changes in party affiliation do you see over the last 50 years? Are things going in the directions you expected?

14.8 Summary

This chapter introduces two new tools: local regression for computing a smooth curve through noisy data, and cross tabulation for counting the number of people, or fraction, in each group over time.

Now that we have a sense of how political alignment as changed, in the next chapter we'll explore the relationship between political alignment and other beliefs and attitudes.

Chapter 15

Political Alignment and Outlook

In the previous chapter, we used data from the General Social Survey (GSS) to plot changes in political alignment over time. In this chapter, we'll explore the relationship between political alignment and respondents' beliefs about themselves and other people. We'll use the following variables from the GSS dataset:

- `happy`: Taken all together, how would you say things are these days–would you say that you are very happy, pretty happy, or not too happy?

- `trust`: Generally speaking, would you say that most people can be trusted or that you can't be too careful in dealing with people?

- `helpful`: Would you say that most of the time people try to be helpful, or that they are mostly just looking out for themselves?

- `fair`: Do you think most people would try to take advantage of you if they got a chance, or would they try to be fair?

We'll start with the last question – then as an exercise you can look at one of the others. Here's the plan:

1. First we'll use `groupby` to compare responses between groups and plot changes over time.

2. We'll use the Pandas function `pivot_table` to explore differences between groups over time.

3. Finally, we'll use resampling to see whether the features we see in the results might be due to randomness, or whether they are likely to reflect actual changes in the world.

We'll use an extract of the data that I have cleaned and resampled to correct for stratified sampling. Instructions for downloading the file are in the notebook for this chapter. It contains three resamplings – we'll use the first, gss0, to get started. At the end of the chapter, we'll use the other two as well.

```
datafile = 'gss_pacs_resampled.hdf'
gss = pd.read_hdf(datafile, key='gss0')
gss.shape
```

(72390, 207)

15.1 Are People Fair?

In the GSS data, the variable `fair` contains responses to this question:

> Do you think most people would try to take advantage of you if they got a chance, or would they try to be fair?

The possible responses are:

Code	Response
1	Take advantage
2	Fair
3	Depends

We can use `values`, from the previous chapter, to see how many people gave each response.

```
values(gss['fair'])
```

```
fair
1.0    16089
2.0    23417
3.0     2897
NaN    29987
Name: count, dtype: int64
```

The plurality think people try to be fair (2), but a substantial minority think people would take advantage (1). There are also a number of NaNs, mostly respondents who were not asked this question.

15.2 Fairness Over Time

To count the number of people who chose a positive response, we'll use a dictionary to recode option 2 as 1 and the other options as 0.

```
fair_map = {1: 0, 2: 1, 3: 0}
```

We can use `replace` to recode the values and store the result as a new column in the `DataFrame`.

```
gss['fair2'] = gss['fair'].replace(fair_map)
```

Now let's see how the responses have changed over time.

15.2 Fairness Over Time

As we saw in the previous chapter, we can use `groupby` to group responses by year.

```
gss_by_year = gss.groupby('year')
```

From the result we can select `fair2` and compute the mean.

```
fair_by_year = gss_by_year['fair2'].mean()
```

Here's the result, which shows the fraction of people who say people try to be fair, plotted over time. As in the previous chapter, we plot the data points themselves with circles and a local regression model as a line.

```
plot_series_lowess(fair_by_year, 'C1')

decorate(
    xlabel='Year',
    ylabel='Fraction saying yes',
    title='Would most people try to be fair?',
)
```

Would most people try to be fair?

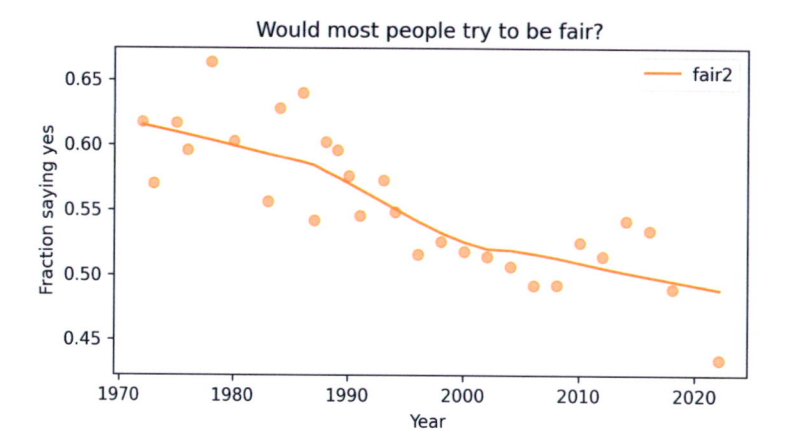

[Figure: Line plot showing fraction saying yes (fair2) declining from about 0.60 in 1970 to about 0.49 in 2020.]

Sadly, it looks like faith in humanity has declined, at least by this measure. Let's see what this trend looks like if we group the respondents by political alignment.

15.3 Political Views on a 3-point Scale

In the previous notebook, we looked at responses to `polviews`, which asks about political alignment. To make it easier to visualize groups, we'll lump the 7-point scale into a 3-point scale.

```
polviews_map = {
    1: 'Liberal',
    2: 'Liberal',
    3: 'Liberal',
    4: 'Moderate',
    5: 'Conservative',
    6: 'Conservative',
    7: 'Conservative',
}
```

We'll use `replace` again, and store the result as a new column in the `DataFrame`.

```
gss['polviews3'] = gss['polviews'].replace(polviews_map)
```

15.4 Fairness by Group

With this scale, there are roughly the same number of people in each group.

```
values(gss['polviews3'])
```

```
polviews3
Conservative    21573
Liberal         17203
Moderate        24157
NaN              9457
Name: count, dtype: int64
```

15.4 Fairness by Group

Now let's see who thinks people are more fair, conservatives or liberals. We'll group the respondents by `polviews3`.

```
by_polviews = gss.groupby('polviews3')
```

And compute the mean of `fair2` in each group.

```
by_polviews['fair2'].mean()
```

```
polviews3
Conservative    0.577879
Liberal         0.550849
Moderate        0.537621
Name: fair2, dtype: float64
```

It looks like conservatives are a little more optimistic, in this sense, than liberals and moderates. But this result is averaged over the last 50 years. Let's see how things have changed over time.

15.5 Fairness over Time by Group

So far, we have grouped by `polviews3` and computed the mean of `fair2` in each group. Then we grouped by `year` and computed the mean of `fair2` for each year. Now we'll group by `polviews3` and `year`, and compute the mean of `fair2` in each group over time.

We could do that computation using the tools we already have, but it is so common and useful that it has a name. It is called a **pivot table**, and Pandas provides a function called `pivot_table` that computes it. It takes the following arguments:

- `index`, which is the name of the variable that will provide the row labels: `year` in this example.

- `columns`, which is the name of the variable that will provide the column labels: `polviews3` in this example.

- **values**, which is the name of the variable we want to summarize: `fair2` in this example.

- **aggfunc**, which is the function used to "aggregate", or summarize, the values: `mean` in this example.

Here's how we run it.

```
table = gss.pivot_table(
    index='year', columns='polviews3', values='fair2', aggfunc='mean'
)
```

The result is a `DataFrame` that has years running down the rows and political alignment running across the columns.

Each entry in the table is the mean of `fair2` for a given group in a given year.

```
table.head()
```

polviews3	Conservative	Liberal	Moderate
year			
1975	0.625616	0.617117	0.64728
1976	0.631696	0.571782	0.6121
1978	0.694915	0.65942	0.665455
1980	0.6	0.554945	0.640264
1983	0.572438	0.585366	0.463492

Reading across the first row, we can see that in 1975, moderates were slightly more optimistic than the other groups. Reading down the first column, we can see that the estimated mean of `fair2` among conservatives varies from year to year. It is hard to tell by looking at these numbers whether it is trending up or down – we can get a better view by plotting the results.

15.6 Plotting the Results

Before we plot the results, I'll make a dictionary that maps from each group to a color. Seaborn provide a palette called `muted` that contains the colors we'll use.

```
muted = sns.color_palette('muted', 5)
sns.palplot(muted)
```

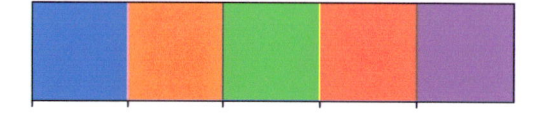

15.6 Plotting the Results

And here's the dictionary.

```
color_map = {'Conservative': muted[3],
             'Moderate': muted[4],
             'Liberal': muted[0]}
```

Now we can plot the results.

```
groups = ['Conservative', 'Liberal', 'Moderate']

for group in groups:
    plot_series_lowess(table[group], color_map[group])

decorate(
    xlabel='Year',
    ylabel='Fraction saying yes',
    title='Would most people try to be fair?',
)
```

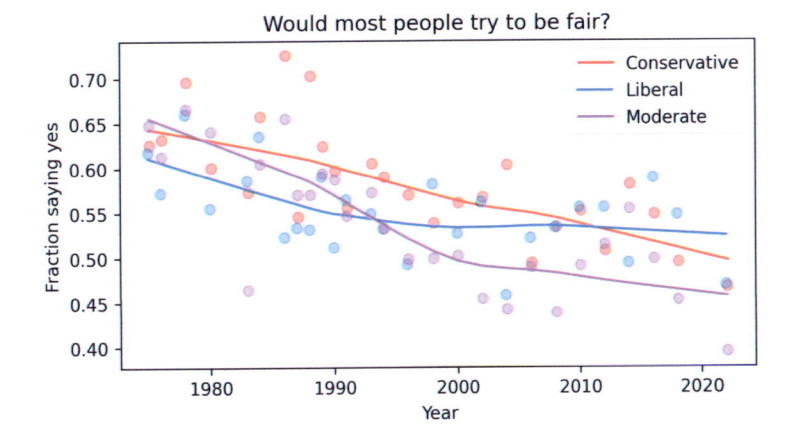

The fraction of respondents who think people try to be fair has dropped in all three groups, although liberals and moderates might have leveled off. In 1975, liberals were the least optimistic group. In 2022, they might be the most optimistic. But the responses are quite noisy, so we should not be too confident about these conclusions.

We can get a sense of how reliable they are by running the resampling process a few times and checking how much the results vary.

15.7 Simulating Possible Datasets

The figures we have generated so far are based on a single resampling of the GSS data. Some of the features we see in these figures might be due to random sampling rather than actual changes in the world. By generating the same figures with different resampled datasets, we can get a sense of how much variation there is due to random sampling.

To make that easier, the following function contains the code from the previous analysis all in one place.

```python
def plot_by_polviews(gss):
    '''Plot mean response by polviews and year.

    gss: DataFrame
    '''
    gss['polviews3'] = gss['polviews'].replace(polviews_map)
    gss['fair2'] = gss['fair'].replace(fair_map)

    table = gss.pivot_table(
        index='year', columns='polviews3', values='fair2', aggfunc='mean'
    )

    for group in groups:
        plot_series_lowess(table[group], color_map[group])

    decorate(
        xlabel='Year',
        ylabel='Fraction saying yes',
        title='Would most people try to be fair?',
    )
```

Now we can loop through the three resampled datasets in the data file and generate a figure for each one.

```python
datafile = 'gss_pacs_resampled.hdf'

for key in ['gss0', 'gss1', 'gss2']:
    df = pd.read_hdf(datafile, key)
    plt.figure()
    plot_by_polviews(df)
```

15.7 Simulating Possible Datasets

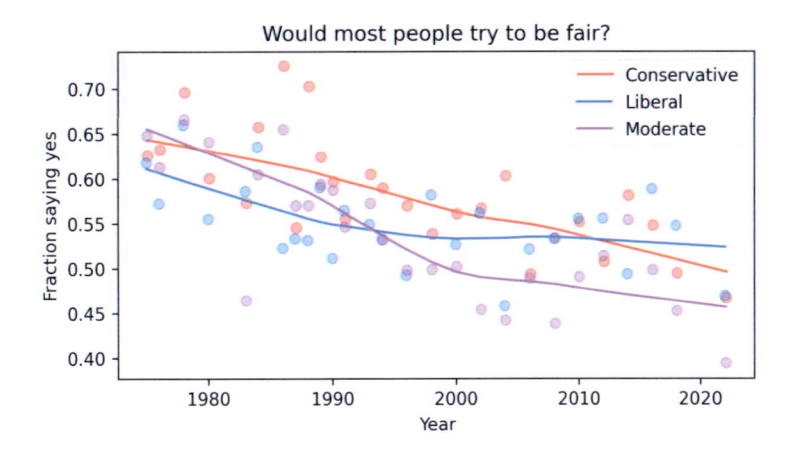

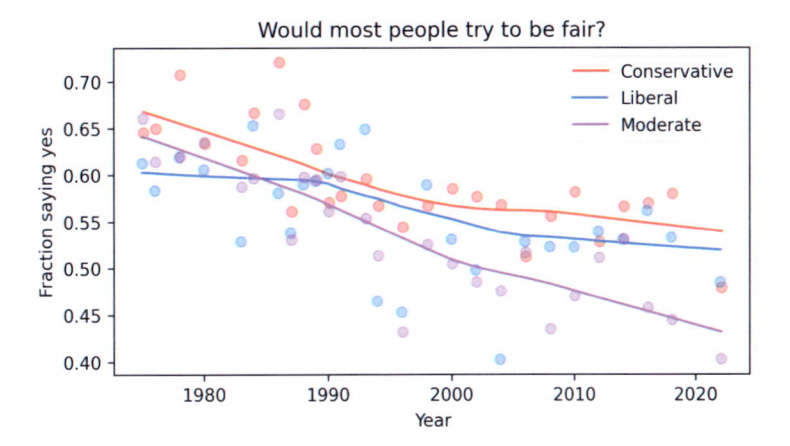

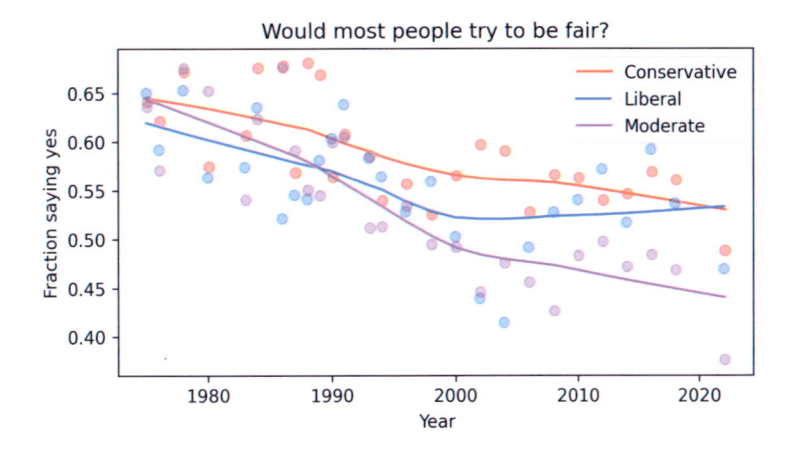

Features that are the same in all three figures are more likely to reflect things actually happening in the world. Features that differ substantially between the figures are more likely to be due to random sampling.

Exercise: You can run the same analysis with one of the other variables related to outlook: `happy`, `trust`, `helpful`, and maybe `fear` and `hapmar`.

For these variables, you will have to read the codebook to see the responses and how they are encoded, then think about which responses to report. In the notebook for this chapter, there are some suggestions to get you started.

Here are the steps I suggest:

1) If you have not already saved this notebook, you might want to do that first. If you are running on Colab, select "Save a copy in Drive" from the File menu.

2) Now, before you modify this notebook, make another copy and give it an appropriate name.

3) Search and replace `fair` with the name of the variable you select (use "Edit->Find and replace").

4) Run the notebook from the beginning and see what other changes you have to make.

Write a few sentences to describe the relationships you find between political alignment and outlook.

15.8 Summary

The case study in this chapter and the previous one demonstrates a process for exploring a dataset and finding relationships among the variables.

In the previous chapter, we started with a single variable, `polviews`, and visualized its distribution at the beginning and end of the observation interval. Then we used `groupby` to see how the mean and standard deviation changed over time. Looking more closely, we used cross tabulation to see how the fraction of people in each group changed.

In this chapter, we added a second variable, `fair`, which is one of several questions in the GSS related to respondents' beliefs about other people. We used `groupby` again to see how the responses have changed over time. Then we used a pivot table to show how the responses within each political group have changed. Finally, we used multiple resamplings of the original dataset to check whether the patterns we identified might be due to random sampling rather than real changes in the world.

The tools we used in this case study are versatile – they are useful for exploring other variables in the GSS dataset, and other datasets as well. And the process we followed is one I recommend whenever you are exploring a new dataset.

Part V

Case Study: Algorithmic Fairness

Chapter 16

Predicting Crime

This chapter and the next make up a case study related to "Machine Bias", an article published by ProPublica in 2016. The article explores the use of predictive algorithms in the criminal justice system.

- In this chapter, we'll replicate the analysis described in the article and compute statistics that evaluate these algorithms, including accuracy, predictive value, end error rates.

- In the next chapter, we'll review arguments presented in a response article published in the Washington Post. We'll compute and interpret calibration curves, and explore the trade-offs between predictive value and error rates.

16.1 Machine Bias

We'll start by replicating the analysis reported in "Machine Bias", by Julia Angwin, Jeff Larson, Surya Mattu and Lauren Kirchner, and published by ProPublica in May 2016.

This article is about a statistical tool called COMPAS which is used in some criminal justice systems to inform decisions about which defendants should be released on bail before trial, how long convicted defendants should be imprisoned, and whether prisoners should be released on parole. COMPAS uses information about defendants to generate a "risk score" which is intended to quantify the risk that the defendant would commit another crime if released.

The authors of the ProPublica article used public data to assess the accuracy of those risk scores. They explain:

> We obtained the risk scores assigned to more than 7,000 people arrested in Broward County, Florida, in 2013 and 2014 and checked to see how many were charged with new crimes over the next two years, the same benchmark used by the creators of the algorithm.

In the notebook that contains their analysis, they explain in more detail:

> We filtered the underlying data from Broward county to include only those rows representing people who had either recidivated in two years, or had at least two years outside of a correctional facility.
>
> [...] Next, we sought to determine if a person had been charged with a new crime subsequent to the crime for which they were COMPAS screened. We did not count traffic tickets and some municipal ordinance violations as recidivism. We did not count as recidivists people who were arrested for failing to appear at their court hearings, or people who were later charged with a crime that occurred prior to their COMPAS screening.

If you are not familiar with the word "recidivism", it usually means a tendency to relapse into criminal behavior. In this context, a person is a "recidivist" if they are charged with another crime within two years of release. However, note that there is a big difference between *committing* another crime and being *charged* with another crime. We will come back to this issue.

The authors of the ProPublica article use this data to evaluate how well COMPAS predicts the risk that a defendant will be charged with another crime within two years of their release. Among their findings, they report:

> [...] the algorithm was somewhat more accurate than a coin flip. Of those deemed likely to re-offend, 61 percent were arrested for any subsequent crimes within two years.
>
> [...] In forecasting who would re-offend, the algorithm made mistakes with Black and White defendants at roughly the same rate but in very different ways.
>
> - The formula was particularly likely to falsely flag Black defendants as future criminals, wrongly labeling them this way at almost twice the rate as White defendants.
>
> - White defendants were mislabeled as low risk more often than Black defendants.

This discrepancy suggests that the use of COMPAS in the criminal justice system is racially biased.

Since the ProPublica article was published, it has been widely discussed in the media, and a number of researchers have published responses. In order to evaluate the original article and the responses it provoked, there are some technical issues you need to understand. The goal of this case study is to help you analyze the arguments and interpret the statistics they are based on.

16.2 Replicating the Analysis

The data used in "Machine Bias" is available from ProPublica. Instructions for downloading it are in the notebook for this chapter.

We can use Pandas to read the file and make a `DataFrame`.

```
import pandas as pd

cp = pd.read_csv("compas-scores-two-years.csv")
cp.shape
```

(7214, 53)

The dataset includes one row for each defendant, and 53 columns, including risk scores computed by COMPAS and demographic information like age, sex, and race.

The authors of "Machine Bias" describe their analysis in a supplemental article called "How We Analyzed the COMPAS Recidivism Algorithm". It includes this table, which summarizes many of the results they report:

All Defendants	Low	High		Black Defendants	Low	High		White Defendants	Low	High
Survived	2681	1282		Survived	990	805		Survived	1139	349
Recidivated	1216	2035		Recidivated	532	1369		Recidivated	461	505
FP rate: 32.35				FP rate: 44.85				FP rate: 23.45		
FN rate: 37.40				FN rate: 27.99				FN rate: 47.72		
PPV: 0.61				PPV: 0.63				PPV: 0.59		
NPV: 0.69				NPV: 0.65				NPV: 0.71		
LR+: 1.94				LR+: 1.61				LR+: 2.23		
LR-: 0.55				LR-: 0.51				LR-: 0.62		

The table summarizes results for all defendants and two subgroups: defendants classified as White ("Caucasian" in the original dataset) and Black ("African-American"). For each group, the summary includes several metrics, including:

- FP rate: false positive rate

- FN rate: false negative rate

- PPV: positive predictive value

- NPV: negative predictive value

- LR+: positive likelihood ratio

- LR-: negative likelihood ratio

I will explain what these metrics mean and how to compute them, and we'll replicate the results in this table. But first let's examine and clean the data.

Here are the values of `decile_score`, which is the output of the COMPAS algorithm. `1` is the lowest risk category; `10` is the highest.

```
values(cp["decile_score"])
```

```
decile_score
1     1440
2      941
3      747
4      769
5      681
6      641
7      592
8      512
9      508
10     383
Name: count, dtype: int64
```

It's important to note that COMPAS is not a binary classifier – that is, it does not predict that a defendant will or will not recidivate. Rather, it gives each defendant a score that is intended to reflect the risk that they will recidivate.

In order to evaluate the performance of COMPAS, the authors of the ProPublica article chose a threshold, 4, and defined decile scores at or below the threshold to be "low risk", and scores above the threshold to be "high risk". Their choice of the threshold is arbitrary. Later, we'll see what happens with other choices, but we'll start by replicating the original analysis.

We'll create a Boolean `Series` called `high_risk` that's `True` for respondents with a decile score greater than 4.

```
high_risk = cp["decile_score"] > 4
high_risk.name = "HighRisk"
values(high_risk)
```

```
HighRisk
False    3897
True     3317
Name: count, dtype: int64
```

16.2 Replicating the Analysis

The column `two_year_recid` indicates whether a defendant was charged with another crime during a two year period after the original charge when they were not in a correctional facility.

```
values(cp["two_year_recid"])
```

```
two_year_recid
0    3963
1    3251
Name: count, dtype: int64
```

Let's create another `Series`, called `new_charge`, that is `True` for defendants who were charged with another crime within two years.

```
new_charge = cp["two_year_recid"] == 1
new_charge.name = "NewCharge"
values(new_charge)
```

```
NewCharge
False    3963
True     3251
Name: count, dtype: int64
```

If we make a cross-tabulation of `new_charge` and `high_risk`, the result is a `DataFrame` that indicates how many defendants are in each of four groups:

```
pd.crosstab(new_charge, high_risk)
```

HighRisk	False	True
NewCharge		
False	2681	1282
True	1216	2035

This table is called a **confusion matrix** or error matrix. Reading from left to right and top to bottom, the elements of the matrix show the number of respondents who were:

- Classified as low risk and not charged with a new crime: there were 2681 **true negatives** – that is, cases where the test was negative (not high risk) and the prediction turned out to be correct (no new charge).

- High risk and not charged: there were 1282 **false positives** – that is, cases where the test was positive and the prediction was incorrect.

- Low risk and charged: there were 1216 **false negatives** – that is, cases where the test was negative (low risk) and the prediction was incorrect (the defendant was charged with a new crime).

- High risk and charged: there were 2035 **true positives** – that is, cases where the test was positive and the prediction was correct.

The values in this matrix are consistent with the values in the ProPublica article, so we can confirm that we are replicating their analysis correctly.

Now let's check the confusion matrices for White and Black defendants. Here are the values of `race`:

```
values(cp["race"])
```

```
race
African-American    3696
Asian                 32
Caucasian           2454
Hispanic             637
Native American       18
Other                377
Name: count, dtype: int64
```

Here's a Boolean `Series` that's true for White defendants.

```
white = cp["race"] == "Caucasian"
white.name = "white"
values(white)
```

```
white
False    4760
True     2454
Name: count, dtype: int64
```

And here's the confusion matrix for White defendants.

```
pd.crosstab(new_charge[white], high_risk[white])
```

HighRisk	False	True
NewCharge		
False	1139	349
True	461	505

16.3 Data Bias

`black` is a Boolean Series that is `True` for Black defendants.

```
black = cp["race"] == "African-American"
black.name = "black"
values(black)
```

```
black
False    3518
True     3696
Name: count, dtype: int64
```

And here's the confusion matrix for Black defendants.

```
pd.crosstab(new_charge[black], high_risk[black])
```

HighRisk NewCharge	False	True
False	990	805
True	532	1369

All of these results are consistent with the ProPublica article. However, before we go on, I want to address an important issue with this dataset: data bias.

16.3 Data Bias

Systems like COMPAS are trying to predict whether a defendant will *commit* another crime if released. But the dataset reports whether a defendant was *charged* with another crime. Not everyone who commits a crime gets charged (not even close). The probability of getting charged for a particular crime depends on the type of crime and location; the presence of witnesses and their willingness to work with police; the decisions of police about where to patrol, what crimes to investigate, and who to arrest; and decisions of prosecutors about who to charge.

It is likely that every one of these factors depends on the race of the defendant. In this dataset, the prevalence of *new charges* is higher for Black defendants, but that doesn't necessarily mean that the prevalence of *new crimes* is higher. If the dataset is affected by racial bias in the probability of being charged, prediction algorithms like COMPAS will be biased, too. In discussions of whether and how these systems should be used in the criminal justice system, this is an important issue.

However, I am going to put it aside *for now* in order to focus on understanding the arguments posed in the ProPublica article and the metrics they are based on. For the rest of this chapter I will take the "recidivism rates" in the dataset at face value – but I will try to be clear about what they mean and don't mean.

16.4 Arranging the confusion matrix

In the previous section I arranged the confusion matrix to be consistent with the ProPublica article, to make it easy to check for consistency. But it is more common to arrange the matrix like this:

	Predicted positive	**Predicted negative**
Actual positive	True positive (TP)	False negative (FN)
Actual negative	False positive (FP)	True negative (TN)

In this arrangement:

- The actual conditions are down the rows.

- The predictions are across the columns.

- The rows and columns are sorted so true positives are in the upper left and true negatives are in the lower right.

In the context of the ProPublica article:

- "Predicted positive" means the defendant is classified as high risk.

- "Predicted negative" means low risk.

- "Actual positive" means the defendant was charged with a new crime.

- "Actual negative" means they were not charged with a new crime during the follow-up period.

Going forward, we'll present confusion matrices in this format.

16.5 Accuracy

Based on these results, how accurate is COMPAS as a binary classifier? Well, it turns out that there are a *lot* of ways to answer that question. One of the simplest is overall **accuracy**, which is the fraction (or percentage) of correct predictions. To compute accuracy, it is convenient to extract from the confusion matrix the number of true positives, false negatives, false positives, and true negatives.

```
tp, fn, fp, tn = matrix_all.to_numpy().flatten()
```

The number of true predictions is `tp + tn`. The number of false predictions is `fp + fn`. So we can compute the fraction of true predictions like this:

16.6 Predictive Value

```
def percent(x, y):
    """Compute the percentage `x/(x+y)*100`."""
    return x / (x + y) * 100
```

```
accuracy = percent(tp + tn, fp + fn)
accuracy
```

65.37288605489326

As a way to evaluate a binary classifier, accuracy does not distinguish between true positives and true negatives, or false positives and false negatives. But it is often important to make these distinctions, because the benefits of true predictions and true negatives might be different, and the costs of false positives and false negatives might be different.

16.6 Predictive Value

One way to make these distinctions is to compute the "predictive value" of positive and negative tests:

- **Positive predictive value (PPV)** is the fraction of positive tests that are correct.

- **Negative predictive value (NPV)** is the fraction of negative tests that are correct.

In this example, PPV is the fraction of high risk defendants who were charged with a new crime. NPV is the fraction of low risk defendants who "survived" a two year period without being charged.

The following function takes a confusion matrix and computes these metrics.

```
def predictive_value(m):
    """Compute positive and negative predictive value.

    m: confusion matrix
    """
    tp, fn, fp, tn = m.to_numpy().flatten()
    ppv = percent(tp, fp)
    npv = percent(tn, fn)
    return ppv, npv
```

Here are the predictive values for all defendants.

```
ppv, npv = predictive_value(matrix_all)
ppv, npv
```

(61.350618028338864, 68.79651013600206)

Among all defendants, a positive test is correct about 61% of the time; a negative test result is correct about 69% of the time.

16.7 Sensitivity and Specificity

Another way to characterize the accuracy of a test is to compute

- **Sensitivity**, which is the probability of predicting correctly when the condition is present, and

- **Specificity**, which is the probability of predicting correctly when the condition is absent.

A test is "sensitive" if it detects the positive condition. In this example, sensitivity is the fraction of recidivists who were correctly classified as high risk.

A test is "specific" if it identifies the negative condition. In this example, specificity is the fraction of non-recidivists who were correctly classified as low risk.

The following function takes a confusion matrix and computes sensitivity and specificity.

```
def sens_spec(m):
    """Compute sensitivity and specificity.
    
    m: confusion matrix
    """
    tp, fn, fp, tn = m.to_numpy().flatten()
    sens = percent(tp, fn)
    spec = percent(tn, fp)
    return sens, spec
```

Here are sensitivity and specificity for all defendants.

```
sens, spec = sens_spec(matrix_all)
sens, spec
```

(62.59612426945556, 67.65076961897553)

16.8 False Positive and Negative Rates

If we evaluate COMPAS as a binary classifier:

- About 63% of the recidivists were classified as high risk.

- About 68% of the non-recidivists were classified as low risk.

It can be hard to keep all of these metrics straight, especially when you are learning about them for the first time. The following table might help:

Metric	Definition
PPV	TP / (TP + FP)
Sensitivity	TP / (TP + FN)
NPV	TN / (TN + FN)
Specificity	TN / (TN + FP)

PPV and sensitivity are similar in the sense that they both have true positives in the numerator. The difference is the denominator:

- PPV is the ratio of true positives to all positive tests. So it answers the question, "Of all positive tests, how many are correct?"

- Sensitivity is the ratio of true positives to all positive conditions. So it answers the question "Of all positive conditions, how many are detected?"

Similarly, NPV and sensitivity both have true negatives in the numerator, but:

- NPV is the ratio of true negatives to all negative tests. It answers, "Of all negative tests, how many are correct?"

- Specificity is the ratio of true negatives to all negative conditions. It answers, "Of all negative conditions, how many are classified correctly?"

16.8 False Positive and Negative Rates

The ProPublica article reports PPV and NPV, but instead of sensitivity and specificity, it reports their complements:

- **False positive rate**, which is the ratio of false positives to all negative conditions. It answers, "Of all negative conditions, how many are misclassified?"

- **False negative rate**, which is the ratio of false negatives to all positive conditions. It answers, "Of all positive conditions, how many are misclassified?"

In this example:

- The false positive rate is the fraction of non-recidivists who were classified as high risk.

- The false negative rate is the fraction of recidivists who were classified as low risk.

The following function takes a confusion matrix and computes false positive and false negative rates.

```
def error_rates(m):
    """Compute false positive and false negative rate.

    m: confusion matrix
    """
    tp, fn, fp, tn = m.to_numpy().flatten()
    fpr = percent(fp, tn)
    fnr = percent(fn, tp)
    return fpr, fnr
```

Here are the error rates for all defendants.

```
fpr, fnr = error_rates(matrix_all)
fpr, fnr
```

(32.349230381024476, 37.40387573054445)

FPR is the complement of specificity, which means they have to add up to 100%

```
fpr + spec
```

100.0

And FNR is the complement of sensitivity.

```
fnr + sens
```

100.0

So FPR and FNR are just another way of reporting sensitivity and specificity. In general, I prefer sensitivity and specificity over FPN and FNR because

- I think the positive framing is easier to interpret than the negative framing, and

- It's easier to remember what "sensitivity" and "specificity" mean.

16.8 False Positive and Negative Rates

I find "false positive rate" and "false negative rate" harder to remember. For example, "false positive rate" could just as easily mean either

1. The fraction of positive tests that are incorrect, or

2. The fraction of negative conditions that are misclassified.

It is only a convention that the first is called the "false discovery rate" and the second is called "false positive rate". I suspect I am not the only one that gets them confused.

So, here's my recommendation: if you have the choice, generally use PPV, NPV, sensitivity and specificity, and avoid the other metrics. However, since the ProPublica article uses FPR and FNR, I will too. They also report LR+ and LR-, but those are combinations of other metrics and not relevant to the current discussion, so we will ignore them.

However, there is one other metric that I think is relevant and not included in the ProPublica tables: **prevalence**, which is the fraction of all cases where the condition is positive. In the example, it's the fraction of defendants who recidivate. The following function computes prevalence:

```
def prevalence(m):
    """Compute prevalence.

    m: confusion matrix
    """
    tp, fn, fp, tn = m.to_numpy().flatten()
    prevalence = percent(tp + fn, tn + fp)
    return prevalence
```

Here's the prevalence for all defendants:

```
prev = prevalence(matrix_all)
prev
```

45.06515109509287

About 45% of the defendants in this dataset were charged with another crime within two years of their release.

16.9 All Metrics

The following function takes a confusion matrix, computes all the metrics, and puts them in a DataFrame.

```
def compute_metrics(m, name=""):
    """Compute all metrics.

    m: confusion matrix

    returns: DataFrame
    """
    fpr, fnr = error_rates(m)
    ppv, npv = predictive_value(m)
    prev = prevalence(m)

    index = ["FP rate", "FN rate", "PPV", "NPV", "Prevalence"]
    df = pd.DataFrame(index=index, columns=["Percent"])
    df.Percent = fpr, fnr, ppv, npv, prev
    df.index.name = name
    return df.round(1)
```

Here are the metrics for all defendants.

```
compute_metrics(matrix_all, "All defendants")
```

All defendants	Percent
FP rate	32.3
FN rate	37.4
PPV	61.4
NPV	68.8
Prevalence	45.1

Comparing these results to the table from ProPublica, it looks like our analysis agrees with theirs.

16.9 All Metrics

Here are the same metrics for Black defendants.

```
compute_metrics(matrix_black, "Black defendants")
```

	Percent
Black defendants	
FP rate	44.8
FN rate	28
PPV	63
NPV	65
Prevalence	51.4

And for White defendants.

```
compute_metrics(matrix_white, "White defendants")
```

	Percent
White defendants	
FP rate	23.5
FN rate	47.7
PPV	59.1
NPV	71.2
Prevalence	39.4

All of these results are consistent with those reported in the article, including the headline results:

1. The false positive rate for Black defendants is substantially higher than for White defendants (45%, compared to 23%).

2. The false negative rate for Black defendants is substantially lower (28%, compared to 48%).

```
error_rates(matrix_black)
```

(44.84679665738162, 27.985270910047344)

```
error_rates(matrix_white)
```

(23.45430107526882, 47.72256728778468)

In other words:

- Of all people who *will not* recidivate, Black defendants are more likely to be be classified as high risk and – if these classifications influence sentencing decisions – more likely to be sent to prison.

- Of all people who *will* recidivate, White defendants are more likely to be classified as low risk, and more likely to be released.

This seems clearly unfair.

However, it turns out that "fair" is complicated. After the ProPublica article, the Washington Post published a response by Sam Corbett-Davies, Emma Pierson, Avi Feller and Sharad Goel: "A computer program used for bail and sentencing decisions was labeled biased against blacks. It's actually not that clear."

I encourage you to read that article, and then read the next chapter, where I will unpack their arguments and replicate their analysis.

Chapter 17

Algorithmic Fairness

In the previous chapter, we replicated the analysis reported in "Machine Bias", by Julia Angwin, Jeff Larson, Surya Mattu and Lauren Kirchner, published by ProPublica in May 2016.

After the ProPublica article, the Washington Post published a response by Sam Corbett-Davies, Emma Pierson, Avi Feller and Sharad Goel: "A computer program used for bail and sentencing decisions was labeled biased against Blacks. It's actually not that clear."

I encourage you to read both of those articles before you go on. In this chapter, I explain some of the arguments presented in the Washington Post (WaPo) article, and we will replicate their analysis.

17.1 The Response

The Washington Post article summarizes the ProPublica article and the response from Northpointe, the company that makes COMPAS, like this:

- ProPublica claims that COMPAS is unfair because "among defendants who ultimately did not reoffend, Blacks were more than twice as likely as Whites to be classified as medium or high risk."

- Northpointe claims that COMPAS is fair because "scores mean essentially the same thing regardless of the defendant's race. For example, among defendants who scored a seven on the COMPAS scale, 60 percent of White defendants reoffended, which is nearly identical to the 61 percent of Black defendants who reoffended."

So ProPublica and Northpointe are invoking different definitions of "fair".

In the previous chapter we explored the first definition by computing error rates (false positive and false negative) for White and Black defendants. In this chapter, we'll explore the second definition, which is called "calibration".

17.2 Calibration

The WaPo article includes this figure, which shows "White and Black defendants with the same risk score are roughly equally likely to reoffend."

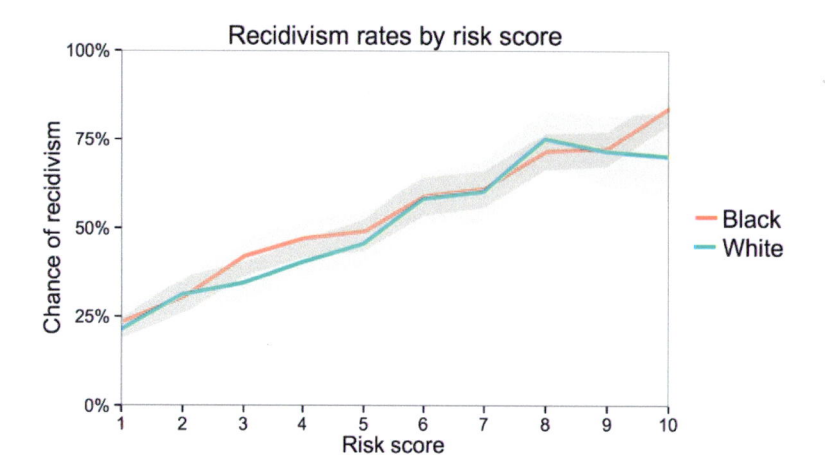

Recidivism rate by risk score and race. White and black defendants with the same risk score are roughly equally likely to reoffend. The gray bands show 95 percent confidence intervals.

To understand this figure, let's start by replicating it.

The following function groups defendants by risk score and computes the fraction in each group that were charged with another crime within two years.

```
def calibration_curve(df):
    """Fraction in each risk group charged with another crime.

    df: DataFrame

    returns: Series
    """
    grouped = df.groupby("decile_score")
    return grouped["two_year_recid"].mean()
```

17.2 Calibration

The following figure shows this calibration curve for all defendants and for White and Black defendants separately.

```
cal_all = calibration_curve(cp)
cal_all.plot(linestyle="dotted", color="gray", label="All defendants")

white = cp["race"] == "Caucasian"
cal_white = calibration_curve(cp[white])
cal_white.plot(label="White")

black = cp["race"] == "African-American"
cal_black = calibration_curve(cp[black])
cal_black.plot(label="Black")

decorate(
    xlabel="Risk score",
    ylabel="Fraction charged with new crime",
    title="Recivism vs risk score, grouped by race",
)
```

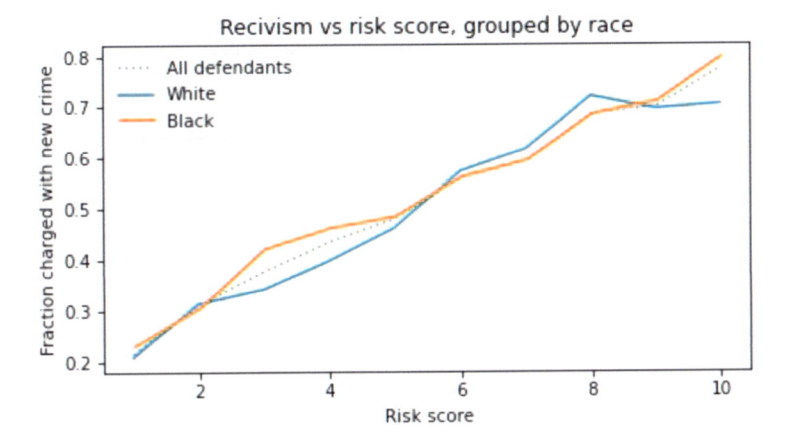

This figure shows that people with higher risk scores are more likely to be charged with a new crime within two years. In that sense COMPAS works as intended. Furthermore, the test is equally **calibrated** for Black and White defendants – that is, in each risk group, the rate of recidivism is about the same for both groups.

The WaPo article explains why this is important:

> A risk score of seven for Black defendants should mean the same thing as a score of seven for White defendants. Imagine if that were not so, and we systematically assigned Whites higher risk scores than equally risky Black defendants with the goal of mitigating ProPublica's criticism. We would consider that a violation of the fundamental tenet of equal treatment.

So we want a test that has the same calibration for all groups, and we want a test that has the same error rates for all groups. But there's the problem: it is mathematically impossible to be fair by both definitions at the same time. To see why, let's go back to the confusion matrix.

17.3 Matrices and Metrics

In the previous chapter, we computed confusion matrices for White and Black defendants. Here they are again:

```
matrix_white = make_matrix(cp[white])
matrix_white
```

	Pred Positive	Pred Negative
Actual		
Positive	505	461
Negative	349	1139

```
matrix_black = make_matrix(cp[black])
matrix_black
```

	Pred Positive	Pred Negative
Actual		
Positive	1369	532
Negative	805	990

17.3 Matrices and Metrics

And here are the metrics we computed from the confusion matrices:

```
metrics_white = compute_metrics(matrix_white, "White defendants")
metrics_white
```

White defendants	Percent
FPR	23.5
FNR	47.7
PPV	59.1
NPV	71.2
Prevalence	39.4

```
metrics_black = compute_metrics(matrix_black, "Black defendants")
metrics_black
```

Black defendants	Percent
FPR	44.8
FNR	28
PPV	63
NPV	65
Prevalence	51.4

If we look at the error rates (FPR and FNR), it seems like COMPAS is biased against Black defendants:

- Their false positive rate is higher (45% vs 23%): among people who *will not* recidivate, Black defendants are more likely to be classified high risk.

- Their false negative rate is lower (28% vs 48%): among people who *will* recidivate, Black defendants are less likely to be classified low risk.

But if we look at the the predictive values (PPV and NPV) it seems like COMPAS is biased in favor of Black defendants:

- Among people in the *high risk group*, Black defendants are more likely to be charged with another crime (63% vs 59%).

- Among people in the *low risk group*, Black defendants are less likely to "survive" two years without another charge (65% vs 71%).

It seems like we should be able to fix these problems, but it turns out that we can't. We'll see why in the next section.

17.4 What Would It Take?

Suppose we want to fix COMPAS so that error rates are the same for Black and White defendants. We could do that by using different thresholds for the two groups. In this section, we'll figure out what it would take to re-calibrate COMPAS – then we'll see what effect that would have on predictive values.

The following function loops through possible thresholds, makes the confusion matrix with each threshold, and computes accuracy metrics.

```python
def sweep_threshold(cp):
    """Sweep a range of threshold and compute accuracy metrics.

    cp: DataFrame of COMPAS data

    returns: DataFrame with one row for each threshold and
             one column for each metric
    """
    index = range(0, 11)
    columns = ["FPR", "FNR", "PPV", "NPV", "Prevalence"]
    table = pd.DataFrame(index=index, columns=columns, dtype=float)

    for threshold in index:
        m = make_matrix(cp, threshold)
        metrics = compute_metrics(m)
        table.loc[threshold] = metrics["Percent"]

    return table
```

Here's the resulting table for all defendants.

```python
table_all = sweep_threshold(cp)
table_all.head()
```

	FPR	FNR	PPV	NPV	Prevalence
0	100	0	45.1	NaN	45.1
1	71.4	9.5	51	78.6	45.1
2	55.1	18.5	54.8	74.8	45.1
3	43.3	27.1	58	71.8	45.1
4	32.3	37.4	61.4	68.8	45.1

17.4 What Would It Take?

The following figure shows error rates as a function of threshold.

```
table_all["FPR"].plot(color="C2")
table_all["FNR"].plot(color="C4")

decorate(
    xlabel="Threshold",
    ylabel="Percent",
    title="Error rates for a range of thresholds"
)
```

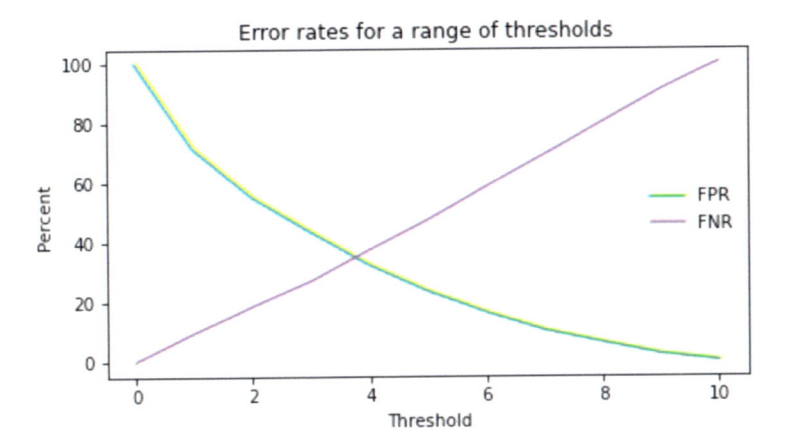

When the threshold is low, almost everyone is in the high risk group; in that case:

- FNR is low because most recidivists are in the high risk group, but

- FPR is high because most non-recidivists are *also* in the high risk group.

When the threshold is high, almost everyone is in the low risk group, and the metrics are the other way around:

- FPR is low because most non-recidivists are in the low risk group, but

- FNR is high because most recidivists are *also* in the low risk group.

The following figure shows predictive values for a range of thresholds.

```
table_all["PPV"].plot(color="C0")
table_all["NPV"].plot(color="C1")

decorate(
    xlabel="Threshold",
    ylabel="Percent",
    title="Predictive values for a range of thresholds",
)
```

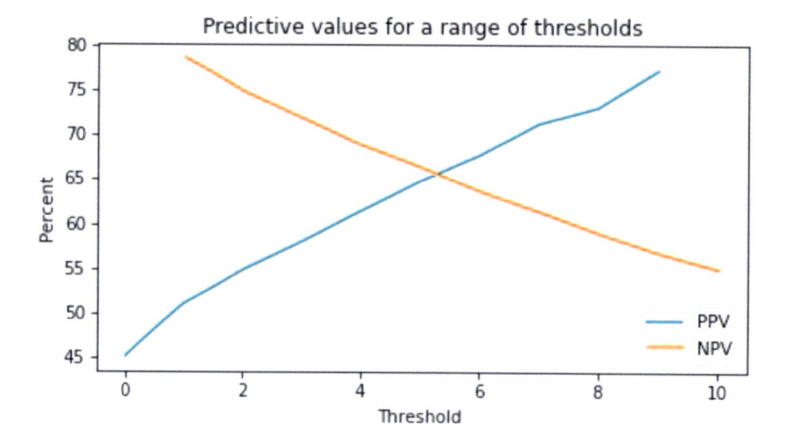

When the threshold is too low, PPV is low. When the threshold is too high, NPV is low.

Now let's compute tables for Black and White defendants separately.

```
table_white = sweep_threshold(cp[white])
table_black = sweep_threshold(cp[black])
```

To calibrate the test, we'll use the following function, which estimates the threshold where a column from the table passes through a given metric.

17.4 What Would It Take?

```
from scipy.interpolate import interp1d

def crossing(series, value, **options):
    """Find where a Series crosses a value.

    series: Series
    value: number
    options: passed to interp1d (default is linear interpolation)

    returns: number
    """
    interp = interp1d(series.values, series.index, **options)
    return interp(value)
```

We can use `crossing` to find the threshold that makes the error rates for White defendants the same as for the general population.

```
matrix_all = make_matrix(cp)
fpr, fnr = error_rates(matrix_all)
```

```
crossing(table_white["FPR"], fpr)
```

array(3.23050171)

```
crossing(table_white["FNR"], fnr)
```

array(3.11998938)

With a threshold near 3.2, White defendants would have the same error rates as the general population. Now let's do the same computation for Black defendants.

```
crossing(table_black["FPR"], fpr)
```

array(5.20752868)

```
crossing(table_black["FNR"], fnr)
```

array(5.01788384)

To get the same error rates for Black and White defendants, we need different thresholds: about 5.1 compared to 3.2.

Now let's see what the predictive values are if we use different thresholds for different groups. We'll use the following function to interpolate columns in the table.

```
def interpolate(series, value, **options):
    """Evaluate a function at a value.

    series: Series
    value: number
    options: passed to interp1d (default is linear interpolation)

    returns: number
    """
    interp = interp1d(series.index, series.values, **options)
    return interp(value)
```

Here's the positive predictive value for White defendants with threshold 3.2.

```
interpolate(table_white["PPV"], 3.2)
```

array(55.26)

And here's the positive predictive value for Black defendants with threshold 5.1.

```
interpolate(table_black["PPV"], 5.1)
```

array(66.17)

With equal error rates, we get different PPV:

- Among White defendants in the high risk group, about 55% would recidivate.

- Among Black defendants in the high risk group, about 66% would recidivate.

Here's NPV with different thresholds for each group:

```
interpolate(table_white["NPV"], 3.2)
```

array(73.04)

```
interpolate(table_black["NPV"], 5.1)
```

array(62.19)

17.5 ROC Curve

With equal error rates, the NPVs are substantially different:

- Among White defendants in the low risk group, 73% went two years without another charge.

- Among Black defendants in the low risk group, 62% went two years without another charge.

To summarize, if the test is calibrated in terms of error rates, it is not calibrated in terms of predictive values.

- If we make the error rates more equal, we make the predictive values more unfair, and

- If we make the predictive values more equal, we make the error rates more unfair.

Fundamentally, the problem is that the prevalence of recidivism is different in the two groups: about 39% of White defendants were charged with another crime within two years, compared to 51% of Black defendants. As long as that's the case (for any two groups) the predictive values and error rates can't be "fair" at the same time.

That's the argument the Washington Post article presented. In the next section, we'll take the argument one step farther by introducing one more metric, the area under the ROC curve.

17.5 ROC Curve

In the previous section we plotted various metrics as as function of threshold. A common and useful way to visualize these results is to plot sensitivity versus false positive rate (FPR). For historical reasons, the result is called a **receiver operating characteristic (ROC) curve**. The following function plots the ROC curve:

```python
import matplotlib.pyplot as plt

def plot_roc(table, **options):
    """Plot the ROC curve.

    table: DataFrame of metrics as a function of
           classification threshold
    options: passed to plot
    """
    plt.plot([0, 100], [0, 100], ":", color="gray")
    sens = 100 - table["FNR"]
    plt.plot(table["FPR"], sens, **options)
    decorate(xlabel="FPR", ylabel="Sensitivity (1-FNR)", title="ROC curve")
```

Here's the ROC curve for all defendants.

```
plot_roc(table_all, color="C2", label="All defendants")
```

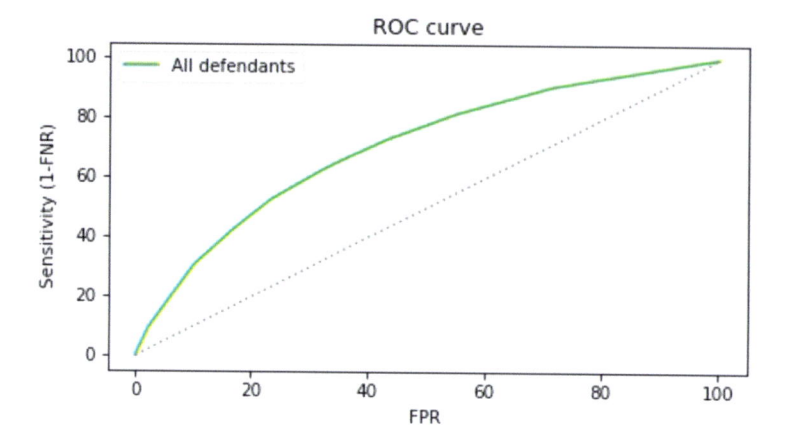

The green line is the ROC curve. The gray dotted line shows the identity line for comparison. An ideal test would have high sensitivity for all values of FPR, but in reality there is almost always a trade-off:

- When FPR is low, sensitivity is low.

- In order to get more sensitivity, we have to accept a higher FPR.

The ROC curve tells us how much sensitivity we get for a given FPR or, the other way around, how much FPR we have to accept to achieve a given sensitivity. The following figure shows the ROC curves for White and Black defendants.

```
plot_roc(table_white)
plot_roc(table_black)
```

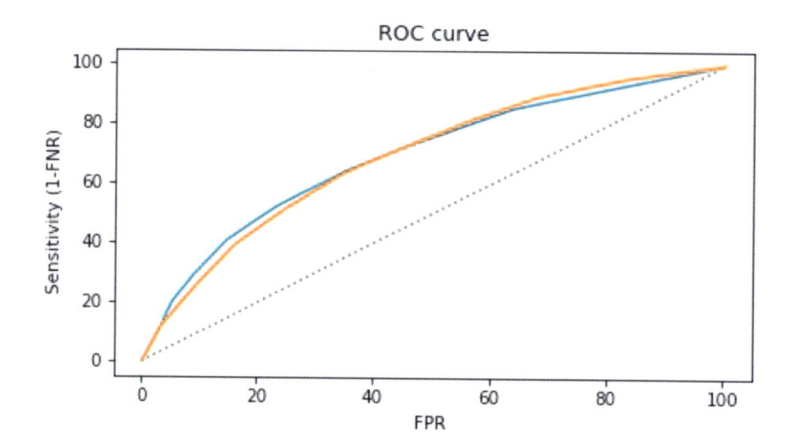

17.6 Concordance

The ROC curves are similar for the two groups, which shows that we can achieve nearly the same error rates (FPR and FNR) for the two groups, as we did in the previous section. It also shows that the test has nearly the same "concordance" for both groups, which I explain in the next section.

17.6 Concordance

The authors of the ProPublica article published a supplementary article, "How We Analyzed the COMPAS Recidivism Algorithm", which describes their analysis in more detail.

As another metric of accuracy, they estimate **concordance**, which they describe like this:

> Overall, [COMPAS has] a concordance score of 63.6 percent. That means for any randomly selected pair of defendants in the sample, the COMPAS system can accurately rank their recidivism risk 63.6 percent of the time (e.g. if one person of the pair recidivates, that pair will count as a successful match if that person also had a higher score). In its study, Northpointe reported a slightly higher concordance: 68 percent.

They explain:

> [These estimates] are lower than what Northpointe describes as a threshold for reliability. "A rule of thumb according to several recent articles is that [concordances] of .70 or above typically indicate satisfactory predictive accuracy, and measures between .60 and .70 suggest low to moderate predictive accuracy," the company says in its study.

There are several ways to compute concordance, but one of the simplest is to compute the area under the ROC curve, which is why concordance is also called the **area under the curve** or AUC. Since we've already computed the ROC, we can use the SciPy function `simpson` to estimate the area under the curve by numerical integration.

```
from scipy.integrate import simpson

def compute_auc(table):
    """Compute the area under the ROC curve."""
    y = 100 - table["FNR"]
    x = table["FPR"]
    y = y.sort_index(ascending=False) / 100
    x = x.sort_index(ascending=False) / 100
    return simpson(y=y.values, x=x.values)
```

The concordance for all respondents is about 70%.

```
compute_auc(table_all)
```

0.7061166121516749

For the subgroups it is slightly lower, but also near 70%.

```
compute_auc(table_white)
```

0.6996145234049567

```
compute_auc(table_black)
```

0.6946519102148443

Different ways of computing concordance handle ties differently, which is probably why we, ProPublica, and Northpointe get somewhat different estimates. But qualitatively they all tell the same story – as a binary classifier, COMPAS is only moderately accurate. However, it seems to be equally accurate, by this metric, for White and Black defendants.

17.7 Summary

In this chapter, we replicated the analysis reported in the Washington Post article and confirmed two of the arguments they presented:

1. COMPAS is calibrated in the sense that White and Black defendants with the same risk score have almost the same probability of being charged with another crime. This implies that it has roughly the same predictive value for both groups.

2. It is impossible for COMPAS to have the same predictive values for both groups and the same error rates at the same time.

And we showed:

- If you design a test to achieve equal predictive value across groups with different prevalence, you will find that error rates differ. Specifically, false positive rates will be higher in groups with higher recividism.

- If you design a test to achieve equal error rates across groups, you will find that predictive values differ. Specifically, positive predictive value will be lower in groups with lower rates of recidivism.

Finally, we derived the ROC curve and computed AUC, which shows that COMPAS has nearly the same concordance for White and Black defendants.

17.8 Discussion

If it is impossible to make a classification algorithm fair for all groups, what should we do?

It might be tempting to forbid algorithms like COMPAS in the criminal justice system, but unfortunately, that doesn't solve the problem. The conclusions we reached in this case study apply to human decision-makers as well, with the additional problem that humans are more unpredictable than algorithms, and can be more biased. As long as we have to make decisions about bail, sentencing, and parole, we will need data and algorithms to inform those decisions, regardless of whether the algorithms are run by humans or machines.

I don't have a solution to these problems, but I will suggest two guidelines: the data we use should be unbiased, and the algorithms should be transparent.

I discussed the problem of data bias in the previous chapter. In this example, we used data about additional *charges* as a measure of additional *crimes*. But not everyone who commits a crime gets charged. If one group is more likely than another to be charged with a crime, the algorithm will be unfair, no matter how it is calibrated.

Of course we should use unbiased data if we can, but if that's not possible, sometimes we can do as well if we *know* the data is biased, in what directions, and by how much. So one thing we can do to make algorithms more fair is to quantify biases in the data we use and compensate for them.

Another thing we can do is make systems like COMPAS more transparent – that is, we should know how they work, what factors they take into account, and what they ignore. Algorithms intended to serve the public interest should be the subject of public discussion, not the trade secrets of a private company.

The use of algorithms in criminal justice, and in many other domains that profoundly affect people's lives, is relatively new. It raises difficult questions about fairness that we have only begun to recognize.

The goal of this case study is to help us measure the accuracy of these algorithms and quantify their fairness. I hope it will contribute to the ongoing debate as we address the many challenges of the criminal justice system and the use of algorithms in our lives.

Further Reading

The first part of this book is an accelerated introduction to Python with emphasis on tools for working with data. One of the benefits of learning Python is that it useful for many other kinds of computing, not just data science. If you would like to learn more about Python, there are a lot of good books and online resources, but if the style of this book works well for you, you might like *Think Python*, also by Allen Downey and published by O'Reilly Media.

If you are interested in scientific computing, you might like *Modeling and Simulation in Python*, published by No Starch Press. It is an introduction to Python focused on modeling and simulating physical systems. It explores a range of topics including population growth, infectious disease, and simple mechanical systems.

The second part of this book is about exploratory data analysis and visualization. If you are interested in exploratory data analysis, you might also like *Think Stats: Exploratory Data Analysis in Python*, published by O'Reilly Media. If you are interested in data visualization, you might like Nathan Yau's blog, *FlowingData*, and his books, *Visualize This* and *Data Points*.

The third part of this book is about statistical inference, that is, using data from a sample to estimate something about a population. We used resampling to quantify the precision of those estimates, and hypothesis testing to consider whether an effect we observe might be due to chance. I am currently working on a book called *Data Q&A: Answering the Real Questions with Python* that applies these methods to questions posted on Reddit's statistics forum.

The methods I demonstrate in this book might be called conventional inference, in contrast to the alternative, which is Bayesian inference. If you are interested in learning more about that, you might like *Think Bayes: Bayesian Statistics in Python*, also by Allen Downey and published by O'Reilly Media.

The Political Alignment case study uses data from the General Social Survey (GSS) to explore political beliefs in the United States, how they differ between groups, and how they change over time. If you are interested in this topic, you might like *Probably Overthinking It*, published by University of Chicago Press, which explores the GSS data in greater depth. It presents a variety of other topics as well, exploring, as the subtitle explains, "How to use data to answer questions, avoid statistical traps, and make better decisions".

Finally, the Recidivism case study explores the use of predictive algorithms in the criminal justice system and explains the metrics we use to assess them. There are many books and articles on this topic, which reflect its importance because of the impact it has on people's lives, and also the difficulty of resolving conflicting requirements of fairness. If you would like to read more on this topic, I recommend Orly Lobel's recent book, *The Equality Machine*, which reviews many of the challenges algorithms pose while also recognizing their potential to do good.

Index

accuracy, 244
age, 100, 119, 137, 196, 199, 201
alignment, political, 210, 225, 228
alpha (transparency argument), 115
AND operator, 88
area under the curve, 265
argument, 58
arithmetic operation, 7
arithmetic operator, 4
arithmetic, Series, 85
array (NumPy), 28
array arithmetic, 29
assignment, 7, 11, 18
AttributeError, 69
AUC, 265
average, 92
axes, 23, 61

bar (Pmf method), 98
bar chart, 98
basket of goods, 32
Behavioral Risk Factor Surveillance System, 113, 171, 195
bell curve, 86, 107, 110
bernoulli (SciPy function), 153
binary classifier, 240
binary variable, 143
birth weight, 80
birthday, 16
birthweight, 199
blinded study, 152
bool, 17
Boolean algebra, 17
Boolean Series, 87, 105, 172, 210, 240
bootstrapping, 169, 173
Boston, 18
box plot, 121

boxplot (Seaborn function), 121, 200
bracket operator, 45, 48, 80, 88, 97, 138, 215
break statement, 40
BRFSS, 113

calibration, 260
calibration curve, 254
call a function, 20
capitalization, 51
case sensitivity, 6
categorical variable, 143, 178
CDF, 98
Cdf object, 99
central tendency, 96
classifier, binary, 240
codebook, 80, 83, 100, 234
coefficient of variation, 162
coin toss, 153
collections library, 55
colon, 35, 39
color palette, 230
color palettes, 220
color sequence (Pyplot), 66
column, 79, 92, 95
columns (DataFrame attribute), 80
comma, 26, 27
comment, 19
COMPAS, 237, 253
compound interest, 8
compression, 91
concatenation, 12, 28
concordance, 265
condition, 38
confidence interval, 155, 180
confusion matrix, 241
conservative, 210
control group, 151, 186

control variable, 202
corr (Pandas method), 176
correlation, 123, 176, 195
correlation matrix, 124
count (Pandas method), 165, 172
Counter object, 55
criminal justice, 237
cross tabulation, 218, 241
cross_tab (Pandas function), 241
crossing function, 261
crosstab (Pandas function), 218
cumulative distribution function, 98
cut (Pandas function), 199

data bias, 243, 267
data compression, 91
data dictionary, 78
data extract, 91
data type, 29
data validation, 81
DataFrame, 79
DataFrameGroupBy object, 138
date, 13
day, 16
debugging, 8, 32
decorate function, 212
decrement, 37
defining functions, 19
Democrat, 222
dependent variable, 137
describe (Pandas method), 84
dice, 93
dictionary, 45, 47
dictionary key, 47
dictionary value, 47
difference in means, 190
discretize, 179
distance, 18
distribution, 85, 93
Double Day, 17
dropna (Pandas method), 120, 136

education, 95, 135
efficacy, 152, 156
element, 25, 26, 35, 45
elementwise operation, 29, 33
empirical distribution, 94
empiricaldist library, 94, 212
empty dictionary, 47

empty list, 27
empty tuple, 26
equirectangular projection, 22
error message, 6
error rate, 257
expect (magic command), 5
exponent, 4
exponentiation, 4, 6, 19
extract, 91

fairness, 226, 252, 253, 267
False, 17
false discovery rate, 249
false negative rate, 247
false positive rate, 247
figure axes, 23
file, 38, 91
file pointer, 38
filter, 88
fit (StatsModels function), 136
fixed-width format, 78
float (data type), 3
float function, 13
float64, 29
floating-point error, 7
floating-point number, 4
formula string, 136
frequency, 54, 70
from_seq (empiricaldist function), 212
full-term pregnancy, 190
function, 7, 19
function call, 20
function object, 20

Gaussian distribution, 107
gaussian_kde (SciPy function), 179
gca function, 23
General Social Survey, 94, 135, 163, 210, 225
Geopandas, 21
Greek letter, 19
groupby (Pandas method), 138, 182, 214, 227
GSS, 94, 135
gun control, 144

haversine distance, 20
haversine function, 18
HDF file, 91, 94, 172, 190
head (Pandas method), 79, 81
header, 35

INDEX

height, 114, 130, 158, 172, 196
hist (Pandas method), 86, 95
histogram, 85, 95
hlines (Pyplot function), 66
hypothesis testing, 185
hypothesis testing framework, 193
hypothesis testing, limitations, 199

if statement, 38
immutable, 26
implicit multiplication, 4
import statement, 5, 14
in operator, 48
income, 102, 135, 137, 164, 179
increment, 37
incremental development, 33
indentation, 39
Independent (political affiliation), 222
independent variable, 137
index, 46
Index (Pandas object), 80
IndexError, 46
int (data type), 3
int function, 12
intercept, 128, 137
interest, 8
interpolate function, 262
interquartile range, 102, 122
inverse (Cdf method), 101
invertible function, 101
IQR, 102, 122
isna (Pandas method), 90

jittering, 116, 179
Jupyter, 3, 5

KDE, 110, 120, 179
kdeplot (Seaborn function), 110, 154, 164, 188
kernel density estimation, 110, 179
key, in dictionary, 47
keyword argument, 58, 86

latitude, 17
LEAP study, 186
legend (Pyplot function), 62
liberal, 210
line of best fit, 128, 131
linear regression, 127
linregress (SciPy function), 127, 136, 177
linspace (NumPy function), 108

list, 26
list concatenation, 28
live birth, 87
locally weighted scatterplot smoothing, 216
location data, 17
log odds, 145
logarithm, 6, 179
logarithmic scale, 71, 122
logical operator, 88
logistic regression, 144, 182
logit (StatsModels function), 144, 182
London, 20
longitude, 17
loop, 35
loop variable, 36
loop, nested, 50
lower (string method), 51
lowess (StatsModels function), 216

magic command, 5
map projection, 22
mapping, 47
marijuana, 146, 182
marker size, 115
math functions, 5
Matplotlib, 23, 60
max (NumPy function), 31
mean (NumPy function), 30
mean (Pandas method), 84, 87, 138
mean, weighted, 90
measurement error, 173, 193
median, 90
method, 42
metric, 239, 257
min (NumPy function), 31
missing data, 81, 90
model, 161
moderate, 210
most_common (Counter method), 55
multiple birth, 89
multiple regression, 137
multiplication, 4, 12
mutable, 26

NameError, 48
NaN, 81, 84, 88
National Survey of Family Growth, 78, 190
natural language, 7
ndarray, 29

negative predictive value, 245
nested loop, 50
newline, 41
noise (variability), 103
nonlinear relationship, 124, 132, 138
norm (SciPy object), 108
normal (NumPy function), 158
normal distribution, 165, 166, 169
normalize, 96, 218
Northpointe, 253
Not a Number, 81
notna (Pandas method), 90
now (Timestamp function), 15
NSFG, 78
null hypothesis, 193
number, 3
NumPy, 5, 28, 84

ols (StatsModels function), 136
operator, 4
operator, update, 37
order of operations, 5
ordinary least squares, 136
overplotting, 115
oversampling, 89, 174

p-value, 189, 194
Pandas, 14, 77
parabola, 141
parental age effect, 204
parentheses, 5, 26
party affiliation, 222
paternal effect, 205
peanut allergy, 186
percentage difference, 31
percentile, 90, 102, 105, 122, 155, 167, 171
percentile (NumPy function), 167
permutation test, 195, 200
Pew Research, 60
pivot table, 229
pivot_table (Pandas method), 229
placebo group, 189
plot (Pyplot function), 60
plurality, 226
PMF, 212
Pmf object, 94
polarization, political, 213, 214, 216
political alignment, 210, 225, 228
political polarization, 213, 214, 216

positional argument, 58
positive predictive value, 245
predict (StatsModels method), 140, 145
predictive algorithm, 237
predictive value, 245, 257
predictor, 137
pregnancy, 78
pregnancy length, 191
preterm birth, 87
prevalence, 249, 263
print statement, 36
probability, 97
probability mass function, 94, 212
Project Gutenberg, 38
projection of a map, 22
ProPublica, 237, 253
punctuation, 52
Pyplot, 60

quadratic model, 202
quadratic term, 139
quantile (Pandas method), 167
quantity, 101
quotation mark, 11, 19

racial bias, 238
random (NumPy library), 107
randomized controlled trial, 151
randomized trial, 186
range, 31
range function, 69
rank, 70
RCT, 151
read_fwf (Pandas function), 79
read_hdf (Pandas function), 94, 163
recidivism, 238
recode, 182, 227
regression, 199
relative difference, 30
relative risk, 152, 187
replace (Pandas method), 84, 219, 227
replacement, sampling with, 169
representative sample, 158
representative sampling, 89, 174
Republican, 222
resample (KDE method), 180
resampling, 151, 169, 226, 232
resampling framework, 160
reset_index (Pandas method), 197

INDEX

rise over run, 73
risk, 152
risk score, 237
robust, 171
ROC curve, 263
rules of precedence, 5

sample (Pandas method), 174, 197
sample statistic, 160
sampling, 92
sampling distribution, 159, 160, 165, 175
sampling weight, 89
sandwich prices, 27, 63
scatter plot, 114
SciPy, 108, 127
Seaborn, 110, 120, 164, 220, 230
semi-colon, 60
sensitivity, 246
sequence, 96
Series (Pandas object), 81, 94
Series arithmetic, 85
set (Python type), 170
set subtraction, 170
sex, 144
shape (Pandas method), 80
Shapely, 21
shuffle (NumPy function), 194
significance, statistical, 203
simple regression, 127, 135
simulation, 154
single birth, 89
skewed distribution, 86, 164, 179
slice, 50
slope, 127, 128, 136, 137
slope of a line, 73
smoothing, 216
smoothness (variability), 104
social desirability bias, 173
solar year, 16
sort (list method), 69
sort_index (Pandas method), 82
specificity, 246
split method, 41
spurious relationship, 202
square brackets, 26
standard deviation, 30, 85, 155, 164
standard error, 155, 173, 180
startswith (string method), 42
statadict library, 78

statistical significance, 203
statistical summary, 30
StatsModels library, 136
std (NumPy function), 30
str function, 13
stratified sampling, 174
strength of correlation, 126
string, 11
string concatenation, 12
string library, 52
string multiplication, 12
strip (string method), 52
summary statistics, 30, 84

tab character, 41
test statistic, 193
The Economist, 28, 63
theoretical distribution, 107
threshold, 240, 258
time, 13
time series, 214, 227
Timedelta, 15
Timestamp, 14
title (Pyplot function), 62
to_hdf (Pandas method), 91
transparency, 115, 267
treatment group, 151, 186
triple-quoted string, 19
True, 17
tuple, 18, 25
tuple function, 26
TypeError, 5, 12, 46, 58

Unicode, 29, 38, 53
unicodedata library, 53
unique words, 50
update operator, 37

vaccine, 151
validation, 81
value, 7
value, in dictionary, 47
value_counts (Pandas method), 82, 170
values (dict function), 68
values function, 211
variable, 7, 8, 11, 19, 92, 95
variable, loop, 36
violin plot, 120
violinplot (Seaborn function), 120

War and Peace, 38
Washington Post, 253
weight, 114, 130, 196
weighted bootstrapping, 174
weighted mean, 90
whisker, 122
whitespace, 40
word frequency, 54

xlabel (Pyplot function), 62

xlim (Pyplot function), 118
xscale (Pyplot function), 71

year, 16
ylabel (Pyplot function), 62
ylim (Pyplot function), 61
yscale (Pyplot function), 71

Zipf plot, 68
Zipf's law, 67

Made in United States
Cleveland, OH
04 June 2025